CALL IT
THE
JONATHAN
KAPLAN
STORY
LIKE
IT IS

CALL IT LIKE IT IS

THE JONATHAN KAPLAN STORY

AS TOLD TO MIKE BEHR

Published by Zebra Press
an imprint of Random House Struik (Pty) Ltd
Company Reg. No. 1966/003153/07
Estuaries No. 4, Oxbow Crescent, Century Avenue, Century City, Cape Town, 7441
PO Box 1144, Cape Town, 8000, South Africa

www.zebrapress.co.za

First published 2014
Reprinted in 2014

3 5 7 9 10 8 6 4 2

PUBLISHER: Marlene Fryer
MANAGING EDITOR: Ronel Richter-Herbert
PROOFREADER: Bronwen Leak
COVER DESIGN: Sean Robertson
TEXT DESIGN: Jacques Kaiser
TYPESETTER: Monique van den Berg
PHOTO SECTION: Robert Plummer
PHOTO RESEARCHER: Colette Stott

Set in 11 pt on 14.5 pt Adobe Garamond

Printed and bound by Paarl Media, Jan van Riebeeck Avenue, Paarl, South Africa

ISBN 978 1 77022 585 5 (print)
ISBN 978 1 77022 586 2 (ePub)
ISBN 978 1 77022 587 9 (PDF)

Disclaimer

Every effort has been made to credit the correct person and/or agency for the images used in this book. Where we may have omitted a name or been unable to find the copyright holder, we ask that the relevant party contact us in order for their name to be included in a reprint edition of the book.

Contents

Foreword

My first encounter with Jonathan Kaplan came in 1996 when, as a young referee fresh out of school, I was invited to touch-judge at an international schools festival at Kearsney College in Natal. I had heard Jonathan Kaplan was due to referee at the tournament and was excited about meeting the rising star in South African refereeing, a guy who was due to referee a Currie Cup game on TV that weekend. The moment came when Jonathan pulled me aside following the game I had touch-judged and, in what I have since discovered is typical of his style, quite bluntly pointed out areas of my performance that needed improving. I felt he was a little prickly and overly critical.

It did not take me long to realise, however, that far from being deliberately aloof or negative, Jonathan was taking a special interest in me as a person and referee, perhaps recognising something in my 18-year-old self before I had even recognised it myself. It was the start of a very special friendship and working relationship.

I watched with growing pride as J.K. went on to become one of the world's most accomplished referees. Our friendship grew as, perhaps prophetically, I ran touch for him in an enormous amount of rugby games, from Potchefstroom to Auckland and from Stadium Australia to Twickenham. And I loved the countless hours we spent on aeroplanes and in hotels and casinos, and on "gentle plods" through some of the world's most glamorous cities, sharing stories and talking about life and rugby.

J.K.'s record at all levels of the game attests to his professionalism and his determination to succeed. This didn't happen by accident. J.K. lives the phrase "a student of the game". I have been fortunate to witness first-hand to what extent he loves the deep intricacies of the game. The passion and energy with which he dives into detailed analyses and deep philosophical conversations on rugby is a testament to his continued love for the game, which has dominated 30 years of his life.

And whether it's a Rugby World Cup semi-final or a Vodacom Cup game in Potchefstroom, it's an illuminating insight into the man to have seen first-hand how his approach to and respect of the participants doesn't change. To achieve the accolades and record number of games at all levels attests to his ability to treat each one of them as being as important as the other. The credibility and respect he has garnered over his 15 years in the professional era is a testament to his character.

There is no question that I am a better referee because of the time I spent with J.K. Much of what I've learnt has been the result of the endless conversations and philosophical debates we've had about the game, but just being around him in a big-match environment, watching him display the courage and the nerve to perform on the world's greatest rugby stages and under the glare of a sometimes rabid media, permeated my subconscious and provided a road map for the psychological resilience required to succeed at this level.

J.K., you have been my beacon in every respect; I only hope I can be the strong and true warrior that you have been.

CRAIG JOUBERT

Foreword

In 1998, when I was Springbok coach, SANZAR's head of refereeing asked me who I and the Bok players thought were the best up-and-coming referees in South Africa at that time. It was an easy choice to make. Jonathan Kaplan, although still a young man, had already established himself as an exceptionally knowledgeable, sympathetic and objective referee, who had a great "feel" for the game. He showed calmness towards and respect for the players and had a wonderful way of speaking to them. There did not appear to be any ego.

He refereed for the players and for the betterment of game and did not appear to think that he, as the ref, was the focal point of the occasion. That in itself was a rarity! We all agreed that he was the best young ref from South Africa at the time. Amazingly enough, SARU had not put his name forward as one of their best candidates. I believe that, thanks to the Springbok squad's recommendation, Jonathan Kaplan was added to SANZAR's list of preferred referees and his career was launched.

One of the toughest jobs for any referee is to remain objective in a hostile environment. Statistics have overwhelmingly proven that all refs are influenced by home crowds. Home teams are almost always penalised less than the away team. This is natural and pertains to all refs. It is not bias; it is just that referees are human and humans generally want to be liked.

One of the most courageous refereeing decisions I ever saw was when J.K. penalised the All Blacks in a home game against Australia in 2000 in a breakdown at the very end of the game. He did not hesitate; he was correct, and he blew what he saw. This gave John Eales the chance to step up and kick the penalty that condemned the All Blacks to a home loss.

Normal refereeing, one would think. It was not. As head coach in over 80 international games, I have seen, time and again, refs who avoid blowing that last tough penalty call that could take the win away from the home side. Jonathan, in the toughest of environments, did not hesitate to make the correct call. J.K. has been courageous, accurate and understated – a world-class referee. He and all rugby-loving South Africans can be very proud of his career.

NICK MALLETT

Foreword

Whenever you discuss a referee, most rugby supporters, players and coaches will have a lot to say, but most of it will probably not be something you'd say in front of your kids. Unfortunately, if your team loses or if you need someone to blame for a bad performance, it is always easiest to blame the referee. Because if it's the ref's fault, you feel better about yourself and your team's performance.

What people don't understand is that without referees, there won't be rugby. How can we play this game that we all love so much without the man in the middle?

As players, we require certain things from a referee. Firstly, that the ref will not favour one team over another; secondly, that he is consistent in his interpretation of the laws; and, thirdly, that he is accurate and doesn't make a lot of mistakes.

There were a lot of good referees in my time, but if I had to pick one to officiate in the most important game I would play, my choice is simple: Jonathan Kaplan. Why is this so and what makes Jonathan stand out? One aspect of Jonathan's refereeing that I hated as a young captain at the beginning of my rugby career but grew to appreciate as a more experienced captain was his self-belief – and probably the little arrogance he had.

Jonathan will always make the big calls and he will call it as he sees it. As a young captain you always want to argue about decisions, but I quickly learnt that you don't question Jonathan's decisions; you only talk to him about trends, because as I said, he calls it as he sees it. Unfortunately you don't get that from a lot of referees, as some of them can be influenced by a persuasive captain or even more so by a big home crowd. The result is that they won't make a big call against a home team in front of their home crowd.

I wasn't always in Jonathan's good books. I remember in 2005, when Os du Randt and I got yellow-carded. I had come in from the side, according to Jonathan, and cleaned out Os with what might have been a bit of a swinging arm. Then, as we landed, Os tried to punch me, but luckily for me he missed. True to Jonathan's nature, he quickly stepped in and sent both of us, two of the most senior Springboks, straight to the cooler without even giving us an explanation.

Jonathan was also the referee in 2008 when we, the Bulls, lost against the Sharks in Durban in the final of the Currie Cup. Afterwards I went to him and told him that I thought he had been outstanding on the day. I could tell that it didn't happen a lot that a losing captain gave him a compliment, but that is the respect I had for him as a referee.

But sometimes I was also in the winning team with Jonathan as the referee, for example when we beat the Chiefs at Loftus in the final of the Super 14 with a record score. A lot of the time a referee would feel bad about a score running away in a final, but this wasn't the case with Jonathan. He allowed us to give one of the best performances ever in Super Rugby.

Jonathan's record speaks for itself. The only compliment that I can add to that is that whenever he officiated a game, the team that played the better rugby on the day would win the match. Because Jonathan didn't make a lot of mistakes, he didn't get influenced by a partisan crowd and he made the big call when he was required to.

VICTOR MATFIELD

Foreword

My first dealings with Jonathan Kaplan were when he was a senior at King David Linksfield, a large Jewish school in the heart of Johannesburg. He was a small but keen rugby player coming through the junior ranks playing mostly scrumhalf, if I remember correctly. Despite being a quick and intelligent player, Jonathan was never going to be big enough to make it as a professional. But wanting to stay involved with the game, it wasn't surprising to see him take up refereeing at a young age.

I can remember Jonathan blowing First-XV games with boys just a year or two younger than him, and it was clear even then that he would go places. He commanded respect, and he was accurate and fair. I like to think these are qualities that have carried Jonathan throughout his career.

Jonathan is the ultimate professional and always has been. I was amazed to see the meticulous records he's kept of each game he's blown, from schoolboy days to Test-match rugby and everything in between.

Intricately constructed databases and spreadsheets have allowed Jonathan to track the rhythm and patterns of his refereeing career, and I have no doubt this attention to detail has made him the standout officiator he was till he retired. It's clear to me that refereeing is not just a job for Jonathan. It's his passion, it's what he gets up in the morning to do and it is what has made him one of South Africa's most respected whistleblowers over the last 20 years.

Generally speaking, referees are a funny lot. Sometimes they will high-five you in the tunnel pre-match or invite you for a beer after the game only to blow you off the park for the opening 40 minutes. Quite often you're left thinking, "I thought we were mates?" as the half-time hooter sounds.

Refreshingly, I've never found Jonathan to be like that; I've never received any preferential treatment and rarely, if ever, argued with his calls.

In the early days it was nothing to see Jonathan blow a Test match with some of the world's biggest and best players on a Friday night at Ellis Park only for him to turn around on the Saturday morning and officiate a First-XV match in Joburg suburbia. I think that diverse apprenticeship, which reached great heights but never denied its roots, has contributed to the respect players have for Jonathan around the world today.

While I'd long been an admirer of his, it wasn't until the New Zealand versus Wallabies Bledisloe and Tri-Nations decider in 2000 that I concluded he was set to become one of the all-time greats. In front of a packed-out Wellington stadium, Jonathan remained focused and made the correct call to award the Wallabies a penalty after the bell. History tells us John Eales calmly slotted the three points to hand Australia a historic win away from home.

It was brave, it was poised and I'm sure Jonathan would tell you, it was downright frightening. Sometimes the scariest thing about an All Black match isn't the 15 men on the pitch but the 30 000 sitting behind the fence making it clear that they don't think much of you.

In my opinion, it was at that moment Jonathan came of age as an international referee. Worldwide only a handful of referees would have had the guts to make that call, and I was incredibly proud to watch a young, up-and-coming South African perform so professionally under pressure.

Considering the company referees have kept over the last 20 years, to have stayed at the top of the tree as Jonathan has is a remarkable achievement. It's been an era of top-quality referees – André Watson, Tappe Henning, Gus Ericson, Peter Marshall and Paddy O'Brien, to name but a few, were all class. Had it not been for these referees reffing at the same time as Jonathan, he may well have been known as the greatest ever – if, in fact, he is not already.

I sometimes wonder if Jonathan wasn't born a galloper, a jockey or at least a bookie in another life. Away from the whistle, it's no secret that he loves the track and a good punt. He has produced some genius at the track over the years, which led to me investing in my first ever horse. By default, I ended up part-owner of two horses with Jonathan, and the pair actually won every now and again, much to my surprise and delight. I look back at that time spent with Jonathan, and our horses, with great affection.

Be it at the races or around a braai, I have always enjoyed Jonathan's company. He is a friendly, intelligent man whom I look forward to chatting with whenever our busy lives cross paths.

It's lucky for the game of rugby that Jonathan chose to be a top-line referee. He's the sort of guy that would have excelled at anything he chose to get into, and I'm sure that post-refereeing he will build a second, successful career should he wish to. Perhaps that career as a jockey is still to come.

I wish Jonathan all the best in the future and look forward to getting a few tips from him at the next Durban July or Melbourne Cup.

JAKE WHITE

Introduction

Enjoy the moment
Have fun
Follow your dream;
The finish is inevitable
— Paulo Coelho

I am an ordinary guy who has lived a blessed life doing the thing I wanted to do all along ... What started out as a hobby blossomed into a long and successful career, which took me to all corners of the earth. I lived my dream, and I did it over and over again!

I live on my own with my two bulldogs, Dexter and Lola, who have been my companions for many years. We share a house with a vast collection of bonsai, which I nurture. Occasionally we have to share our space with others (not what you're thinking), when I (or other alpha males who like to hold the tongs in smoky environs) have the odd braai.

I have been blessed with a wonderful, loving, supportive family and many friends. Some have been transient in my life; others have added much colour to my existence. My hobbies include road running, horse racing and all card games.

My philosophy in life is to create the best possible outcome from any given starting point. To learn and be aware. To challenge myself and those around me. To be grateful for my successes as well as my failures, as I have found pain to be the best educator and driver.

I am a firm believer that nothing is coincidence – that everything is connected, that all roads meet and that there are cosmic galaxies out there that remind us that our problems are so trivial in the greater scheme of things ... I am by no means perfect – I have made mistakes and will, no doubt, continue to make them in the future.

Ultimately I would like others to look back and say that I maximised my time here and made the world a better place in my own small, humble way.

This is my story.

1

No stone unturned

It was ironic. I'd run many really tough marathons and ultra-marathons – the Foot of Africa (one of the toughest 42s in South Africa), several Comrades, the Long Tom, the Korkie and Two Oceans. Hell, I'd even run back-to-back marathons!

I'd reffed in a massive hail storm in Glasgow where it felt as if golf balls were raining down on me, and in -18 wind chill with driving sleet in Christchurch, where my assistant Andy Turner started to get frostbite on his nose. Once I blew a Super Rugby match with flu until I nearly collapsed and medics treating me in my dressing room battled to find my pulse.

But my greatest physical challenge began not on a rugby field or a marathon course, but on my Vespa, going up a hill. Into a tractor.

I was on my way home on my little blue scooter after doing some chores and enjoying a coffee at Jason's Bakery in town. I was in third gear, going at about 60 on upper Strand Street near the old rock quarry. Halfway up the hill I became aware of a stationary tractor about 30 or 40 metres away. It was parked up against the kerb, facing in the direction I was heading. And the driver was sitting motionless in his seat.

I barely noticed it – it was not in my way. But then it started moving, and surprisingly fast for an old tractor. Fast and right across my path. I couldn't believe it! The idiot was doing a U-turn without looking behind him.

With only seconds to think, I started calculating my escape. But there was none. The pavement was too high and the tractor, which had now stalled, was blocking the road.

All this time I was breaking hard. And cursing. Even if they had tried, the cops couldn't have set up a better roadblock.

By this time I had slowed down to about 20 or 30 kays, but a collision was inevitable. The options were flashing lightning-fast through my head while the scene in front of me played out in slow motion. Should I hit him square? Or drop the Vespa and broadside into him Speedway-racing style? Should I hit him on the big tyre? Or the small one ...?

Bang!

I picked the small tyre because it was protruding furthest from the body of the tractor. Compared to the speeds I normally drove, this was a snail's pace, but it was enough to send me flying. I landed in a crumpled heap on the tar next to my scooter. But I was up immediately, dusting off my knees and cursing the driver.

"What the hell do you think you're doing?" I shouted at him.

He just stared back. A fiftysomething municipal worker, he was as white as a sheet and so shocked he couldn't talk. I felt a stinging around my left knee. When I looked down, there was a cavernous hole just beneath my patella. It looked a bit like a cleaved chunk of meat on a butcher's block. Except that the meat was white. As white as my tibia, which had been part of me for 44 years. Yet here we were, face to face for the first time. Pleased to meet you, *boet*!

Strangely, there was no blood, no pain. Just a stinging sensation. And then one thought barged through my mind. Not, "Shit, you're lucky, Jonathan." But, "Shit, there goes my World Cup!"

It was Tuesday 19 July 2011, and my flight to New Zealand for my fourth – and swansong – World Cup was on 30 August. I had fought so hard to get there, to make World Cup 2011 the cherry on the top of my career.

The tractor driver was bewildered, panicked speechless about the consequences of not paying attention. But he didn't have a clue how far-reaching they actually were. The World Cup was not just another tournament. For me, it represented four long years of sacrifice and commitment, of keeping fit and performing at the highest level. Four years of working hard for one last crack at proving that I was still one of the best international refs around. That I was capable not only of holding my own, but of having a really good tournament and being there at the business end of the competition.

I tried to walk, but I was feeling a bit wobbly. I looked at my leg again and saw blood dripping down, staining my shoes. I hobbled to the side of the road and collapsed onto the pavement. Adrenaline started to kick in big-time. I pulled out my cellphone and called my friend Allan Turner, who worked a few minutes away.

"*Boet*, I've had an accident on my scooter." I was calm and thinking clearly. "I've got a deep cut on my leg. I need you to come now. I need you to take me to hospital."

I was together enough to see that there was nothing wrong with the tractor. The driver was okay too – I was the only one hurt. Then, for the first time I noticed a skinny bloke hovering near me, a pedestrian who had witnessed the accident while strolling up the hill.

"*Meneer. Hier, meneer.*"

His weather-beaten face spoke of a hard life. His clothes told me he could be living on the street. He offered me his dirty handkerchief.

"*Dis vir die bloed, meneer.*"

I was thinking germs and started to say no, but he was a Good Samaritan giving up a possession to stop my bleeding. He bandaged my knee with care and attention and the bleeding temporarily stopped.

Then Allan arrived.

"What the hell happened, Jonathan?"

He wheeled my bike to the side of the road and locked it. Then I stood up and hobbled to his car. We sped back down Strand Street towards Christiaan Barnard Memorial Hospital four blocks away.

I texted my mom, who was visiting my brothers Gary and David in Canada. I kept it brief and just said that I'd had a scooter accident. I had a cut on my leg, but everything was fine.

My then girlfriend, Lisa, wasn't answering her phone, so I texted her too. Allan pulled up outside the emergency unit just as Lisa called me back. She was on her way. I walked into the hospital still unsteady, treading on the ball of my foot. I called André Watson, SA Rugby's manager of referees and my boss since 2004.

"I've had an accident and I've got this cut on my leg, but I'd still love to do the Bulls/Free State game tomorrow." Obviously, it was the adrenaline talking. "I'm at the hospital and I think they can give me some painkillers and tape me up and I'll be good to go."

André was business as usual. "Get back to me within the hour. I need to organise a replacement as soon as possible if you can't make it."

By now one of the nurses had already got me onto a trauma board. An ER doctor in green theatre scrubs approached me. The doctor had overheard my conversation with André.

Recognising me, he said, "Ah, Mr Kaplan, let's have a look at your knee ..."

Removing the bloodied handkerchief, he summed it up clear as a whistle.

"One thing I can tell you for sure is that you won't be reffing at Loftus tomorrow. You've got a serious wound. There may even be ligament and tendon damage. And you are definitely going to need plastic surgery."

Bullshit, I thought. I walked away from the accident!

Off he went to attend to the next emergency. I noticed that Allan was mesmerised by the bloody mess that was hidden by my Good Samaritan's hanky.

"Jeez, Jonathan! That does *not* look good."

He looked like he could hurl but rallied to snap a photo. Allan knew me well enough to know it would be excellent war-story material for my next braai.

"Are you in pain?"

It was sore, but not unbearably so. I had been in hospital for food poisoning once and that had been 10 times worse on the pain scale.

A smiley, happy nurse, all white, gleaming teeth, breezed in. "I'm going to give you some happy drugs."

I told her to take it easy with the needle (typical male), and she injected me in the ass. I didn't feel a thing. Within minutes, though, I was happy with everyone. I felt serene. I loved all the nurses. I loved life. I even loved my wound.

But every now and again the illusion slipped, just enough for me to detect the unease lurking in the back of my mind. I sensed that something wasn't right.

Lisa arrived just as they were wheeling me in to have an MRI. She, too, snapped a pic and then raised her eyebrows. I could tell she didn't like the look of this at all.

But the MRI results brought at least some relief. There was no ligament damage, no broken bones. Just bone bruising. That was a good sign. My World Cup was still on. But I would need surgery.

Back in trauma I called André and told him that he needed to find a replacement. I would be missing out on some Currie Cup matches and two very important warm-up Test matches between France and Wales and Ireland and England, but it would be a small price to pay if I could make it to New Zealand.

My thoughts were interrupted by the arrival of a plastic surgeon, whose first priority was some oke who'd put his hand into a meat grinder. That sounded a lot worse than my little scratch.

Dr Mark van der Velde popped his head round the white plastic curtain to introduce himself. He was a fit-looking, balding fella, just like me. He told me that he would be back once he was finished with the meat-grinder bloke. Thanks to the Pethidine, I wasn't hassled. While I waited, Lisa told me that if my recovery was a priority, she strongly recommended surgery under local anaesthetic. She had played sport at the highest level and had had her fair share of sporting injuries and operations. Mark returned and I told him of my World Cup dilemma. He explained to me that if every second of every day was important, I would recover quicker if I opted for a local anaesthetic.

By now I was thinking: I'm going to leave no stone unturned, starting right now. I implanted the mantra in my mind: No stone unturned ...

By the time I left the hospital, the foundations of my recovery would be in place. *Whatever* it took, I was going to the World Cup.

"Are you ready?"

"Let's do it!"

I was still cruising on Pethidine, but I was also plotting my recovery. How many days left to the World Cup? How many weeks? When would be the last match I could ref to test-drive my knee before I flew out? I was already visualising everything quietly and calmly in my head as they wheeled me into theatre.

Mark interrupted my thoughts by telling me he had to inject the local anaesthetic straight into the wound. "Fucking hell! That's going to be painful."

"Yes. The beginning is sore. But bite the bullet for a few seconds and the pain will go away."

I asked for a hand towel to bite down on and the nurse held my outstretched hand while Mark cleaned the wound. Then he stuck the needle deep into it. It was *sore*. I was biting down hard on the towel and squeezing the nurse's hand so tightly, I apologised and let go.

"Not to worry. It's nothing compared to a mother delivering her baby."

I felt Mark fiddling around in the wound. Pushing. Pulling. Prodding. It wasn't sore, just a little disconcerting. Then he looked up and gave me the bad news.

"Your patellar tendon is half severed. It's been cleaved in two and one half is flapping around."

He explained that the patellar tendon is actually a ligament that connects the bottom of your kneecap to the top of your tibia. Your patella is attached to your quadriceps muscles by the quadriceps tendon. All working together, they straighten your knee. Injury to this tendon makes walking or running very challenging, and braking or turning suddenly is impossible. Mine was cleaved halfway to the middle from the right-hand side.

Later, when my Vespa went in for repairs, I learnt from the mechanic that there had been a lot of blood on the leg shield. My knee had broken and penetrated the shield's plastic covering with enough force to leave a dent in the shield's aluminium section. The fracturing plastic must have provided an edge sharp enough to cleave open my knee and cut through my tendon like a scalpel.

I felt a rush of anxiety. "What does that mean?" Suddenly the Pethidine was not helping that much.

"It's a significant injury. You can already feel how it's affected your walking. You won't be able to run. Even if you could and you tried to stop suddenly or change direction, your knee would just buckle. You would collapse on the ground. Recovery time is a minimum of eight to 12 weeks."

My reaction was denial. Bullshit! I was confused. "I thought the MRI was clear? I only have six weeks, Mark. Not eight. Find a way to speed up my recovery. I need to get there. Give me the tools to get there. If my leg fails in the first game, I will deal with that. I don't mind breaking down, even if it means another bad injury and another operation. Just get me to my fourth World Cup. I don't care how you sew it up. Double, triple, whatever you have to do so that I can get on that plane. Sew it up so that I'm ready to board on the 30th. So that if I do everything right, follow all your advice, there's a chance that I will ref at the World Cup …"

I didn't really give Mark an opportunity to question my thinking – I just wanted him to find a way. He could have said that I was being too ambitious and that I was asking too much. He could have played it safe. But he just went back to work. Along the way he distracted me with small talk and questions about the nuances of rugby.

In between the pulling and stitching, I repeated myself.

"I don't want to know that I can't make it, Mark. You're not allowed to tell me that I can't make it. You have to tell me how I'm *going* to make it."

About 45 minutes and 35 stitches later, Mark was done. He told me what to do and to come back in seven to 10 days.

"My secretary will call you to make an appointment."

It was 19 July 2011. I would test my leg on 27 August at the last-chance saloon – reffing a schools game – where I would know whether I could board the flight to New Zealand on 30 August. I would have a few days to strengthen up before my first game on 12 September – Tonga versus Canada. I would blow the opening whistle, and I would leave the results of my endeavour to the universe.

I hobbled out of Christiaan Barnard on crutches. Six weeks to the World Cup, eight weeks of recovery time …

No stone unturned.

2

A constant childhood

I don't think anything in life is preordained. But my mom, Tikvah, believes my rugby career was written in the stars.

She was just 20 years old, two years out of matric, when she gave birth to me in Durban's Parklands nursing home. It was 7.15 p.m. on 7 November 1966. True to her name – Tikvah is Hebrew for hope – she battled bravely for 12 hours to deliver me, as my head was very wide with no give (I was big-headed even in those days!). But eventually the obstetrician used a scalpel and forceps to haul all 8.6 pounds of me into this world. And as I arrived, the doctor exclaimed that my head was the shape of a rugby ball. In 16 years of practice, he said he had never seen anything like it.

My mom wanted to name me David, after her 13-year-old brother who was knocked down and killed while riding his bicycle just weeks before her matric exams. But even though two years had passed since then, her loss was still too raw, so she called me Jonathan Isaac instead, which in Hebrew means "God has given laughter". And of course, Jonathan was David's best friend in the Bible.

Apparently, I was a very alert baby. At three months old I lay in her arms while she read a fashion magazine and seemed to understand when she pointed out a model's eyes, ears, nose and mouth. Those early recognition skills, my mom said, were the genesis of my later ability to scan a field or a room and take everything in like a photocopier.

She may well be right. I do have an ability to recall detail, particularly mindless detail, when it comes to facts, scores, dates, etc. I don't think it's remarkable, but my friends are often amazed by my memory, especially when I can recall scenes from matches I reffed a long time ago.

My mom was from an academic family, so she read and talked to me a lot. By the age of 10 months, I could count to 10. A cloth book was my first toy, and it never left my side. I also played for hours with a six-piece puzzle, which I managed to assemble correctly by the time I was one. By that age, I also knew my cars. I pointed them out from the back of my mom's Volvo as she drove around Durban. I knew the difference between a Valiant Regal, my dad's car, and a Volvo, as well as a Chevy and my favourite, a Mustang. I also knew a Datsun when I saw one. The only car I couldn't nail was a Morris Minor, which I called a taxi. Later my mom discovered that I was identifying the cars by the shape of their headlights.

My dad was from a traditional and quite conservative Jewish family with staunch Orthodox values. He is a generous, roll-up-your-sleeves, hard-working, upstanding citizen, and respectful of others. I got my determination, respect for tradition and strong work ethic from him – the "ginger in my beard", I call it.

My earliest childhood memories are from the age of four. One crystal-clear memory I have was of my dad, Mervyn, giving me the biggest hiding of my life. I was playing at the top of the driveway of our Gainsborough Drive home in Durban North with Gary, my middle brother, who was then three. I decided to be naughty and run down the long driveway towards the busy road, which I knew was strictly out of bounds. Gary's mistake was to follow his big brother.

Our domestic worker, Constance, diligently reported us to my dad, a pharmacist, when he returned that night from his Musgrave Road pharmacy. He promptly gave us both a hiding and sent us to our room. I was typically defiant, and said it didn't even hurt. Gary, however, was so scared that he started crying even before he got his smack.

The significance of this moment is that it contains two key values that were constant while I was growing up: discipline and love. My dad wanted us to comprehend that the road was dangerous and that by making one simple mistake, we could be dead. The lesson was duly learnt. My mom came to our room before we went to sleep that night to reassure us. We Kaplans never went to sleep angry or fighting, she told us. There could be disagreements and arguing, but when you went to bed at night, all that had to stop and you had to know that you were loved. It was a moment that remains etched in my memory.

That unconditional love was why I always felt like Superman – like I had been born brave. It brought a whole bunch of possibilities to my life. As long as I knew I had that foundation and that I was a valuable entity, a valuable person, then *anything* became possible.

Although I would be separated from my brothers when I was 10 for four life-defining years, we remained extremely close. Our relationship with one another would always be constant, and we would always be there for each other. No other triumvirate has more love and respect and desire to be together than the Kaplan brothers. So although my brothers have lived in Canada for the past 16 years, we remain deeply connected. They will always be rocks in my life and my career, as I am a rock to them. And despite being the smallest, I will always be their big brother, leading, I hope, by example.

Although I wasn't aware of it at the time, my parents' marriage had started to unravel before my youngest brother, David, turned one. When I was five-and-a-half, my dad, by mutual decision, moved out with just his golf clubs and the hi-fi. I wanted my parents to be together and for us to be a family, but in time I also accepted that it wasn't to be. They weren't getting along, and separating was the best decision that they could have made for us and, more importantly, for themselves.

I wasn't aware of their separation having any dramatic emotional impact on me. Instead, it allowed me to weigh up my mom and dad's divergent value systems and adopt the best from both. It was a beautiful gift that shaped my life. But it was a pity their marriage didn't work out, as the family history suggested they were destined to be together.

From my dad's side of the family, the "journey" started when my great-grandfather, Wolf, who was born in Russia in 1869, left the country (using a dead man's passport, whose surname was Kaplan) to avoid 25 years in the army and settled in Durban, initially living on a banana plantation to survive.

Once he had scraped together enough money, he returned to Russia to fetch his wife and child. When the boat docked in Beira, Mozambique, he bought first-class tickets to Durban – if he had bought any other class of ticket, he would have been denied entry back into South Africa. Not being able to speak English, he eked out a meagre living, eventually owning a tearoom in a building called Tinsley House in Musgrave Road. His son Harry, my grandfather, was born in Durban in 1905, and was put through varsity and became a pharmacist. He played rugby for Pirates in Durban and was vice-captain when they won the Wylie Cup. He obtained a gold medal and was top of his year in his final exams at the University of Natal.

On my paternal grandmother's side, Jechiel came to South Africa aged 17, a stowaway in the hold of a ship where many of the refugees subsisted on herring and potatoes for the duration of the three-week journey. Very few of them survived. Jechiel met a South African girl called Hannah and they had five kids, one of whom was my gran, Ida. Hannah's family was from Calitzdorp and were ostrich farmers.

My mom's father, Maurice Ehrlich, was Polish, born in Warsaw in 1911. His entry into South Africa was facilitated by Razelle, who had absconded here with another man, and once she was naturalised, the rest of her clan was allowed into the country. They left a Europe devastated after World War I and arrived in South Africa on the Union Castle line in 1922.

My granny Sonja was born in Ponevezh, Lithuania, in 1922. As a result of the Russian pogroms and rampant anti-Semitism in those days, her family left that country in 1926 on a United Baltic Corporation ship and sailed from Libau to Cape Town via Southampton.

My gran's family spent time in Wolmaransstad in North West province. They were also desperately poor, and as a result, her father became involved in diamond digging. My gran eventually ended up in Doornfontein, opposite Ellis Park Stadium!

My maternal grandparents met in Muizenberg while they were on holiday and settled in Durban, where my grandfather, a book-keeper, eventually became a hotelier. And here is the twist in the story ... out of all the buildings he could have bought in Durban, he bought one called Tinsley House, the same building in which my great-grandfather from my dad's side had had his tearoom!

Who would have thought that nearly half a century later, the descendants of these two families would meet, get married and produce three very good-looking little boys: Jonathan, Gary and David.

Sadly the fairy tale ended in divorce, which proved challenging in my formative years. We were constantly moving around, never staying in one place for more than four years. It was the forerunner of the constantly peripatetic life I would lead further down the track. I only really settled down when I was 35 and moved to Cape Town.

We had already relocated twice by the time my parents got divorced. And soon afterwards we moved again, this time into my grandparents' house in Lonsdale Drive, Durban North, where my mom was raised.

When I was eight, we moved once more, this time because my grandparents wanted a bigger house. We lived in the Riley Road, Berea, house until I was 10. My grandpa Maurice died from leukaemia at Tinsley House, now an old-age home, when he was in his sixties.

I was a super-competitive kid. According to my mom, I was that way from the moment I opened my mouth and worked out how many spoonfuls of food I was prepared to eat, which up until the age of eight was ProNutro and strawberry yoghurt. Whether it was marbles, Monopoly or card games, or playing hand tennis with my buddies, I was always keeping score.

One of my great pleasures was playing chess and cards with my dad. He taught me how to play and never just let me win, but I eventually started beating him fair and square. By the time I was 10, I was good enough at chess to win Natal junior colours and compete in the South African Junior Chess Championships, thereby following in my dad's footsteps.

One of the main themes of my childhood was plenty of opportunity to test the waters. My parents allowed me to try my hand at anything I fancied: tennis at Circle Tennis Club; swimming lengths early in the morning under my dad's watchful eye; karate, where I got my green belt. Eventually, through a process of fun and elimination, I found my niche in cricket and rugby.

Rugby, however, was my first love. I started playing Bumble Bee rugby at Berea Rovers, where I ran around like a wild thing with the other boys all trying to get hold of the ball and afterwards was given an ice cream as a reward for my efforts. The ball seemed more like a brick, but it was great fun.

Being chubby and extremely short – shorter than the shortest girl – I wasn't athletic enough to play in the backline. So I made hooker my position and took to it like a duck to water.

I loved it, because I was always up against someone bigger than me and I relished the challenge. I wasn't stronger than my opponents, but I was a very good striker of the ball and would often win tightheads. Those were the days when the ball used to be fed in straight down the middle ...

Watching club rugby with my dad was how I preferred to spend my Saturday afternoons. Almost every Saturday my dad and I set off for Kings Park to watch a double-header. Club rugby was our Super Rugby. Season tickets in the main grandstand on the halfway line for seats T19 and T20 gave us a gold-circle view. And the group of knowledgeable, die-hard rugby supporters around us educated me. I will never forget those special days, and hope in future to go back and show them how much I've learnt.

Watching Natal play Currie Cup matches at Kings Park was always special, but one of the abiding memories of that time was my first Test match at the ground when I was nine. It was July 1976, and the Boks beat the All Blacks 16-7. I had to sit on a temporary stand consisting of scaffolding and remember how it shook when Gerrie Germishuys ran around Bryan Williams to score a very important try. The ref in that match, Gert Bezuidenhout, would pop into my life during my matric year in a very significant way.

In 1977, my mom announced that she'd met this man called Les and was moving to Johannesburg to be with him. I was playing outside when my parents called me into the lounge to break the news. They sat me down and very matter-of-factly informed me that Gary and David, who were then eight and six respectively, were going to Joburg with my mom. They were not being given a choice in the matter. But they felt I was old enough to decide whether I wanted to go with my mom or stay with my dad.

They told me that I didn't need to make a decision immediately, and that I shouldn't feel as if I would be letting either one of them down, no matter whom I chose to live with. They assured me that they would respect whatever decision I made. I wanted to get back to my game, so I decided right there and then to stay with my dad. I didn't want him to be lonely. My brothers would have my mom and I would have my dad. I also didn't want to leave my school or my friends. But my main reason for staying was that I didn't want to abandon my dad.

There was no trauma attached to this watershed moment. Although I probably should not have been making this decision at 10, I found it quite empowering that my parents were already treating me like a young adult. As it turned out, though, my decision would result in a rather painful experience.

3

Moving on

In the four years I lived with my dad, I learnt to occupy my time. I had had to make a decision way beyond my age, but because I was resourceful, I was going to find a way to cope. I made up my mind to keep busy. I made sure that I had a good time at school and then spent the afternoons with my friends. And when my dad came home, he and I spent time together.

After school, my dad's housekeeper, Beauty, looked after me. Every afternoon she used to make me a snack, and my favourite was fried eggs on toast or peanut-butter sandwiches with a cup of tea. Then I played cricket or hand tennis with my friends in the neighbourhood. I filled my days with the things any normal 10- to 12-year-old would do, and I enjoyed frequent sleepovers at friends' houses.

I remember my lifelong friend Stephan Charnas and I would clear the chairs out of the TV room, put on boxing gloves and smash each other sideways during our usual Tuesday-afternoon play date.

My dad did his best for me as a single parent. He was trying to make a living while also trying to be both a dad and a mom. He did a great job. But there were times when I missed my mother and my brothers. And there was the up and down on the plane between Durban and Joburg as an unaccompanied minor for four years, which challenged me as much as the constant relocations did. There was also the emotional push and pull between my mom and dad, and the subtext of whose way was best.

But generally, I was a happy boy. I loved having TV dinners with my dad, and he spoilt me with Beta videos we'd watch while eating takeaways. I loved TV series like *Hawaii 5.0*, *Petrocelli* and *Charlie's Angels*.

But I especially couldn't wait for Saturdays at Kings Park. This rugby ritual with my dad meant a lot to me. I started dreaming about playing on this hallowed ground one day. First prize would have been for Natal in the

Currie Cup, because that was the big-deal tournament while Bok rugby was in isolation. My other sporting dream was to maybe run Comrades one day. You can't grow up in Durban and not want to run Comrades.

One night at around 4 a.m., my dad got a call from my gran, who said that Harry, my grandpa, was not moving. I was sleeping next to my dad and could sense his panic. He leaned over to me, kissed me and told me not to worry, but he had to go. While driving to my grandparents' house, my dad hit and killed a bird. Later, I thought that the incident symbolised that my grandfather had already passed on.

When my dad got back, he told me the news and then broke down in my arms. It was the first time I saw my dad cry. He sobbed uncontrollably, and for a moment, *I* felt like the dad.

In order to broaden my knowledge of our Jewish heritage, my dad sent me on a camp, called Bnei Akiva, with other Jewish children at the end of the year. Getting there involved a train trip, and at the camp you had to put up your own tent and make your own bed. Breakfast consisted of blue, hard-boiled eggs, and our daily routine was generally to be as naughty as possible in as short a space of time as possible. But we did learn about our heritage and culture, and I got to mix with Jewish people my own age. Three things stand out from that trip:

1. I received R50 in pocket money for the three-week trip and came back with about R180, courtesy of my klaberjass and other card exploits.
2. I made a catastrophic error by rubbing my eyes after putting a healthy dose of mosquito repellent on my body and cannot describe the agony and helpless feeling of not having an adult to help me cope with the pain.
3. And after enduring cold showers for the first two weeks, I decided to abandon that plan and arrived home with a new 'tan' that gave me a decidedly 'Asian' look. It took my dad an hour to wash all the dirt off me, and the colour of the bath water when I was done was nothing short of dark brown.

My dad went on lots of dates, and sometimes his girlfriends slept over (one at a time, of course). But when I was 12, my dad, who was then 38, met Terry, a 24-year-old woman from Joburg. It was love at first sight. My dad is one of the most conservative, cautious people I know, but after three dates, he proposed to Terry on New Year's Eve. She took her time to accept – all of 48 hours! They are still together to this day, 35 years later.

My first birthday

Grade 1 schoolboy

I made my debut playing Bumble Bee rugby at Berea Rovers

Cross-dressing? Not really, I was dressed up for a play for the Jewish festival of Purim

My dad's wedding to Terry in 1978. That's me on the left, next to Terry, with David in front of my dad and Gary on the right

My bar mitzvah in November 1979

Graduation at UCT in 1989

My touch-rugby team in the early 90s. We actually won this tournament!

Managing UCT at the Varsity Under-20 Rugby Champs in Durban in 1990

Still looking fresh at Camperdown 70 kilometres into the 1994 Comrades

My first Rugby World Cup experience was as a young, enthusiastic spectator in my home country in 1995, when the incomparable Jonah Lomu set the rugby world alight

On touch in the game where David made his first-class debut for Natal against the Leopards. What a special occasion!

One of the few times I got to wear a green and gold jersey as a ref. Argentina vs England A at Franklin's Gardens, Northampton

Posing with Willie the Whistle, Tappe Henning and Ian Rogers before England played Argentina at Twickenham in 1997. It was the first time I got to wear my Test blazer

With Johan Meeuwesen, Bobby Cazaneve and Ian Rogers in Argentina for a series against England, 7 June 1997

Three of the smallest chests in front of the mighty Mount Aconcagua, Argentina, 1997

With Fijian Waisale Serevi, the greatest rugby Sevens player ever

Kelvin Deaker, Carl Spannenberg and me on a fine day in Hamilton, New Zealand

Having dinner with Giulio di Santis, Mark Lawrence and Phil Botha in Rome in February 2000 before the first ever Six Nations match

Bledisloe! My brothers David and Gary trying to blend in with the All Black crowd in Wellington, New Zealand, 5 August 2000

Ed Morrison wishing me good luck before the Test between New Zealand and Australia in 2000

Soaking it all up after the match

Terry gave birth to twin baby girls in the two years that followed, and I developed a few issues with my dad, who now had to split his time between his new wife, their babies and me. Terry was thrown in at the deep end, having to cope with a new stepson, who at 12 was growing up fast, two babies and a new husband. This caused a bit of friction in the household. My dad really wanted his marriage to work, and I didn't blame him. But something had to give. He put a lot of time and energy into his relationship with Terry, and I began to feel marginalised, especially after having had him all to myself for those first two years.

I didn't blame anyone for what happened. As I said, my dad and Terry are still married – they were meant to be together. They loved me and it was never their intention to hurt me. I nevertheless felt very sad and lonely at the time.

I also felt disappointed that my dad was not able to sense my level of unhappiness and do something about it. Unfortunately I wasn't able to talk to him about how I felt and, for two years, the pressure built. Then one morning the dam burst.

The moment came on 22 November 1980, the first anniversary of my Bar Mitzvah. I was close to breaking point. That Saturday morning, my dad was at work. I was downstairs studying for my last exam when my mom called to find out how I was. We made small talk for a while, but she sensed my unhappiness. She asked if I wanted to come and live with her and my brothers in Joburg, and I just cracked and burst into tears. And in an instant I made a decision. I had reached the edge emotionally. I loved my dad. My dad had been everything in my life. But it was time to move on.

My mom promised that she would fly to Durban to pick me up from school on the Monday. But instead, on the day, my dad arrived in his Valiant. The 10-kilometre drive home was one of the most emotionally draining moments of my life. He kept telling me, "I wish you had told me; I wish we had spoken about it." And I kept replying, "You never listened to me. In all the time I wanted to say it, you never listened to me."

For the rest of the way there was just a stifling silence. And a sadness that this was the end of a chapter. Me sitting in the back of my dad's car wishing I had been able to talk to him about my pain. Wishing I had been able to confront the things that had been making me angry and sad.

Part of me wanted to talk more in the car, but there was really nothing to say. The decision had been made. I just wanted my mom to fetch me so that we could leave.

4

A humble beginning

Reuniting with my brothers was hugely emotional. Although it felt strange initially, things were once again the way they were supposed to be – all of us together, united under one roof.

My mom wanted me to attend King David Linksfield with my brothers. But because of my late enrolment, I got shoved into a Standard 7 (Grade 9) class, where I felt completely out of place. I didn't let it get me down, though.

Although I wasn't the best chess player on the team, I won colours and captained a side that was always at the top of the Southern Transvaal schools' log. I had a passion for the game and spent hours alone in my room playing against myself on the computer. I also won colours for service to the school, which was a forerunner of things to come, where I would commit huge chunks of my time serving the game of rugby.

I played cricket and soccer at King David, and although I wasn't particularly good at either of them, I considered myself a decent all-rounder and always contributed 100 per cent.

As in primary school, rugby remained my passion. But although I played right up until matric, it gradually sunk in that I wasn't big enough to make it as a player in any position. Right through high school I felt I was a small boy among growing men.

It's tradition at King David to watch the senior team play after finishing the other matches, and from the sidelines I became aware that the first team always needed a linesman. So I took the gap and volunteered to run touch for them. From Standard 8 onwards I was always there, the bloke in his blazer and tie running touch for the first team. Although I wasn't *in* the first team, I was part of the first-team environment and close to all the action.

Generally, I was happy at King David, although I subscribed to the principle that if you sacrificed yourself to any clique, you were automatically beholden to it. I didn't want to be beholden to anyone other than myself, so I stayed on the periphery, preferring to mind my own business. That way I maintained a wide circle of friends and avoided being sucked in by the different cliques that tended to form in high school.

One of my greatest disappointments at school was when I was not nominated to be a prefect. It was something I thought I could do really well, and it hurt when my name was not on the nominees' list for our year.

To me it seemed as if my true worth had gone unnoticed. It turned out to be one of the key moments in my life, as I resolved right there and then that I would succeed in whatever I set out to do, and I would do so on the highest platform for as long as I could. No matter that others were blind or oblivious to my qualities, *I* knew what I was capable of.

Come valedictory night, I was awarded a trophy for service to the school. For me, it was their way of acknowledging my contribution to King David.

In matric, I finally drew a line in the sand with my stepfather, Les, who had, up until then, been distinctly inadequate as a stepfather.

Although he never tried to bully me emotionally, he did press my buttons. One night at his parents' house, where we were observing Shabbat, matters came to a head. I can't remember exactly what he said to me, but it was something confrontational. Instead of just taking it, like I had so many times before, I snapped. I challenged what he had just said, and when he didn't respond, I got up and stormed out, making it clear that I didn't give a damn about the consequences.

It took a great deal of personal courage to confront an adult in an adult environment. It was a moment when thinking and talking morphed into taking action. It was the moment where I declared: "I will not take your shit any more."

In that moment, I stood up for my brothers and myself. They later told me how proud they were of me.

By that time I was 17 and had been reffing men twice my age for a while, so I had some experience exercising my authority. I had my mom to thank for that, because she had opened the door that would change my life forever.

It started with a broken nose in Standard 9, when I was playing scrumhalf for the third team against Athlone High. I got the ball from the back of the ruck, made a break and then got held up. I was facing the wrong way, but my legs were still pumping forward. The next thing I knew, someone had clocked me on the hooter – a good target, given my ethnic background – and blood was spurting out. I finished the game with my nose somewhere on my cheek.

Later, when my mom came to fetch me, she said that it was the last time she was taking me for X-rays. She suggested that because I enjoyed running touch, I should give reffing a try. I said fine, but she must set it up. I didn't feel like making any arrangements or phone calls.

Convinced it was the way to go, my mom set the wheels in motion early in my matric year when she informed me that she had called Ellis Park and got a number for Gert Bezuidenhout, the bloke who had reffed the first Test I'd watched at Kings Park. After hanging up his whistle, he had become the chairman of the Transvaal Referees Society.

My mom told me that when she called Gert's office, they thought *she* wanted to become a referee. They told her that they didn't accept women. When she informed them that the appointment was for her 17-year-old son, they said I was too young to be a referee. But, typical of my mom, she convinced them to give me a chance.

Accompanied by one of her fashion-world friends, Steven Rich, my mom navigated her way nervously to Rosettenville, where the referees' meeting was being held. It was getting dark and she was unfamiliar with the south of Johannesburg, which she perceived as being dodgy.

We eventually reached our destination without mishap and I went inside and introduced myself. I was attending my first ever referees' meeting! I felt a bit like a fish out of water with all the premier-division refs dominating the floor and discussing all sorts of laws and applications. And I really stuck out. I had turned 17 just three months earlier and looked even younger than that. And I was still small compared to my peers.

Of all the guys in the room, only one was youngish. He introduced himself as Ian Anderson and immediately took me under his wing. Ian was in his twenties and had just finished varsity. He immediately struck me as an intelligent, switched-on bloke.

After the meeting, Gert walked me back to the gloomy parking lot, where my mom was waiting with Steven. She started the car but I told her to wait, as Gert wanted to talk to her. Gert chatted away, telling my mom he thought I had what it took to make a good referee, and that he would start me in my first match the following month. He advised her to buy me a law book to study. And then he told her what a mom would like to hear: "Your son will be a Test referee one day."

I don't think any of this meant much to Gert at the time. He had no idea how I would pan out. I think he was just making conversation and being polite. But it resonated with my mom. As we drove off, she turned to me and said, "One day you will ref at Twickenham, my boy."

"Mom," I replied, "if I ever get to ref a Test match at Twickenham, I promise you, I will kiss you *on* the field."

5

The first game

It was a month after I had signed up as a fully fledged member of the Transvaal Referees Society. I'd studied my law book and there I finally was, all 5 foot 8 of me, a 17-year-old teenager still writing matric, reffing 30 okes, some of whom were old enough to be my father.

The match itself was nothing to write home about. Wits versus Kempton Park was typical of most fourth-league encounters: a bunch of guys out to blow off some steam on the park. There was nothing elegant or sublime about it.

The students won 23-7, but what stands out about 24 March 1984 more than anything about the game was that I was the most excited person on the field. My mom had given me a lift to the ground, and I arrived not knowing whom to greet, where to change, what protocols to observe, where to handle the toss or even which field we would be playing on. But I didn't lack confidence!

The cherry on the cake came after the game, from a Wits player who made a point of engaging with me. "I just wanted to say that you are the best ref we have ever had," he told me. "I know you're young, but just keep it up ..."

Even though they were playing against each other, the players had banded together to help me achieve the best possible outcome – or so it had seemed, anyway. My debut could have been a blowout. It could easily have been such a nightmare start that it discouraged me completely. But instead it was a landmark game that came complete with a sign ... something was telling me, "Just keep going, *boet*, just keep going."

I refereed 15 games in my first year of reffing. I was starting out at the bottom, in the fourth league, where most of the players were dirt trackers, old-timers, part-timers, and blokes who couldn't or wouldn't train any more. They were there for a Saturday run-around and afterwards a few beers in the pub to wash away their troubles.

I may have looked like a 12-year-old without a hairbrush, but I was learning fast. Wanderers against Edenvale was a good case in point. Within 10 minutes, I had six players in the bin, every one of them for a damn good reason. It was one of those afternoons where everyone was letting out their frustrations. Very quickly I drew a line in the sand. They weren't taking me seriously. Clearly, they underestimated me. It took six yellows until the penny finally dropped. Then they settled down and we had a fairly decent game of rugby.

Watching all this from the sidelines was none other than Hugh Bladen, the former Transvaal and Junior Springbok flyhalf who would go on to become a renowned TV commentator. After lunch and a few beers at the Wanderers Club, he and his buddies strolled across to my patch. I must have made an impression. Hugh would tell his mates in later years, when I was making a name for myself, that Wanderers was where he had first spotted Jonathan Kaplan – laying down the law.

I reffed Police and Jeppe at Arthur Bloch Park in Mayfair. The men were all working class and blue collar, but they embraced me, the Jewish kid from the affluent northern suburbs, because they recognised that I was there to facilitate a good afternoon of rugby. I like mixing with people from all cultures and backgrounds, and the few beers I was able to enjoy in the pub afterwards helped round off a good run and a job well done. Like she often did, my gran was filling in for my mom, who was working that day. She also didn't like driving the dark, unfamiliar streets and was out of her comfort zone. By the time she arrived to pick me up, I was mildly pissed. I reached the car trying my hardest to act like I was sober. My gran, to her credit, didn't bat an eyelid. How many other league refs had to be taken to their matches by their mothers or grans?

Reffing had become a hobby, but I was taking it very seriously. I knew that I had an aptitude for scanning a field, comprehending a situation, discerning right from wrong, and helping to create a good spectacle. It was fun and re-warding, but I was also sensing that perhaps this was something I could take to the next level.

At the end of 1984, I matriculated with distinctions in history and geog-raphy. I felt as if I'd lived a sheltered Jewish life, so instead of going to varsity, I decided to do my obligatory two-year national service with the idea of broadening my cultural horizons and allowing myself some time for self-discovery. It didn't quite work out as planned. I encountered a fair amount of anti-Semitism and racism in the army, which I found repulsive. The years 1985 and 1986 were not a very progressive period in my life and did not shed any light on what I would like to do next.

But army life was not without its seminal moments. While undergoing basic training, we were required to go to the range for target practice. I was useless. I didn't want anything to do with the military in general, and killing specifically, so I shot my bullets at a variety of "alternative" targets. My score was 46 out of a possible 120 – I was the third worst shot in the whole group. I was thrilled. The guy next to me got 117 out of 120, and he was thrilled too. He got a *baaltjie* for his efforts.

I was fortunate that I was treated differently from the other troops, primarily because I was a rugby ref and had to "work" every Wednesday or sports day. Sometimes, as the day wore on, the heat got more oppressive and the drinks in the bar tastier, my seniors would ask me to ref their games too. Sometimes I would referee three games in a row.

In addition to defence-force leagues, I was reffing Tukkies *koshuis* matches and a range of army and air-force championships. And I was loving it. The more I reffed, the more I realised that I had to grow, I had to get scars, I had to learn to communicate better with players and manage situations differently.

At one of these games, the Air Defence Week in Dunottar, I saw one of the worst injuries ever. A wing, who had run down the touchline, was tackled into touch and, as the players rolled over each other, the flag, which had been stuck into the ground with a spike, was dislodged and found its way through the back of the wing's left knee – in the one side and out the other. The bloke was in agony, and even I could barely look at the wound without feeling sick. All I could say was, "*Vasbyt, tjom!*" However, it wasn't enough to deter him from a few drinks later that night at the "dance". The wonder of modern drugs, or the bravado of a great war wound?

On top of my defence-force responsibilities, I still managed to find the time and energy on some Wednesdays to shoot through to King David, ref a junior game and then watch the first team. On one particular Wednesday I was reffing King David under-15A, with my brother David playing hooker (much like his older brother). David was always extremely respectful of me and never used our relationship to gain any favours. He also discouraged his teammates who wanted to manipulate the old-boy connection. Jonathan will never screw us, he told them, but he will also penalise us every time we break the law.

After reffing that match, I moved across to watch the King David firsts play. But the ref didn't pitch, so they asked me to stand in. Greenside, with, if I recall correctly, James Small on the wing, were leading when King David hit back, against the run of play, to score two tries and reduce the lead to eight. A King David player went down injured in the last minute with the score at 18-10, and the coach – a Mr Viljoen, I think – took the opportunity to chance his arm with me.

"Come on, Johnny," he urged. "Just give us a few more minutes."

I looked at him, cocked my eyebrow and allowed for a pregnant pause. I blew the final whistle straight after the conversion.

Gradually, as my two years of national service rolled on, I developed a reffing philosophy with three basic principles: judgement, flair and nerve.

Judgement is the ability to understand the law, and to tell right from wrong.

Flair is the ability to add colour to a game, and it involves player management, emotional intelligence or EQ, communication and non-verbal skills. Those skills include excellent preparation. Flair will determine whether players walk back down the tunnel saying that it had been a good game or a great game. Flair is the ability to squeeze the pips out of the lemon so that you give players the best possible environment to exhibit their skills. The more risks one takes, the greater the ability to create something special.

Nerve is something you can't teach. Nerve is a trait in individuals who can act under pressure. You often find players who are able to reach a certain level but can't go any further because the pressure is too great. The same applies to refs. Some people feel comfortable in a challenging environment, others panic.

Reffing also required a decent level of fitness. And at that point, I was the fittest I'd ever been. Not just because of basic training and lots of reffing, but because I had discovered road running towards the end of 1985. Me, the chubby little hooker, could now pound the road. And, like reffing, I was loving it.

In the last two months of 1985 I ran six races of between 15 and 32 kilometres. In 1986, I went ballistic and ran 44 more races, including eight marathons and ultras.

By the time I wound up my national service, two of my sporting dreams were coming into sharp focus. One of them was the Currie Cup. I wasn't going to play it. But bursting with pride over my promotion to third league at the end of 1986, I was beginning to believe that I had what it took to ref in that league one day.

The other was running Comrades. It's a long, long way to run. But I was loving road running so much that by the time I enrolled for a Bachelor of Business Science degree at the University of Cape Town (UCT) in 1987, it wasn't a question of *maybe* running Comrades, but *when*.

6

Varsity

I was pacing up and down the touchline like a frustrated bull terrier that couldn't get to the dogs on the other side of the fence. I was imploring my boys to tackle, defend, tackle ... Then, against the run of play, we scored a try and took the lead.

I could barely contain myself. The match was well into the second half, and if we could just hang on to our lead, Oslers, UCT's under-19B side, were still in the hunt for the league trophy.

It was going to take a massive effort. We were playing Defence at Silvermine, and compared to *my* boys, they were brutes. It was David versus Goliath. But my players were special, a rag-tag bunch who had grown to believe in themselves and the team. We had to use whatever competitive advantage we could find and lever that against something very traditional in order to achieve results. I used a bit of amateur psychology, telling the men that no other team wanted them, so we became a tightly knit unit that realised our best chance for glory lay in the realm of passion, opportunity and a deep-seated drive to prove our worth.

I recognised that in order to beat teams that were bigger and stronger than us, we would have to use two other factors to win: fitness and desire. Other teams had players with better pedigrees, but we tackled them into submission, fuelled by the desire to succeed. I ensured that the group was always present and suffering together, whether it was during general fitness sessions or "koppestamp".*

---

* A shortened version of a game where players get the opportunity to test themselves physically in a role-playing situation.

27

We took our more illustrious opponents out of their comfort zones and straight into the realms where we were strongest. My gut feel was that most of our boys had a story, and when they recognised it in one another's eyes, they played well above themselves.

And with silverware in their sights, they were playing out of their skins. Beat Defence and it was just two more wins to lifting the trophy for the first time ever in the Western Province (WP) under-19B league's 38-year history.

With eight minutes to go, Nick Davies, who played flank at Michaelhouse, went over to seal our historic win. This try followed an astonishing performance in which our players had been pushed off the ball at every scrum and had made three times as many tackles as our opponents, but still managed to subdue the gargantuan Defence team. Later, my captain Ashley Kantor told me that when Davies crashed over, he felt Silvermine Mountain shake, almost as if the gods were expressing their joy.

I was so proud of these players. The names Formby, Wepener, Allen, Becker, McDonald, Wood, Kantor, Fish, Old, Whitmill, *et al.* may mean nothing to the greater rugby fraternity, but they will always have a special place in my heart.

In search of a new rugby challenge, I had started coaching the Oslers part-time in 1988, my second year at UCT. That season we were what the Oslers had always been: plain bloody average. Then, the following season, the boys had started playing for one another and believing in the mantra that together we could achieve something special.

I'd like to credit it to my coaching, but I have to put my hand up and confess that I was pretty clueless. Even though I had completed my level-one and level-two coaching courses, I didn't have the skills or the experience to be a good coach. In fact, without the help of Dr Cecil Moss, I probably would not have passed my level-two course!

All I was was a coordinator, motivator and bullshitter. My biggest skill was fishing players out of bars and getting them to practice. Getting them fit and battle hardened.

Several of the players knew their limitations but still wanted to play just for sheer love of the game. And that's all you could ask for at that level. Like Barry Whitmill. The spirit of the team was embodied in a player who wasn't deemed good enough initially, but who, through dedication, perseverance and massive output, displayed the qualities that the team would need to achieve its potential. As we chased the trophy, this motley crew proved to me that the passion to play rugby could sometimes count for more than school pedigree. At this level, if you were fit and focused and had that glint in your eye, there was every chance of success.

And my players had exactly those qualities. They won their last two matches and the league was ours. Later, at the Western Province Annual Awards dinner, I reminded myself that I always had to be honest about this moment – that I was not a coach. Certainly not one fit to sit at the same table as the UCT's first-team coaches Alan Solomons and Gus Enderstein, or the legendary Dr Cecil Moss.

Although sport took up a lot of my time, I had also enrolled at UCT in 1987 to obtain a Bachelor of Business Science degree. But I didn't enjoy maths and stats, so the following year I switched to BA Social Science, majoring in economics and psychology. Later, I topped that up with a postgraduate diploma from UNISA in marketing management.

I was particularly lazy on the academic side of university life. I enjoyed the carefree days far too much, and I often found myself in trouble when exam time arrived. A case in point was Economics II in 1988, where I needed 71 per cent to pass the final exam. I realised I would have to put in an all-nighter, and a friend recommended that I take a dietary supplement called Thinz to keep me awake. I worked through the night, took a little refresher before the exam, and passed. I do remember, however, that I found it extraordinarily difficult to fall asleep that night.

Out on the rugby field, I was also gaining refereeing experience in the third league, this time as a Western Province Referees Society ref. In my first year at UCT, I also reffed under-20s and UCT's internal league and got my first taste of reffing Sevens rugby. By the end of 1988, I was promoted to the second league. The next year I was invited to join the UCT Rugby Club Committee, where I met the administrator and under-19A coach, Rob Wagner, a former Villagers captain and flank. We forged a strong friendship that continued long after I graduated.

During my two-year tenure as res rugby coordinator, I had one of the most embarrassing moments of my life. At the end of 1989, I was in a committee meeting where we decided to award Robbie Brink, who would go on to play flank for the victorious Springboks at the 1995 Rugby World Cup (RWC), the most improved player of the year gong.

I left the meeting to go and visit my brother David in res, where we bumped into Robbie. He informed us that he was too busy studying for exams to attend the awards dinner. After basically telling him that he was getting the award, he decided to come.

But when they announced the winner at the dinner, the award went to Paul Johnson instead. I was absolutely gobsmacked. And incredibly embarrassed.

After the ceremony I asked Rob Wagner how he could have done that to me, and he explained that they had changed their decision after I'd left the meeting. Robbie laughed it off and never held it against me. But for some reason I have not been able to shake that memory. Whenever I see Robbie, I cringe with embarrassment.

In 1990, my final year at varsity, I reached a milestone when I ended the season as a first-league ref. It was a proud moment. It had taken me just seven long seasons to achieve that status.

And having the opportunity to ref my *boet* David made my graduation year even more memorable. By now he was good enough to play hooker for Province's under-20 probables against the possibles at UCT.

David was going well, but in the final trial match before selection, it broke my heart to see him going down injured towards the end of the first half. I could tell that he was in pain and unsure about his leg. But I told him to get up; I didn't want anyone thinking he was a "soft Yid". So I said, "David, you've got two minutes left and one more scrum, so just try to run it off. Get up, get up!" I wanted him to show the others that he was tough enough for this level of rugby.

David got up and scrummed one more time. When I blew the half-time whistle, I noticed him hobbling off. Later scans showed a torn anterior cruciate ligament, which required surgery. Sadly, David never cracked that level again for Province. But I did get to be a part of his finest hour, halfway through the 1990s, one that still means a lot to the Kaplan family.

In 1988 I finally realised one of my big dreams and ran Comrades in the colours of UCT. The next year, I repeated the feat. I can't describe how it felt to accomplish a dream I had nurtured for so many years. All the training (well, not *that* much training, actually), all the suffering, came to a head when I finished that first race. It was one of the greatest feelings ever. When I climbed that last little hill on entering the stadium in Pietermaritzburg, the tears just started running down my cheeks. And then I heard my dad, who was waiting patiently for me among the masses, shout, "Well done, my boykie!" That snapped me – I turned into a blubbering mess. Ninety kilometres in 9 hours 40 minutes. I LOVED it!

I thought I might add that I beat South African and world ultra-marathon legend Wally Hayward home. He was previously undefeated and had won the race five times. Perhaps I should also add that he was 77 when I beat him! He attempted the race again the next year, and he made it with a few minutes to spare before the gun went off. For me, his was one of the greatest sporting achievements that I have witnessed.

Make no mistake, I was by no means a good runner. In fact, I was a bit of a plodder, but I nevertheless ended up as the captain of the UCT Road Running Club for two years. In 1990 I was also made manager of UCT's athletics team for the intervarsity championships at Rand Afrikaans University, which was a lot of fun.

I'm a bit embarrassed to admit this, but there was only one time in my life where I felt I had trained really well – at the back end of 1990, as I was finishing varsity life. Throughout my running career, and, indeed, my life, I'd got by by doing the bare minimum. However, during this period I smashed all my personal bests with the help of some of my more talented – and hard-working – running friends. My 37:30 for 10 kilometres and 56:57 for 15 kilometres were probably the standout achievements of an otherwise pretty average running career.

I was feeling the fittest I'd ever felt. When the 1990 Winelands Marathon came round, I was confident enough to attempt a sub-three-hour run. It is one of the tougher Cape marathons, but everything was going according to plan. Until the 35-kilometre mark, when I ran one hill too hard and hit the wall. My legs turned to jelly and every step was a mission. Eventually I was reduced to walking the final three kilometres. I still managed to cross the finish line in 3:09. But it was bitter-sweet, because I knew I'd blown the chance to run a sub-three. I was so finished, I collapsed on the grass. It was the first time I ever ended a race so blown. It was not a pretty sight ...

When I graduated at the end of 1990, I packed everything I owned into my trusty little white Daihatsu Charade, which my brother had won in a King David raffle. My mom gave it to me, because I had just got my licence. The ± 140 000 kilometres on the clock showed it had served me well.

As I left the mountain behind me on the N1, I knew that this was the end of a major chapter in my life. I had loved UCT, which, with its awesome history and special character, had provided me with the perfect springboard to continue my journey. I had forged friendships there that would last me a lifetime, and I had enjoyed my rugby, my running and my social life. Oh, yes, and I got a degree ...

But I had a strong feeling that I was not leaving Cape Town forever. I didn't know when or how I was going to return; I just knew that I would.

7

Another level up

I could not have packed more into my four years at UCT if I tried. It was massively rewarding ...

But I did take my eye off the ball in my final year when it came to securing a job. So when I arrived in Joburg in January 1991, I was playing catch-up. Although work was supposed to be plentiful, it took me six months to land a decent job at Afcom, a packaging company, in the south of the city.

Things didn't get off to a good start on the field either. My new bosses at the Transvaal Referees Society decided that they needed to assess my reffing before they entrusted me with any first-league games, so I had to revert to blowing second league for a while. That was how the system worked in those days, and it frustrated me, as I felt more than capable. But I went with the flow and after a few matches the society that gave me my first break deemed me worthy to blow first league.

That first year turned out to be a good testing ground for my resolve. By then I was aware that there was a considerable amount of thuggery in Transvaal club rugby, but it took me a few games before I got my first real taste of it, with Randfontein at home to Wits.

Randfontein was a mining-town club with a proud rugby tradition. But they were still coming to terms with the new South Africa and its approaching democracy when Wits arrived with a multiracial team of dynamic young players who were starting to make a name for themselves.

Determined to teach the "communist students" a rugby lesson they wouldn't forget, Randfontein bossed their way to an 18-3 lead before their old legs started to tire against the much younger students.

As Randfontein's frustrations mounted, so, too, did the penalties, which got slotted one after the other by the sharp-shooter boot of Wits fullback Gavin Lawless, who was destined for higher honours.

At 18-12, Wits scored a try and converted to go 18-all. Then they got another penalty to go 21-18 up. In the final 15 minutes of the game, the students scored another converted try and looked like they would easily hold on to their 27-18 lead. Then things got out of hand.

With about 10 minutes to go, Randfontein's No. 8 knocked out the Wits flank for being offside. I had no choice but to show the culprit a red card. So I was completely astonished when the several-thousand-strong home crowd gave the bloke a standing ovation as he left the field!

After that, the whole mood of the game shifted. Realising they were not going to win it fair and square, Randfontein resorted to blatant thuggery. I considered calling off the game, but I didn't think that was what the students wanted.

To their credit, Wits refused to be bullied. I heard their forwards captain, Robbie Wray, one of the smallest guys on the field, urging his guys to be brave and stand together against the onslaught. But they lost two more players before the final whistle. One, John Cunningham, got hit so hard in the mouth that his lip instantly inflated to the size of a tennis ball. John McCarthy, a talented flyhalf from King Edward VII School, also had to go off after being *klapped*.

As I blew the final whistle and walked off the field, I was very aware of the hostile environment. Then Wits captain Ashley Shafto said something that made me realise I had naively underestimated just how intimidating the pitch had become.

"Don't worry, Jonathan," he said while walking next to me in a protective manner. "Just keep walking. I've got your back." Unfortunately the atmosphere didn't improve after the match. When Randfontein wouldn't allow Wits's black manager into their pub, the students quite rightly kicked up a stink and left in protest. By then I had also had enough, and I, too, left in disgust.

One of the good things about returning to the Transvaal Referees Society was that I was reunited with my friend Ian Anderson, who had worked his way up the ladder and was now a highly rated provincial referee. Thanks to him being in the right place at the right time, I got my first taste of provincial rugby, even though I was still reffing club rugby and was only ranked number eight out of the 10 first-league refs in Transvaal.

When Ian received his green-and-gold blazer, a lunch was held in his honour. By then he was the premier referee in the province and well respected by the rugby hierarchy, including Transvaal rugby supremo Louis Luyt. During the lunch, Luyt told Ian that his Transvaal number-three ref, Jan Senekal, had hurt his hamstring and he needed to replace him for Northern Transvaal B against Western Province B at Newlands. Without missing a beat, Ian said, "Send Jonathan."

Luyt being Luyt, the decision was made there and then and I got the call. I didn't have a clue why I got to be the lucky one. I was thinking, "I'm only number eight; there are a whole bunch of more experienced guys above me, so maybe they think I've got potential."

Whatever their logic, I was incredibly excited to be given my first opportunity to ref a Currie Cup curtain-raiser in a legendary rugby stadium in front of a big crowd. The match was also a bit of a homecoming for me, as the Province side, coached by Alan Zondagh, contained quite a few former UCT players who had played when I was coaching. Guys like Robbie Brink, Tank Lanning and Bishops prodigy Michael Ehrentraut, a great player who, despite having heaps of talent, never made it to the big league. The sensational, hard-tackling centre Tinus Linee, who would later win Bok colours, was a beast on defence, knocking himself out on one occasion with his kamikaze tackling.

Northern Transvaal B also had some serious players: Johan Roux, Chris Rossouw and Conrad Breytenbach would all later go on to become internationals, and there were several others who would become Bulls legends.

Without a doubt this was a huge step up from the first-league club games that I was used to. These were serious rugby players that I would be reffing. But Newlands was empty when I ran on. There were, like, three people and a dog in the stands.

However, all that was quickly forgotten as I got caught up in the intensity of reffing my first big one. In fact, I was so focused on the game that I didn't even register the stadium filling up to capacity. So much so that when I blew the final whistle, I was surprised by the massive cheer that went up.

What lingered about that game was the feeling of a job well done. The Transvaal Referees Society had sent one of their lieutenants, committee member Alwyn Vortmann, to babysit and rate me. He scored me 80 out of 100 and concluded his assessment with the following remark: "A game really well refereed. On this showing, Jonathan deserves another chance."

But it was Paul Dobson's report that meant a lot to me. As the chairman of the WP Referees Society, he voluntarily decided to evaluate my performance, and he was generous with his praise.

"Dear Jonathan, it was good to have you back in the Western Province. I could see that the members felt quite a bit of pride that you were back here and that you did well. You did referee well and it was a good match. You gave the guys a chance to play ... you clearly have a good career ahead of you."

In addition to recognising an element of my repertoire that I pride myself on, Paul also listed seven points that he thought would be of use to me in future. The one I found most interesting concerned my interpretation of the advantage law.

"Your advantage was a bit like a curate's egg. Good in parts, though at times you stretched it too far and at other times you were too quick. Your judgement of advantage needs careful thought. On the other hand, I was also pleased that you did not waste people's time waiting for advantage when the other team was on desperate defence ..."

Paul was a perceptive student of the game. Striking the right balance when I played advantage was the one aspect of refereeing that challenged me, and it would continue to demand my attention in the years ahead. I still have Paul's assessment report.

I must have ticked the right boxes, because I was given two more top-level games in 1992: Transvaal under-20 against Western Transvaal under-20, and Free State B, featuring one of my favourite hookers, Wessel Lightfoot, versus Natal B, where Joel Stransky and Hugh Reece-Edwards ran the show.

The following year the trend continued and I notched up my debut first-class match when I reffed Eastern Province (EP) against the SA Barbarians at Ellis Park in the M-Net Night Series. Some big names in that encounter were Garth Wright, the fulcrum of the EP side, James Dalton for the Barbarians, with Allister Coetzee at scrumhalf.

Before the game, while trying to gain access to the dressing room of the players, one of the EP players told me that the ball-boys' changing room was around the corner. I was small and short, but never before had I been confused for a ball boy!

Eastern Province were leading comfortably at 24-12 with four minutes to go when the Barbarians got a penalty, which was fired over by Police flyhalf Jackie Krause. I'd reffed him often in club matches and was aware that he had a cannon of a boot.

At 24-15, the Barbarians took the ball up after the kick-off and went through so many phases I lost count, eventually scoring a try close to full time. Krause converted to make it 24-22 with just a few seconds on the clock.

The Barbarians managed to master the kick-off again, moving up all the way to the halfway line. But no matter how hard they battered away, EP stalled them there. Then suddenly the ball came back to Krause, who slotted a monster drop in excess of 50 metres to win the game in dramatic fashion.

I was given two more first-class games in 1993. One was Northern Transvaal B against Western Province B at Loftus, where the Bulls exacted revenge for the previous year's defeat. And the other was Northern Universities and SA Barbarians in a curtain-raiser for the Springboks versus France Test at Loftus, where everyone bought into the spirit of the game and the crowd got dished up a fantastic 60-46 feast of rugby.

As much as I was enjoying this introduction to the top tier, ironically it was a club-rugby match that stole the show in 1993. Roodepoort, in a pre-season warm-up, were playing at home against Old Greys, the champion Free State club coached by former Springbok flank Klippies Kritzinger.

With 20 minutes to go, Roodepoort, captained by the notorious apartheid hit-squad member Calla Botha (who, incidentally, was always very nice to me), were comfortably leading 41-16. Then, all of a sudden, things clicked for Old Greys and they went on a try-scoring rampage – half a dozen of them – until they were 47-41 up with just two minutes to go.

Roodepoort, however, got their mojo back and scored a converted try to clinch the match by a single point. Kritzinger, who was close to tears, came to me after the game and said it was one of the best games he had ever been involved in. It was a special match, as it contained some razzle-dazzle rugby, a comeback of note, a dramatic ending and was played in fine spirit. Plus it had almost reduced a Springbok legend to tears! For me, those elements were much more important than any prestige associated with an appointment.

8

Memorable games

I had a very different interaction with Roodepoort later in the season. They were at home to a talented Pirates outfit coached by former Transvaal eighth-man Kenny Smit.

The game was going along swimmingly when suddenly Roodepoort turned ugly. In the side were Calla Botha and Calla Barnard, and their hit-squad colleague Ferdi Barnard, who would later confess to the 1989 assassination of anti-apartheid lawyer and activist David Webster. Also in the side was bouncer-turned-hitman Nigel McGurk, a friend of mine who, years later, would be implicated in the killing of mining magnate Brett Kebble.

One thing led to another and Roodepoort started picking up some yellow cards, then one, two, three red cards. The last was for Calla Barnard. I didn't see him take out the opposing hooker as the scrum broke up, but my touch judge fingered him. An old bloke from the fourth league, he reported Barnard for punching and headbutting. By then the game had turned into one of the most intimidating rugby matches I'd ever experienced – and probably ever will. It had already crossed my mind several times that the moment would come when I would have to abandon the game, but that was the last resort, so instead I showed Barnard a red.

The crowd was giving the touch judge a hard time, which pissed me off, because blokes like him gave up their time so that players could have an enjoyable game of rugby. After the match I checked in with him and told him I had no reason to doubt his judgement, but that he had to be sure of his facts because he was going to be grilled at Barnard's disciplinary hearing. To his credit, the old guy stood his ground.

Barnard approached me after the game and said the touch judge had made a "*kak*" decision, that he was innocent, scout's honour. In all my dealings with

Barnard he'd been as respectful as he was then. I wasn't made aware of his reputation until years later, but I didn't think knowing would have made any difference to how I handled him. I told him there and then that I hadn't seen anything because I was following the ball, but I had no reason not to believe my touch judge.

Later Kenny Smit commended me for holding my nerve. "Jonathan, you are the first ref to ever stand your ground here, and today was one of the most intimidating environments I have ever been in. Well done. I take my hat off to you."

Surprisingly, I also got support from Roodepoort chairman Lodie Toerien, who, in his post-match speech, addressed the elephant in the room head-on. "There are a couple of people here who want to point the finger at you, Jonathan. But I want to stand up as chairman and say I thought you had a good game. I want to thank you for your contribution this afternoon."

That, for me, signified true leadership. Here was a guy prepared to confront the ugly truth that his players had gone way beyond their mandate and needed to be reined in. In spite of what Lodie said, however, Roodepoort sowed doubt in the touch judge's mind by telling him that he was old and blind and out of his league.

But Pirates had an ace up their sleeve: they had recorded the game. So there it was as clear as daylight for all on the disciplinary committee to see. Roodepoort were taken to task, vindicating not just the touch judge's call but each and every one of the red cards I had handed out.

Often, though, tough calls in club games were not that clear-cut. Most of the time there was not a camera filming the proceedings. And that could really mess with a junior ref's head. Like when Police played Germiston Simmer, which was the closest I came to being threatened by a player.

I spotted the Police lock punching as the ball emerged from a scrum. I could see multiple blows hammering into the Simmer prop, who was totally exposed in the scrum. That was an old tactic in those days. At least I thought it was the lock. The truth was I couldn't see exactly who the offending arm was attached to. But intuition and training made me 99 per cent sure that it was the lock.

I called him over and showed him a red. He pleaded innocence. And when he saw that I wasn't going to back down, he offered a vague apology and actually requested a yellow card! So I told him to take a walk. Not surprisingly, Police lost 15-28.

As I was leaving the field, the other Police lock approached me from behind and placed his hand threateningly on my shoulder. He was the biggest player on the field, but I looked him in the eye and told him to remove his hand. But he persisted, telling me he wanted to have a word with me. "Get your hand off my shoulder," I repeated, not quite knowing what I was going to do if he didn't comply. Just then a Police captain and fellow referee, Ronnie Abrahams, intervened, telling his player to leave me alone.

At the post-match drinks I was told that if the upcoming disciplinary hearing suspended the lock I had red-carded, he would have to forfeit his selection for National Police Week. I wasn't sure whether it was a ploy to throw me off my stride, but it had the necessary effect.

For days afterwards I agonised over my decision and whether I had made the right call. One night I shared my self-doubt with my gran over coffee and rusks, not sure what course of action I should follow. Being an excellent listener, she allowed me to unpack and explore all my doubts, all my ethical dilemmas and all my options right into the wee hours. And she left me with this: "You did your best, my Jakes. It's good that you think about these things and question so intensely. But just let it be. By the time you get to the hearing, you will know what the right course of action is."

A week later, at the disciplinary hearing, I refused to be intimidated by the lock's entourage of lawyers and didn't deviate from my version of events. And I left proud that I had manned up without allowing doubt to weaken my resolve.

But it wasn't over yet. The lock appealed his four-week suspension. It threw me a bit. Someone had to be suspended for the punching, but maybe it really hadn't been the lock. Maybe that's why he was appealing … Maybe I should just make a phone call and let this bloke enjoy Police Week.

At the appeal hearing, presiding officer Gert Augustyn, who was vice-president of Transvaal Rugby Union, cut straight to the chase. Augustyn asked: "Man to man, let's just be honest … did you punch the prop or not?" Eventually the lock acknowledged that he had, and the ban was enforced.

I felt both relieved and vindicated, but no joy at denying this player his special week. The discomfort of those few weeks was not something I wanted to repeat in a hurry. Outsiders don't realise that there are times when doing the right thing can be emotionally draining.

At the same time I accepted that if I was in it for the long haul, then those scars were necessary. If I wanted to make the big league, where my resolve would be tested again and again, then I was going to have to earn my stripes.

Years later I was to receive an email, via a friend of a bloke I don't remember reffing or meeting, that highlighted the challenges I had to overcome.

There was a time in South Africa not that long ago when our university campuses were hotbeds of anti-apartheid activism and police were frequently "operating" there. I was a cop then and proudly representing Bobbies on the left wing (no pun intended!). So imagine what happened when Joburg Police played Wits University in a first-league rugby encounter? It was violent. Brutal. Ugly. And one day a fresh-faced young Jewish referee, smaller than our scrumhalf, took control of such a match. We expected him to be quite incapable of controlling our forward pack, not known for a delicate approach when playing against students. Well, we were quite wrong and I was very impressed. Why? Because he understood the laws and communicated clearly, fairly and firmly. His name, we discovered after the match, was Jonathan Kaplan. Today he stands head and shoulders above all his peers as the finest rugby referee ever. And we salute you on a great career, Kappie. Take a bow!

On a lighter note, I was asked to do a "Beeld Trofee" under-15 semi between Menlo Park and Potch Volkies in Pretoria on a Saturday morning. I drove through, practising my Afrikaans on the way. When I arrived, there was a little more pomp and ceremony than I had expected. There was even a match programme for the day that listed the names of all the players and beneath them the words: "Skeidsregter: Johantan Kapluyn." I felt completely part of their special day!

By the end of the 1993 season, at the age of 26, I was promoted to one of the provincial panels along with Tappe Henning and Andy Turner, where we joined André Watson, who had already made the cut a few months earlier. We were going to be fast-tracked as youngsters with potential in order to infuse fresh, new blood into an ageing group of referees.

It was a significant development for any young, up-and-coming ref, because up until then, selection had been based on a one-union, one-ref system that had bogged down panels with dead wood from smaller unions.

Buoyed by my selection, I decided to broaden my reffing experience by travelling around the UK and Europe. But after reffing 18 low-level club games for the London Referees Society over a period of five months, I returned to South Africa in early 1994 a little demoralised, as I had not progressed as much as I'd hoped.

But it was nothing compared to the shattering news that I received while overseas – my friend Ian Anderson had been killed in a car accident. It was a huge loss for me personally, but it was also a major loss for the game of rugby. Ian had had it all and would have become one of this country's finest international referees.

What added to my grief was the knowledge that before his death, Ian had been nominated to ref his first big Test, between Scotland and New Zealand, at Murrayfield. But he was deemed too green by the powers that be, and the Test was given to Freek Burger (in addition to the England versus New Zealand Test a week later).

It made me so sad to think that Ian and his family never got to experience that joy before his passing. Ian was of Scottish descent and would have fulfilled his lifelong dream. Freek did a good job, but in truth Ian would have done his country equally proud.

The 1994 season saw me reffing C-section Sport Pienaar rugby in places such as Cradock, Newcastle, Upington, Nelspruit, Lichtenburg and Pietersburg (now Polokwane). I absolutely *loved* those experiences. I found the people of those small towns very welcoming and warm. With little resources at their disposal, they did a great deal for the "soul" of South African rugby. Some of my fondest memories come from those games.

I wrapped up my season reffing the President's Cup final as the curtain-raiser to the highest-scoring Currie Cup final ever, in which François Pienaar's Lions thumped Free State. Overall, it was a good experience. But nothing I reffed in 1994 could compare to the excitement I felt in October when I quit my marketing job at Nike, where I worked after Afcom, and packed my Charade once again, this time for Durban.

I was heading there to start a new company called Triangle Transport – with my brothers. I was a month away from my 28th birthday and the last time we had all been together was when I was 15. It had been a long, long wait. But finally the reunion we'd all dreamt of was about to happen. We would reclaim the time we'd lost in our childhood in our shared digs in Lambert Road.

9

Reffing in the big leagues

Back in Durban, it didn't take me long to realise that the Natal Referees Society differed markedly from the Transvaal Referees Society. I believed I had something unique to offer as a ref, something different from the blokes who had gone before me. But I had felt pigeonholed at the Transvaal Referees Society, where questioning and challenging the old order was perceived as a threat. I felt that if I didn't allow myself to be moulded into a yes-man, my career would go nowhere fast.

The Natal Referees Society was the complete opposite. And the bloke in charge of refs, Phil Botha, was a breath of fresh air. He believed in me and what I could bring to the party and encouraged me to express myself on the field. Phil also recognised early on that I had the right qualities to become a top international referee.

That season I made my mark in the B-section, reffing matches across the country, which was a step up from Sport Pienaar. I also enjoyed reffing a few cross-section games (between A-section and B-section teams), which included some Springboks. By the time I blew my final whistle of the season, I was convinced that I was ready to fulfil my dream of reffing Currie Cup.

That was affirmed when I opened my 1996 season with a friendly in Kokstad between Natal and Free State in front of 6 000 townsfolk and farmers braaiing on the side of the field.

In my first taste of the big league, James Small and Helgard Müller had a full – and apparently typical – verbal go at each other during the match, expressing their lack of regard for the other's mother. I let it slide because I could see there was no venom involved. Behind all the posturing, they still respected each other as players.

Instead what stuck with me for a long time after that game was one of the best tries I'd ever seen. Natal recycled the ball over and over during a two-minute passage of play. Relentlessly, it went back and forth through the hands until, finally, prop Adrian Garvey finished it off.

That game also dished up a massive hit. Ollie le Roux, all two tons of him, now in Natal colours after defecting from Free State, got the ball while moving at pace. Os du Randt, in his prime, lined him up and stopped Ollie dead in his tracks with a tackle so ferocious that it sent him into reverse at the same speed at which he'd arrived.

Not long after that friendly, I also got my first Test match. Nothing big or glamorous, but my first step on my Test journey – Zimbabwe hosting Namibia at the Police grounds in Harare. I found all the pre-match pomp and ceremony quite surreal. It wasn't something I was used to. And it drove home the message that national pride was at stake that afternoon.

Namibia's 19-18 win was not pretty, and was only decided by Michael Booysen's drop kick two minutes from time. However, that didn't rob the moment of its significance, either for the players or for me. For the rest of my career, 3 May 1996 would remain one of those special milestones.

After the final whistle, Namibian coach Henning Snyman came over to me and gave me his tie as a memento of my first Test. I said I was looking forward to seeing more of him as I progressed, to which he responded that he was dying and would not be around for much longer. Such a poignant moment!

Two months later, I reffed my first and only Craven Week, held at Stellenbosch. I'd always had a soft spot for schools rugby, but this tournament was the pinnacle. Yet as special as it was, the cherry on top that year was becoming a full-blooded Currie Cup ref.

My first appointment that season was a real homecoming: Western Province against Northern Free State at my much cherished Newlands. Province predictably romped home 73-12, and to mark the occasion, I issued my first Currie Cup red card, to a player who had stamped on Joel Stransky's head.

That score had nothing on Northern Transvaal's 147-8 obliteration of South Western Districts in Pietersburg, which broke the record for the most points scored in a Currie Cup match. In the process, Jacques Olivier touched down seven times to break the record for the most tries scored in a Currie Cup game. And even though he was on the losing side, eighthman Anton Leonard made a big impression on me.

As did my biggest Currie Cup match that year, which came to me by default the day after I had run my fifth Comrades. After a tough up-run of 90 kilometres on the Monday, I got a call the following day from Freek Burger telling me he was putting Ian Rogers and Tappe Henning on ice for underperforming and wanted me to do Ian's game between Free State and Northern Transvaal in Bloemfontein on the Saturday.

Talk about being caught between a rock and a hard place. I was so stiff I could barely manage a hobble, but there was no way I could turn down an opportunity like that. So I said yes and sought the help of my mate James Fleming, who was the Natal under-20 physio. Twice-a-day treatments and anti-inflammatories did the trick, and by the Friday I was able to run again, albeit with a great deal of discomfort.

Although my legs were still stiff, I managed to make it through the game. In the final minute, with Free State barely in the lead, I awarded a penalty to the Bulls on the halfway line. I might have been green at Currie Cup level, but I didn't blink. However, apparently one of the Free State *ooms* in the president's box was so shocked he spat his false teeth out. By the time he popped his teeth back in, the kick had missed and Free State had won by 27-25.

I also remember refereeing a Currie Cup match between the Lions and Border at Ellis Park round about this time. Rudolf Straeuli was the captain, and after the toss I asked him to stay behind. I reminded him that although I knew many of his teammates quite well, I expected them to show me the same respect they showed any other ref and to not be too familiar with me on the pitch. Lo and behold, a minute into the game I penalised Border at a ruck, and James Dalton shouted at the top of his voice, "Good call, Johnny ... Good call!"

It was a long afternoon ...

One of my biggest learning curves of that season occurred during a Student World Cup game between England and France at Rand Afrikaans University. It was a game that really rattled me, yet provided a great opportunity for growth. I have advocated that all referees need these kind of games, and the vulnerability that goes with them, in order to achieve their maximum potential.

Around the 58th minute, I detected a mood shift in the game, which up until then had been niggle free. Four minutes later, all hell broke loose. I'd never experienced anything like it. All of a sudden there was a full-on, free-for-all brawl involving every player on the field barring the English halfback, a really small bloke like me, who was standing next to me with the ball in his hand, and the French wing, who had also decided it was in his best interests not to get involved.

What was quite scary was that it wasn't handbags either, but vicious kicking and punching, which involved everyone off the benches as well. It was like a gang fight, and it was a disgrace.

I realised straightaway that this was not a brawl I or my assistants could extinguish, and we had to wait a full two minutes for the red mist to fade. By then the pitch resembled a battlefield, with bleeding players everywhere and three of them out cold on the grass.

Part of me wanted to call off the game at that point, but my intuition told me that it would be a good idea to allow everyone the opportunity to try to regain their dignity. Luckily, after reading the riot act to both captains, the game proceeded reasonably smoothly until the end.

France thumped England, but there was nothing to feel proud of. They say that there is no love lost between the two countries, and I'd just experienced the nastiest manifestation of that. Without a doubt it was the most vicious and longest explosion of violence I would ever witness on a rugby field.

At the end of 1996, I got my first big Test-match experience when I reffed England A versus Argentina at Franklin's Gardens, the home of Northampton. Our liaison officer, Pete, was doing a "sterling" job transporting us around England, but sometimes his timing was completely off. This match day proved to be no exception. Not familiar with the town and the potential traffic implications, we arrived three and a half hours before kick-off at a pitch-dark car park with a padlocked gate and no one around! We started to question whether we were even at the right venue, but eventually Franklin's Gardens came alive.

It turned out to be a tough match for me, with the England players trying to prove that they deserved higher honours. It took me out of my comfort zone and I didn't get to relax for one second. It was exactly what I needed in respect of my growth curve – the exposure to different rugby cultures and experiences, where expectation was different from my home country.

Another test of character presented itself on that tour when I ran touch with Ian Rogers for Tappe Henning when he reffed England against Argentina at Twickenham. It was a huge occasion for me, not just because of the venue, but also because it was the first time I got to wear my Test blazer.

It was a close game, with the crowd groaning regularly at England's poor finishing. But halfway through the second half, England finally managed to keep the ball and recycle it through about half a dozen phases before scoring the best try of the match.

In the build-up to the try, however, I had spotted Martin Johnson punching one of the Argentinian players. It was a no-brainer and out went my flag. You can imagine the booing that erupted!

Intimidating for some, but for me it was water off a duck's back. I had realised long before that reffing was not a popularity contest. And I was definitely no shrinking violet when it came to making big decisions. The only things that mattered to me in that split second when I had to make my call were balance and accuracy. As long as I got that right, I could take the heckling.

That Test experience was also memorable for a couple of events off the pitch. At the post-match function, Ian, a great ambassador for his country, walked up to one of the tables and, in the best Queen's English, loudly and boldly proclaimed, "Good day to you all, my name is Ian Rogers, how wonderful to meet you." Tony Spreadbury looked over at Tappe and me and said, "Good God, he is more English than us!"

In those days, the post-match functions were usually quite stiff affairs, and protocol was observed quite strictly, more so at Twickenham than anywhere else. At some stage during the evening's events, a dude dressed to the max would stand up and announce, "Pray, silence … blah blah blah," and the speeches would start. Captains and chairmen of the unions would have their say (usually the same old stuff), and then the players would be free to enjoy their dinner in suit and tie. (Incidentally, in my opinion, Steve Borthwick of England and Brian O'Driscoll of Ireland always delivered the best and most entertaining post-match speeches, combining intellect, linguistic skill and a good dose of humour.)

On this occasion, everything was going according to protocol, when the captain of the Argies got up and spontaneously invited one of the new caps, Omar Hasan Jalil, to sing a song to mark the occasion for the audience. There was a stunned silence. This was completely out of the ordinary and not in kilter with what had preceded.

After a fair amount of encouragement and whooping from his teammates, the big, burly young prop got up and proceeded to sing "Nessun Dorma" absolutely brilliantly, with such power and vigour that he almost blew the speakers in the room. He eventually had the whole room waving white serviettes in the air, like a deranged and delirious crowd cheering on the Pittsburgh Steelers, and received a standing ovation befitting a man who had scored the winning try in a Test match. Awesome!

10

Obstacles and opportunities

Reffing at Kings Park was always an occasion, but one match that will always hold a special place in my heart was Natal versus the Leopards in 1997. Not because I was reffing, not because it was a rugby spectacle, but because my brother David got a promotion from Natal B, where he had been a stalwart for the last four or five years.

I'd reffed David dozens of times as a King David schoolboy and, more recently, for his club Crusaders, which was one of the most powerful club sides in the Natal league. But the last time I had reffed him at this level was at UCT seven years previously, when a torn anterior cruciate ligament put paid to his dreams of ever playing for Western Province under-20.

His comeback from that horrible injury was a testament to his courage and determination. I was proud of him for persevering since then, overcoming many disappointments and finally being rewarded with a provincial jersey.

But what made his first-class debut even more special was that our dad, who had to wrestle with his religious conscience to pay tribute to his son's moment of glory, was there watching from seat T19. It was a Friday night and my father was a strictly observant Jew. For him, at the time, the start of Sabbath was cast in stone. Not just for him, but for his boys as well. But tonight he had made peace with God, and just as well, because this would be the first and last time the opportunity presented itself.

David, a hooker with the ball skills of a back, put in a solid display at the heart of a rampant Sharks pack, enough to be my Man of the Match. And as was his way whenever I was the ref, he didn't expect any special treatment, neither for himself nor for his team. Unfortunately, David never got another game with the Sharks, but at least he'd had his moment.

Another clear memory from that season was when the Lions hosted the

Hurricanes at Ellis Park with Christian Cullen at fullback, one of the most naturally gifted rugby players I would ever ref. The Canes managed an early 22-3 lead, but the Lions clawed their way back to 35-34. Then, in the dying minutes, they conceded a penalty and gifted the New Zealanders a 37-35 victory.

After the game, Kobus Wiese came up to me and said, "Johnny, why did you penalise us? A New Zealand ref would never have penalised *them* in that situation ..."

I didn't respond. The question he had asked me was symptomatic of a general feeling among the players of that era that refs reffing in their home country favoured their own teams in 50:50 situations. But for me it was not about my personal allegiance or who I thought should win the game. It was about reffing to the best of my ability without sacrificing my impartiality. And if I had to make a brave or controversial decision, I would do so. Clinically, without blinking. That was the only way I could face myself in the mirror the next day and be proud of the way I went about my business.

That year I joined colleagues Ian Rogers and Johan Meeuwesen on a memorable tour to Argentina for their series against England. To this day, it remains my favourite tour. The open spirit of adventure and friendship was the best I would experience. Ian was the de facto leader of the group. His friendly and open manner forged many opportunities for us to meet different people and experience some breathtaking parts of the country, including the Andes, Mount Aconcagua and the Iguazu Falls.

We experienced first-hand the warmth of the locals, who were often quite poor in respect of possessions but rich in their warmth for their fellow human beings, particularly given that we were complete strangers. And we enjoyed many strong coffees, late nights (they only start eating at 11 p.m.!) and, of course, the tango.

I forged a lifelong friendship with Grizz Wylie, the legendary former All Black coaching Argentina at the time, and his wife Jenny. We were also treated royally by the referees Caito Etchebehere and Bobby Cazaneve, as well as Efraim Sklar, a referee from Argentina who had blown in the 1995 Rugby World Cup, and his family.

One vivid memory I have of that tour is of us sightseeing at the base of Aconcagua in the Andes, where I wandered off from the group to take a leak in the snow. While I was concentrating on the patterns I was drawing in the white powder, an Andean Condor, one of the rarest birds of prey and claiming one of the biggest wingspans of any bird, glided over me, no more than 10 metres above the ground. It was an awesome sight. I wondered whether it was checking me out as a tasty snack!

In the lead-up to the Test matches, I refereed a couple of club games, and at one stage in one of the matches, the captains asked me to slow down, pointing out that this was not a Super 12 rugby game!

I ran touch for Ian in the first Test and reffed the second Test, which Argentina won 35-13. It was a bizarre turnaround, as they had lost the first Test by a similar score – 20-40. This sometimes happens with teams that do not have time to prepare adequately before a Test.

Back home I was thrilled when I got the awesome opportunity to ref the British & Irish Lions against Free State. After their 52-30 victory, the Lions' manager, legendary England and Lions prop Fran Cotton, rated that match as one of the greatest midweek games of a Lions tour. I was very proud to have played a part in it.

By now, my brothers had both immigrated to Canada and in July I decided that I would visit them to see first-hand where they lived. So, well in advance of my trip I told my boss, South African ref manager Freek Burger, about my plans, even though I wasn't employed by the South African Rugby Union (SARU) on a full-time basis at that stage and they were only paying my match fees. I would have three weeks off and then resume my Currie Cup duties on my return. I was very keen to gain as much experience as possible at that level, and from a SARU point of view it was not only desirable, but necessary if they wanted to further my career.

But when I returned from Canada expecting to have a busy September, I discovered I hadn't been allocated a single game. Confused, I asked Freek what the deal was. He explained that his secretary must have got my leave dates mixed up. Despite my protests, he said he wouldn't change the schedule. It was apparently more important to adhere to the "error" than do what was in the best interests of my career, the Currie Cup and the organisation. I found that absurd.

I don't dwell on obstacles, so I got over my disappointment and anger and turned my attention to the one big game I had been allocated, in the last round of the Currie Cup in October: Western Province versus Northern Transvaal at Newlands. Both sides were brimming with Boks and they were both in the running for the finals, so it had all the potential to be a massive game.

The night before the match I did something out of character and joined my mate Juicee at a club called All Bar None, where I had one of those spontaneous big nights you tend to regret in the morning. By the time I got to bed at 3 a.m., I was well and truly pickled.

I felt a little ragged the next morning, but by that afternoon, I had plenty of petrol in the tank.

Province, coached by Harry Viljoen, romped home 52-34. I felt I had nailed the game, having facilitated a fantastic fixture in which the players were able to go big. I'll elaborate on this in more detail later, but by pushing the right buttons, and getting the players to trust me early on in the match, I helped orchestrate a magical fixture that included big brutal hits, non-stop action, flat-out endeavour and a series of breathtaking, brilliantly crafted tries – my kind of game!

That night I went to sleep a happy man, feeling I had reffed one of the games of my life. I didn't realise it then, but nothing would top this encounter. To this day, it remains my favourite Currie Cup game of all time.

The next morning I joined Steve Strydom, the chairman of SA Rugby Referees, for breakfast. I could tell that Steve was pleased with me. In a low tone, he said: "Don't tell anyone, Johnny, but you're getting the Currie Cup semi-final. After yesterday's performance, you deserve it."

My first Currie Cup semi – I could hardly believe it! And although I heard no more about it over the next few weeks, I wasn't concerned – the semi was mine. Steve told me that they would make it official at a SARU meeting on the Sunday night preceding the semi. But the call never came, and I battled to fall asleep.

Monday arrived and there was still no word. I tried to quell my anxiety and anticipation with reason. Obviously there would be a perfectly good bureaucratic explanation for the delay. But by Tuesday, my patience had worn thin.

Finally, Steve called. "I want to be the first to tell you, Johnny, but we have decided not to give you the semi."

I was so stunned, I found it difficult to take in Steve's lame explanation about "horses for courses", let alone his assurance that my time would come. For the remainder of the week I struggled to come to terms with the disappointment, oblivious that this was just the beginning of a series of disappointments I would endure in my job. It was a massive blow that was tough to comprehend. André got my semi and the final as well, and that was that. I would have to get over it and move on.

As I was preparing to put the finishing touches to the final manuscript, I received an astonishing Facebook message from a friend of mine now living in Perth that revealed exactly why my first Currie Cup semi-final had been so unceremoniously taken away from me. For 16 years I was never quite sure why I had been denied this appointment.

James Sheriff, a provincial referee from the Lions who had served on the national panels in the mid-90s, told me that the Lions coaching staff (of which he was a part) had been doing a fair share of research on referees, analysing their personalities and refereeing styles. In that year, there had been a great deal of discussion around which referee would suit the Lions in their quest to win the premier domestic trophy.

Initial appointments made by Steve and his selectors had me down to ref the one semi involving the Lions. Apparently Louis Luyt, then president of SARU and the Lions, asked whether my appointment was in the best interests of Lions rugby. After some discussion, it was decided that André Watson "seemed to favour the Lions based on stats and penalty counts". On the basis of those discussions and that information, I was yanked from the game and Watson replaced me. James told me that he could never have discussed this with me at the time; in his words, "this should never have happened".

This astonishing revelation further corroborated my belief that on occasion I was not given a fair crack. More importantly, it brought into question whether or not this had happened before and, if so, how often? Which referees had been compromised in the selection process? And what was the net effect on their respective careers? How far had this gross interference stretched – was it just a South African issue or did the tentacles extend further afield?

But something even more important to me than the semi had been revealed: and that was the fact that *they knew I could not be buckled*! This makes me super proud, prouder than refereeing any semi-final, and goes a fair way towards tempering the sheer disappointment I felt at the time.

These types of disappointments are inevitable; it was just the manner in which they were handled that was unacceptable. My character, my sense of purpose and my long-term vision of what I wanted to achieve allowed me to be able to accept the landscape and find a way of negotiating my way around the obstacles. This was very much a case of losing the battle to win the war!

11

Taking responsibility

It's a match no one will remember. It is a cold, blustery winter's day with driving rain and a pumping northwester. The stands are pretty empty, adding to the sense of desolation. It is June 1998 and Ireland, who are touring South Africa, get a line-out seven metres out from the Western Province try line in the dying minutes of a dour friendly played at a wet Newlands. The tourists had been looking at a 6-12 defeat, but were now in a promising attacking position with the potential to win the match.

Lock Malcolm O'Kelly catches the ball cleanly and I see the Irish backs joining in to drive the maul towards the try line. I penalise them for joining the line-out too early, the Irish complain, but I've made my decision. And Province hold their lead until the final whistle.

Afterwards, Ireland's manager, Donal Lenihan, was spitting mad at me. He obviously felt I'd robbed his team of an opportunity to win the match. The legendary, hard-nosed lock of the 1980s was so angry that I steered clear of him. Any conversation at that point was going to be heated and would solve nothing. It was a pity, because as a boy he had been one of my favourite Irish players when he toured here with the Lions. I would have enjoyed having a beer with him.

Later, while running through the tape of the match, I realised that the Irish were quite entitled to feel disappointed. I'd made a mistake. The replay clearly showed Ireland throwing the ball in to a 13-man line-out, which included six of their backs. The backs who'd joined the drive had, in fact, joined from the back of the line-out and not from the backline, where I thought they'd been positioned.

I had to put up my hand and admit that I'd missed the move and perhaps prevented the Irish from putting Province under pressure. Maybe I'd even affected the outcome of the match. I was guilty of poor concentration at an important juncture of the game.

The next step would be challenging but necessary. To remain true to myself, I couldn't sweep this under the carpet. I picked up the phone, called the Irish management and apologised for my mistake. I also asked them to convey my apology to the team and explain that my error had been neither malicious nor deliberate.

I don't like making mistakes, but I'm philosophical about it. Mistakes are part of the territory, part of a learning curve. Before my Ireland blunder, I'd reffed the Highlanders against the Reds in Dunedin in my first Super Rugby tour match. I made no controversial calls in that game and there were no protests afterwards, but I knew I'd reffed poorly.

I was clearly capable of handling a game at that level. It wasn't as if I was a bad ref or that I didn't have the skills. I just hadn't prepared well and hadn't identified incidents on the field. I wasn't confident, my body language was average, I was too staccato in my communication and I couldn't get the game to flow. This was borne out in a poor assessment report. It hurt, and for a while I was angry with my assessor, Bob Francis of New Zealand. But there was nothing wrong with his assessment. What was really irking me was that I'd been appointed to ref only three games in that Super 12 season and I'd already wasted one opportunity to make a good impression.

In those days, referees were given an average of only three Super Rugby games per season, as opposed to the players, who were playing between 11 and 13 games per season. It was unrealistic to expect us to have the same match sharpness as the players, or to grow our skills at the same pace. The result was that it felt like I was playing catch-up that whole season.

I also found the travelling insane that year. In the space of three months – from the end of February until late May – I made three trips to Australia and New Zealand. I boarded a plane and flew to one time zone to ref a Round 1 game in Dunedin and run touch for a Round 2 match in Christchurch. Then I flew back to South Africa to a different time zone for 10 days and returned to Australia for three weeks for Rounds 5 and 6, running touch twice and reffing a game in the third week. Then it was back to South Africa for two weeks before returning to Australia in May for two more weeks to run touch once and ref my third and final Super 12 game between the Waratahs and the Hurricanes.

It was ridiculous. The switch in time zones was torture, especially when you flew east. It also had a huge impact on my social life. I missed special occasions, braais, and time with my family and friends, who mean a lot to me. In order to stay in touch, I had to develop a different way of living, always having to let people know when I was back in town.

That's the psychological challenge of being an international ref. Players travel in groups where they have their mates and enjoy group activities and are never alone. They are a family on the road.

At that stage, refs travelled in pairs, which often cemented good friendships; one of these was Ian Rogers, who had been on the provincial panels for many years and was an articulate and outspoken supporter of referees' interests. He was a fine referee and I respected him; he was a bit of a mentor to me. Ian always said that if you were going to cock it up, then at least do it with conviction.

He and I had not seen much of each other since the Super Rugby season had started in February. I was about to depart for the match between the Waratahs and the Hurricanes in early May when I heard the shocking news that Ian had cancer. After taking a knock in the Brumbies/Hurricanes game in late April, he had gone for physio, where they'd found a lump that required further investigation. X-rays then revealed a tumour the size of a tennis ball on his lungs.

I got to the hospital as fast as I could. There, I asked Rod Gurr, the president of the Natal Referees Society, when Ian would be able to start reffing again. Never, he replied. Ian would be lucky if he lived through this. Devastated, I visited Ian, who broke down in tears, telling me that he was too young to die and that he was worried about how his young family would cope.

It was a raw experience talking to a friend who had just been told he was on death's doorstep. Only a few months before we were travelling around New Zealand together chatting about how we were going to change the world.

As stunned as I was by the news, life had to go on. In May, I finally got my chance to show that I could handle a big final when I was chosen to ref the first ever Vodacom Cup final, between Griquas and the Lions.

In a one-sided game, Griquas thrashed the Lions 57-0. It was the crowning achievement for the team from the Northern Cape after a few years under the captaincy of Luther Bakkes and the astute coaching of André Markgraaff. They had bought some very underrated players like Edrich Lubbe, Rob Markram, Albert van den Berg, Kobus van der Merwe, Philip Smit, André Vermeulen and Dawie Theron into the squad, and the gamble had paid off.

Next, I got some top-flight exposure when I reffed the Emerging Springboks giving Wales a 35-13 hiding in Sasolburg. Come August, I witnessed one of the greatest Test comebacks of all time, and one of my favourite rugby moments ever. I was the fourth official on the side of the field, but I remember very clearly the epic comeback that started from a Joost van der Westhuizen try after the Boks had trailed New Zealand 5-23. Further tries by Bob Skinstad and James Dalton sealed an improbable, but very special, victory. It was a privilege to have been so close to it.

I also reffed a number of Currie Cup games in that 1998 season, some of which were memorable, like Griquas' record 87-14 victory over Border. But it was Griquas narrowly going down to Boland 13-17 at Wellington on 24 August that proved to be one of the watershed games of my career.

With four minutes to go, Boland made a break and scored a try. As I was following up, I suddenly felt this unbelievable stabbing pain in my left knee. It was weird, because I was more carthorse than athlete. I never got niggles or injuries. But this sudden pain came out of the blue, and it was so severe that it stopped me dead in my tracks whenever I tried to run.

It took a supreme effort, but I managed to hobble through the closing minutes of the game. As I walked off the field, I sensed that this was not something I was going to be able to run off by the next Saturday. There was something very wrong with my knee.

Back home in Durban, my physio sent me for X-rays, which revealed that I had split my articular cartilage. The prognosis was shattering: an operation was the only way to fix my knee. And even then there were no guarantees that I would be able to continue my reffing career.

I withdrew from my next Currie Cup appointment without telling my bosses the full extent of my injury. There was no way I was going to have an op in the middle of the season. So there and then I decided to take a gamble. I was due to ref Western Province against Boland on 5 September, which was less than two weeks away, and I was going to figure out a way around my injury.

Over the next few days I developed a way of running so that my left heel did not hit the ground. That way I could move around pain-free without anyone detecting that I was carrying an injury. It was a massive risk. I could only pull this off as long as no one realised that I was injured.

My plan was to use the Province/Boland derby as an acid test. If I made it through that match, I would take it one game at a time until the end of my season. If I broke down, then so be it. That would be a signal that I must stop.

But until then, my first prize was having the op at the end of the season so that I could keep my career rolling.

Why did I do this?

I had been asked to make important decisions from a very young age and, as a teenage referee, I had had to stand my ground in hostile environments. I was therefore comfortable and happy to take responsibility for my actions, and I understood the value that flows from navigating my own destiny ...

What I had learnt over time was that where there is a will, there is a way.

12

Losses and gains

The Newlands derby was an acid test for my knee. Province were the reigning Currie Cup champions, boasting 11 Boks, but Boland had improved their game considerably under Rudy Joubert and his predecessor, Nick Mallett.

Within the first four minutes, Toks van der Linde thundered over under the sticks for Province's first try. Here we go, I thought. Predictably, this would be the floodgates opening. I was right. Sort of. Instead, it was an electrifying Boland who stunned the Newlands faithful with a dizzying five-try spell in the next 27 minutes. I wondered whether Province had ever conceded five tries in a first half in a Currie Cup game at Newlands.

During a scrum in the first quarter, I saw Dale Santon and Toks van der Linde having a scuffle. When things settled down, I called the two of them over and, to Toks's big surprise, Dale claimed that Toks had called him a "Hotnot". Toks had recently returned home from New Zealand, where he had been accused of racially slurring a woman. I suspected it might have been a move on Dale's part to unsettle WP or distract them, and it could easily have done so. I neutralised the incident and later learnt that it had been a ruse that both characters speak fondly of today.

Province got a sniff in the second half, but Boland played out of their skins to record a brilliant 39-25 victory that will go down in the history books as one of their finest moments ever. It was almost a fairy-tale ending, where grit, character and determination won the day for the underdog.

Without a doubt, this will go down as one of my favourite Currie Cup games.

In mid-September, Tappe Henning and I boarded a plane to fly to Sydney for a World Cup qualifier involving Samoa, Tonga, Fiji and Australia. I ran touch for Tappe in the Samoa versus Tonga game, which started with me flagging a late tackle by a Tonga centre. Tappe yellow-carded him. About 25 minutes later, the same player committed another dangerous tackle, except this time he nearly decapitated his opponent. There were no ifs or buts; it was a clear-cut decision. Tappe reached for the red in his pocket, and then something unexpected happened. Two Samoan players, captain Pat Lam and Inga Tuigamala, rushed up to Tappe. "Please don't send him off," they begged. "This is how we play our rugby."

Unbelievable! This was a Test-match qualifier to establish who would go to the World Cup, but still the beautiful spirit that permeated Pacific Island rugby triumphed over the advantage to be gained from the opposition losing a player for the rest of the match. Where else in world rugby would a captain beg a ref not to red-card an opposition player?

At the end of the tournament, I reffed Fiji in a 32-15 romp over Tonga in Brisbane and returned happy with my performance. I now knew I could ref a few more Currie Cup games without breaking down. Game by game, my decision to tough out the season was being vindicated.

In October I got my first crack at a Currie Cup semi-final, between WP and Griquas. I was thrilled about this opportunity after the previous year's bitter disappointment.

Before the match a massive thunderstorm had broken out, which drenched the field and made it very difficult to play a free-flowing game. With Griquas coach André Markgraaff's astute game plan in tatters, he tried to get the game postponed, to no avail. Western Province won 27-11, thanks to their greater savvy on defence and the big-match temperament of their Boks.

Even as an impartial ref, with no allegiance to any player or province, I still couldn't help but feel sorry for Griquas. That match marked the end of a fairy-tale season for them, which included a number of giant-killing victories. And it would probably be a long time before they ever got another shot at winning the Currie Cup.

Personally, though, I was a step closer to the end of my season. Just one more challenge remained overseas, in Ireland, where I reffed Romania and Georgia on 18 November in another World Cup–qualifying tournament. The match itself was not that memorable, with Romania edging in 27-23, but what followed at the post-match function was.

I was a few tables away from members of the Irish team, including Donal

Lenihan, who might still not have put my Newlands mistake behind him. My mate Owen Doyle, the Irish ref manager, a bloke whom I really respected, came to me and said, "Go on, Johnny, why don't you just go and talk to Donal? It's a great opportunity to break the ice."

So I got up, walked over to Donal and tapped him on the shoulder. I told him that although we'd started off on the wrong foot, hopefully we could move past it. Donal was quite taken aback, but he stood up nevertheless and, towering above me, we made a bit of friendly chit-chat and that was that.

Later that week, Donal came over to me at another post-match function and said, "Jonathan, you don't know how much your gesture meant to me. Please accept this autographed Irish rugby jersey as a token of our friendship." His thoughtful response to my gesture was a telling reminder of why I loved being involved in the game that meant everything to me.

I flew back to South Africa proud that I had successfully navigated one of my toughest career challenges. But it wasn't over yet. My surgeon, Dave Pollock, had warned me that there were no guarantees after surgery. I may not be able to run again. For all I knew, Romania versus Georgia could have been my last major assignment.

With all due respect to both teams, it was not the way I wanted to end my career. I had a Currie Cup semi-final and a Vodacom Cup final under my belt. I'd also reffed several Test matches and a brace of international standard games. Now I was within touching distance of a World Cup.

Incidentally, it was around this time, shortly after my 32nd birthday, that my silver streak started to manifest. Now located next to my ever-widening bald patch, people often ask me about it. I have no idea how or why it started, but the hair there has slowly got more wiry and silvery. I have always regarded it as some sort of defect, but others have come to identify me with it.

My injury, and my hair, paled into insignificance, however, when, on 26 November, Ian succumbed to his disease. I knew he didn't have long, but his death only six months after his diagnosis was humbling – as was Ian's acceptance of his fate in the weeks before he passed away. Even though he had fought a good fight and tried alternative treatments, he told me near the end that he had come to terms with his mortality. His words would have a profound effect on my outlook on life.

Ian's cremation was a celebration of his life. In my eulogy, I acknowledged him as a special person and a gifted referee with exceptional man-management skills. Nevertheless, it was an emotional day and at times I was in tears. Rugby had lost one of its top referees and I had lost both a friend and a respected colleague.

I will never forget Ian. But he was gone, and there was nothing I could do about it.

13

Kicked in the balls

It was August 1999, and Province were playing the Bulls at Newlands. My left knee was like new after having had surgery in December, and I was back in the swing of the Currie Cup competition. The ball came back from a midfield ruck to Bulls scrumhalf Conrad Breytenbach, who looked like he was going to run it.

In anticipation, I stepped towards his defensive line when, suddenly, he opted to kick instead. But he then slipped in the process, sending the ball flying, not downfield, but rocketing right at me. With no time for evasive action, it hit me square and hard in the nuts, dropping me like a sack of potatoes.

I couldn't breathe, let alone blow my whistle. But I nevertheless made a feeble attempt to get back on my feet and blew play to a halt. Not that the players needed to hear the whistle. They'd seen what had happened and had stopped playing.

I was on my knees, battling to catch my breath, when Bulls prop Pierre Ribbens decided to put me out of my misery. As if injured, he went down on his haunches a few metres away. He understood that I was trying my best to recover in front of a packed Newlands, if not with my balls intact, then at least with a little dignity.

That brought Dr Henry Kelbrick, all 150 kilograms of him and laden with bags, rumbling towards us from the bench on the opposite side of the field. Puffing and panting, he came to an impressive sliding stop next to Pierre.

"*Wat makeer*, Pierre?" (What's the matter, Pierre?) I heard him ask.

"*Niks*, doc ..." (Nothing, Doc ...)

Henry looked at him as if to say, "Then what the hell did I just run across the field for?"

"*Dis die ref*, doc ..." (It's the ref, doc ...)

Quickly realising that I didn't want any hands-on treatment, as it were, Henry pretended to treat Pierre while advising me from a distance on how to recover. It was all quite ridiculous. When we restarted the game, Pierre reminded me that I "owed him one".

It was just one of those random things that can go wrong on a rugby field, but, when I looked back on 1999, it was quite symbolic, as it summed up a full year of being knocked down, dusting myself off and getting back up again.

My season had started off well enough. I had breezed through my Vodacom Cup games in early 1999 without any hint of pain and discomfort in my knee, and then survived one of the longest Super Rugby tours known to man – a torturous six and a half weeks on the road.

I left South Africa on a three-week tour to perform one reffing and two touch-judging jobs for Tappe and Andy Turner. Then the tour was extended by a week when I was asked to stay behind for another touch-judging appointment, this time for André. Then I also touch-judged for André in the semis and then the final, which prolonged the trip to just over six weeks. Considering that I only refereed one game during that period, it was extraordinary.

Known as the Tour from Hell, this is what it looked like:

Durban–Johannesburg–Perth–Sydney (stopover)–Christchurch–
Dunedin (ref Highlanders 9 v ACT Brumbies 8)–Auckland (touch
judge Blues v ACT Brumbies)–Napier (touch judge Hurricanes
v Waratahs)–Wellington–Sydney (touch judge Waratahs v Crusaders)–
Brisbane (touch judge Reds v Crusaders)–Christchurch–Dunedin
(touch judge final Highlanders v Crusaders)–Christchurch–Sydney–
Perth–Johannesburg–Durban.

Interestingly, while running touch for Tappe in the Blues versus Brumbies game, he tore his hamstring just before half-time with the score 16-0 in favour of the hosts. I took over, and with no real change in conditions at all, and no wind to speak of, the final score was 16-22 to the visitors.

Perhaps just a case of the Brumbies playing better in the second half, but I always wonder whether this was not a classic case of two different refereeing styles making a different imprint on a game.

Prior to my Tour from Hell, I did two shorter Super Rugby tours. During the second one, in the mid-season clash between the Waratahs and the Blues,

I made a seemingly insignificant poor call. It was nothing more than a blip on the Super Rugby radar, but, curiously, it would develop into a fascinating saga. One side of it has long been in the public domain, and although it is parochial and inaccurate, everyone is entitled to their opinion. In Chapter 25 I will share my side of the story and you can draw your own conclusions.

It all began in April 1999 in Sydney, 14 minutes into the first half when the Blues were leading the Waratahs and I blew what I believed to be a Tahs knock-on from general play. Half the players from both sides stopped playing, but the rest played on, with the Tahs sweeping 70 metres up-field to score a "try". Of course, I had to call them back and the try was not awarded. But the Tahs had not knocked on and they lost the match.

Afterwards, some of the Sydney press claimed that my error had cost the Tahs the game. As always, I felt bad when I made a mistake, however important or unimportant it might have been in the context of the game. I didn't like feeling that I let coaches and players down. So sensationalising my error in the press simply magnified my regret. I beat myself up for weeks afterwards until I came to terms with the fact that making mistakes was human. And refs, believe it or not, *are* human! It would take a few seasons before the media-circus blame game, which some coaches and players liked to milk, became water off a duck's back.

By now I was being paid to do the job I loved, because in November 1998, André Watson, Tappe Henning, Carl Spannenberg and I had become South Africa's first professional refs. The move from amateurism to professionalism had initially met with a lot of resistance. It was typical of the old guard who, as usual, was lagging behind the times. By the time serious negotiations got under way at SA Rugby in early 1998, Australia and New Zealand's refs had been professional for 18 months.

I sensed that SA Rugby's new CEO, Rian Oberholzer, supported the move, but he nevertheless wanted ref management to justify the expenditure. And Steve Strydom's resistance didn't help our cause. He claimed that paying us more was not going to make us more professional, which was an absurd argument, to say the least. There was no job that could, or would, accommodate us being on the road for six months of the year.

His position was that in *his* day they got by perfectly well without getting paid. It frustrated the hell out of me. The rest of the rugby world had moved on and was fully professional – how could you justify an argument by referring to the way things had been done in the past? Yet here he was, stuck in the past.

I thought it was a simple enough matter and I said as much to Rian during one of our meetings: "Rian, in the 1998 season I was away from home or out of the country on rugby business for a total of four months. I have two degrees, I co-own my own transport business ... Please tell me, is there a business or boss out there that you think would accommodate me being away for a third of the year? Would you be able to give one of your salaried employees that much time off work? And judging by next year's schedules, half of the year off?"

Long story short, at the end of 1998 we signed the contracts and became professional referees.

Not long after that, I was chosen alongside Tappe Henning to go to the 1999 Rugby World Cup as a touch judge. André Watson was chosen as a referee. I was going to experience one of the biggest events of my career in rugby union, but I was disappointed that I hadn't made the cut as a ref. I felt I was worthy. I was more than good enough.

But my disappointment quickly subsided once I became conscious of the bigger picture. Whichever way you looked at it, it was an honour and a privilege to be part of any RWC.

Disappointments were part and parcel of the careers of professional sports-people, and I had no doubt my time would come. So I resolved to take a positive attitude into the World Cup. I wanted to mix with as many of my peers as possible and learn as much as I could to ensure that I became a better, more complete referee.

My disappointment was also tempered by the knowledge that a whole bunch of young, up-and-coming refs like Scott Young, Steve Walsh and Alan Lewis had also missed the cut – even though we all had the ability to perform at the highest level. So we all shared the same disappointment.

Come the end of September I packed my bags and departed for Wales and the 1999 Rugby World Cup. Once settled in, I set out to follow my philosophy of "inclusivity" and tried to get to know all of my overseas colleagues. Regret-tably, Steve, Tappe and André seemed to retreat into a little laager, having dinner together every night and speaking Afrikaans to each other in front of the rest of the group. Although I respected their choice, I wasn't really interested in joining them. I also didn't think it was a good advert for South African rugby. After all, hadn't we been in isolation long enough?

I also chose not to train with the South African refs in the mornings, pre-ferring the evening sessions instead, which they resented. I was soon told that I wasn't a "team man". My friends from other shores, however, warmed to my willingness to mix, socialise and learn from them. They also recognised that I didn't want to be part of a clique. On one occasion, the great Derek Bevan stood next to me as we were ordering drinks at the bar. He looked me straight in the eye and said: "Boyo, I can see exactly what's happening here. You have our full support."

I ended up running touch in three matches, all in Wales, which was a pity. Because the tournament was co-hosted by Scotland, France and England, travelling to and officiating at other venues would have greatly added to my RWC experience.

When I eventually boarded the aircraft to fly back to South Africa, I felt happy that I'd been part of that unique experience. It was a great tournament, exceptionally well run, with many exciting matches, yet I couldn't wait to get home. That was a terrible feeling for a person who sees opportunity in every situation, no matter how bleak. But the truth was that all I had to show for the 1999 World Cup was the enduring friendships I'd made.

Back in South Africa, SA Rugby ref manager Freek Burger requested a meeting, where he dressed me down for the stance I had taken with the South African contingent. I asked him why he was attacking me without first asking for my view on the matter. It stopped him in his tracks. So I explained my viewpoint by saying that I didn't see any value in withdrawing into a laager when we all had such a fantastic opportunity to enjoy a cosmopolitan environment for a limited period of time. He didn't seem to get it, and I left the meeting feeling more frustrated than ever.

But every cloud has a silver lining … Some time later I became privy to a conversation that had taken place between Springbok coach Nick Mallett and Kiwi Tim Gresson, the International Rugby Board (IRB) judiciary committee chairman and the South Africa, New Zealand and Australia Rugby (SANZAR) chairman and selector. The occasion was a cocktail party after South Africa beat New Zealand in the play-off for third place at the Millennium Stadium.

Tim asked Nick, "Who do you think is the best young ref in South Africa right now?" Without blinking, Mallett (who was not a close friend of mine) said, "Jonathan Kaplan."

"Funny you should say that," Gresson replied, "because we also believe Kaplan is the best. But every time we put his name in the hat, SA ref management say they have many better than him back home."

14

The first ever
Six Nations match

It was all a bit surreal. Three months earlier I hadn't been deemed good enough to ref at the World Cup, but here I was now, in Rome in January 2000, to ref the opening match of the inaugural Six Nations Championship, between newcomers Italy and the previous year's Five Nations champs, Scotland. What a break!

The Five Nations Championship originated in 1910 and became the Six Nations in 2000, when Italy joined England, Scotland, Wales, Ireland and France in the competition. It is easily one of rugby's most prestigious annual tournaments, and I was the only South African appointed to ref in it that year.

It was a big occasion, one I'd been working towards for a long time. It was my big break, and it was up to me to prove that I could cut it at that level.

The build-up was fantastic. I arrived in Rome 10 days before the Test along with one of my touch judges, Mark Lawrence, who would become one of my favourite travelling companions on overseas tours. Mark was disciplined and organised, while I was spontaneous and unconventional. We had the makings of a great team.

We spent our first day in Rome sightseeing on foot, which would become a tradition of mine whenever I reffed in a foreign city. In the days leading up to the Test match, I also refereed several warm-up matches that would get me into the groove, so to speak. For the first match we were driven about 500 kilo-metres to a snow-bedecked Parma by Italian referee Giulio de Santis, who had scant regard for speed limits and solid white lines. There I reffed the Italian Cup final, in which Viadana beat Piacenza 32-14 on a field resembling a muddy cabbage patch. Both teams were loaded with foreigners from Argentina, South

Africa and New Zealand, and the 4 000 passionate Italian fans loved it. I was glad for the run after several months of inactivity.

Then it was time for more sightseeing, which included exploring ancient Roman ruins in the countryside on horseback. My horse was called William, a really dopey animal that always lagged behind the others, which suited me just fine, as I'd always been a bit nervous around horses. Mark, on the other hand, bragged about what a great horseman he was, so he was given Francesca, who summarily threw him off and did a quick back scratch while Mark contemplated his ego.

After that little adventure, I reffed a Wednesday match between the Italian under-21s and under-25s on a bitterly cold evening to test my application of the new laws, an experiment that resulted in much chaos.

That night we had dinner with members of the Roma women's rugby side, and afterwards Mark treated them to some of his magic tricks, which made them very suspicious of our integrity for the upcoming Test.

Mark's dodgy linguistic skills were a great source of amusement. He thanked everyone, every day, in Spanish, to which they would always reply, "*espanõl?*" And then, to cap it, every time we were asked something, for some reason only known to him, Mark would respond by saying, "*ciao*". For example, if he was asked whether he would like to go to the Vatican City, he would say, "See you later."

To add to the merriment and camaraderie, my old friend, Natal refs manager Phil Botha, arrived in Rome. It was great motivation to know that he was there to support me. More than anyone, he knew just how much this opportunity meant to my career.

The Thursday before the Test I met with coaches Brad Johnstone of Italy and Ian McGeechan of Scotland to discuss the new laws and their application. As it turned out, it was one of the most co-operative meetings I had ever had with coaches. Johnstone and McGeechan felt the same, and they said as much during a BBC interview on match day.

Why, you may ask, do we meet with coaches at all? In this particular case, there was a set of previously untried law variations that needed explaining, but in any event, the real value in these meetings is that they lay the foundation for the trust that is needed to develop a platform for a good game.

I have often found that this interaction between coach, captain and referee leads to a better rapport on the field as a result of the understanding that is reached off it. Any misconceptions, historical issues and inconsistencies within the game can usually be discussed freely, and sometimes quite robustly. The result is the players run onto the field with a clear understanding of what is expected of them.

The meetings are not compulsory, but I always made a point of trying to ensure that they took place. Even when coaches appeared to be happy that I was officiating their game, I would still find a way of having a coffee with them prior to the match.

But back to my first Six Nations Test. On the morning of the big day I had breakfast with Mark and my other touch judge, Joel Dume of France, and then gave a couple of interviews to the BBC and a rugby show hosted by ex-Scottish eighthman John Beattie.

After a light lunch and with an hour to spare to kick-off, we arrived at Stadio Flaminio, a 25000-seater rugby stadium, where I met some legendary Scottish players like fullback Gavin Hastings and flyhalf John Rutherford, as well as England scrumhalf turned journalist and commentator, Nigel Starmer-Smith.

Following a quick inspection of the field and a chat with match commissioner John West of Ireland, probably one of that country's most famous referees, I headed for the change rooms for a chat with the teams.

I couldn't believe how the time had flown since I arrived at the ground. The next thing I knew I was on the field trying not to sing along to a rousing rendition of "Flower of Scotland". Instead, I took a moment to centre myself. I was aware that the big day had arrived. It had taken 17 years since I first reffed as a schoolboy, but here I was, at a big turning point in my career: almost two decades of my life condensed into 80 minutes. The anthems were over. Now it was time to fly!

Fortunately, I felt totally at ease throughout the game, which was everything I expected of a Six Nations Test. I felt well prepared and my calls were straightforward and clinical, and Mark and Joel backed me up well. There were no dramas.

The only curve ball occurred midway through the first half when Scotland, captained by John Leslie, son of All Black legend Andy Leslie, went over Italy's try line after what appeared to some to be a knock-on. Fortunately I was well positioned and correctly adjudicated a try.

Out to prove their international pedigree, Italy played some impressive rugby, which had the Italian crowd of 20000 in raptures. Erratic kicking by the Scots and a brilliant Man of the Match display with the boot by Argentine ex-pat Diego Domínguez handed Italy a historic 34-20 victory. Domínguez's three drop goals in the second half not only demoralised the Scots, but also added to his match total of 29 points, a tournament record.

Afterwards Phil, Mark and Joel all told me they thought I had nailed the match. Back in my change room, France's Marcel Martin, the director of the 1999 and 2003 Rugby World Cups, knocked on the door to congratulate me on a job well done. And later, back at the hotel, my assessor, Brian Leigh of England, ticked all my performance boxes.

To cap it all, Italian captain Alessandro Troncon and Scottish skipper John Leslie were effusive in their praise at the post-match function, saying that I had reffed a great game. While they were talking, I noticed Brian raise his glass in agreement, as if to say, "Well deserved, mate; here's to your future."

The accolades were a great motivation, but I took them with a pinch of salt. This Six Nations Test had not been particularly challenging. That said, it was a huge break and I knew I had not let anyone, including myself, down.

That night, Mark, Phil, Joel and I celebrated into the wee hours, so much so that when Mark turned in at 5.30 a.m., he refused outright to meet the Italians for a prearranged breakfast at 10 a.m. I barely managed to drag myself downstairs to fly the flag, and then took it easy for the rest of the day. The next morning I flew out of Rome, mission accomplished, wondering if this was as good as it would get for the season.

My next stop was Paris, where Mark and I were due to run touch at the weekend for Stuart Dickinson, who was reffing France against England. We spent the week sightseeing in Normandy, visiting the beaches the Allies had landed on to start the end of World War II and eventually passing through the greatest little village I can remember, Honfleur.

On the Sunday I reffed a third-division club match between Maisons Laffitte St Germain and Plaisir in front of the 400 spectators who had braved the wet weather. Plaisir won the match 24-7, and despite the conditions, the game was played in a fantastic spirit and at a rollicking pace. As I walked off, the crowd gave me a standing ovation. It was the first time that happened to me and I felt quite chuffed. Perhaps it helped that I was an international referee officiating a third-division match ...

Unfortunately, Stu didn't enjoy the same reaction when he reffed in front of a packed Stade de France. He reffed well for most of the match, but then made one error that may have cost French centre Richard Dourthe a try. England won the match 15-9.

In the bus that took dignitaries to the post-match dinner, things turned nasty when some of the French blatantly passed rude comments on Stu's refereeing abilities. The worst was when Dourthe's mother went up to Stu's wife Fiona and ranted about what a crap ref her husband was.

It left a bad taste in my mouth. It was an unprovoked attack. Whether fuelled by ignorance, disappointment or anger, it was just not on. At that level, you should be able to show a bit of respect and maintain your dignity.

I felt sorry for Stu and Fiona. No one deserved that. The incident highlighted the burden refs carry whenever they invite family to support them. There's always the risk that they would bear the brunt of the abuse meant for you. I could handle it. It went with the job. I would brush it off as a fan who was upset and didn't know how to deal with his disappointment. But it's different for family when fans sitting near them verbally abuse the ref. They are your blood and they want to defend you. And that can get complicated, even out of hand.

That ugly incident aside, by the end of my first Six Nations tour, I couldn't imagine that I would ever have another one as memorable.

My overseas Super Rugby appointments came to an end when I ran touch for André in the freezing-cold final, which the Crusaders narrowly snatched from the Brumbies 20-19. Then I flew on to Buenos Aires to run touch, again for André, in a Test between Argentina and Ireland. It was probably the most extended journey I ever undertook, just to run touch for two rugby matches: Durban to Joburg, Joburg to Sydney, Sydney to Canberra, Canberra to Sydney, Sydney to Joburg, Joburg to Cape Town, Cape Town to Buenos Aires, Buenos Aires to Cape Town, Cape Town to Durban.

I was finished by the time I got back. People do not always understand the effects of jet lag and life on the road. All I wanted to do was sit at home and unwind with my dogs. Or sit at a coffee shop, on my own, doing a crossword puzzle, which was weird because, in effect, I was just doing what I would have been doing on the road anyway.

Players feel sorry for themselves because they travel so much. But they don't come close to southern hemisphere refs. In 1999, I went on 133 flights and was away from home for 186 days. The following year it was 123 flights, but I was away from home for 216 days!

I think I was flying even more than an international airline pilot – without the downtime. People say, "What a great job; you get to travel all over the world." That's true. I've seen the world with rugby, and it's been fantastic. But travel can quickly become a bind, and then a burden.

The thing is, you can't say you are tired when you land. You've got to perform. And that takes its toll. A lot of southern hemisphere refs stop reffing Super Rugby not because of the workload, but because the travelling kills them and their lifestyle. The northern hemisphere refs have it relatively easy, as their travels often involve 24-hour turnarounds.

But, like road running, the pain was worth the gain. In July I flew to see my dad in Toronto, where he had lived since the late 1990s in order to be closer to my brothers. It was his 60th, and he'd laid on a cruise to Alaska for the whole family. It was awesome to be reunited with them, and the cruise from Vancouver to Anchorage and back along the Inside Passage was unforgettable and worth every air mile.

We partied, we feasted, we gambled and we did a fair amount of sightseeing. I also snagged the third largest king salmon ever caught off a boat at Ketchikan, Alaska, the salmon capital of the world. My fellow passengers were so impressed, all of them wanted their photo taken with my catch. The Alaskan fisheries department later sent me documentation to prove the record catch, just in case my mates back home didn't believe me. And then for years afterwards sent me questionnaires so that they could update my fisherman's profile – which didn't exist!

Revitalised by an unforgettable family holiday, I boarded my next long-haul flight without any concerns about jet lag. Vancouver–LA–Auckland on United Airlines turned out to be one of my best flights ever. The food was great, the movies were great … I was great. Because I was on my way to ref the biggest match of my career: a Bledisloe Cup clash between the All Blacks and the Wallabies in Wellington. It didn't get any bigger than that.

15

Bledisloe

Five days before I refereed the biggest Test of my career, between the All Blacks and World Cup champs Australia, I landed in Wellington, New Zealand. I was over the bloody moon that Scotland versus Italy in January had turned out to be only a precursor to how good things could get.

As you'd have expected, the air of anticipation in Wellington was electric. Three weeks earlier in Sydney, the same sides had clashed in one of rugby's all-time thrillers, which the press had dubbed the Match Played in Heaven.

That match had opened at breakneck pace, with the All Blacks screaming into a 24-0 lead after just seven minutes' play. But never-say-die Australia gradually clawed their way back into the game, going into a 36-34 lead with about two minutes to full time. Then Jonah Lomu got the ball and went round Stephen Larkham to clinch the match 39-35 for New Zealand. Each team had scored five tries in that spectacle, and I knew fans would be gagging for a repeat.

To make that possible, I would have to find a way of facilitating a great match in which my lack of experience would not be exposed. André had reffed the previous Test, probably one of his best performances. He had raised the bar and the onus was now on me to meet that challenge. His was going to be a hard act to follow, but I was quietly confident that I was not only capable, but if I applied myself, anybody's equal.

I'd lined up some special support. Back in June, when I was given this plum appointment, I decided I wanted Gary and David to share it with me, as they had been my staunchest supporters through thick and thin.

My wingmen flew in on the Thursday and found me in my hotel room preparing for a coaches' meeting with All Black Wayne Smith and Wallaby Rod Macqueen. There was a lot of back-slapping and hugging. I was happy that Gary and David were finally there to experience the occasion with me. We'd been emailing one another and talking about this moment for weeks. I can't describe just how it felt to have their support and to know how proud they were of me. As Gary had recently told me in an email, they had looked on with pride for 17 years as I quietly and methodically plotted my way to this point. In the process, he said, I had inspired them with my self-belief in spite of the doubting Thomases along the way.

Wanting to acknowledge my brothers, I gave them VIP treatment all the way. Following the coaches' meeting, I took them to dinner with my two touch judges, Scotland's Rob Dickson and England's Ed Morrison, who had reffed the 1995 World Cup final. Joining us was my assessor Jim Irvine from Ireland, who had warmed to me as a person and recognised that Saturday's match had the potential to cement my arrival as an international referee.

Everywhere my brothers and I went in Wellington, I was treated like some kind of celebrity. Fans wanted to interact and have their picture taken with me. It was weird, to say the least. I preferred flying under the radar – the fame thing doesn't do it for me. But it gave my brothers a kick, and that was good enough for me. Gary and David also accompanied me to the pre-match cocktail party, where they were thrilled to meet some of the legends of the game.

Later that evening, I made sure they would be able to accompany me to WestpacTrust Stadium on the day of the match. I wanted them to be with me in my change room, which was next to the All Black and Wallaby dressing rooms, so that they, too, could experience the buzz I got before a big match. They overheard me making these arrangements and the looks of delight on their faces said it all.

The following morning's build-up was intense. I had an acute attack of the butterflies, and my brothers' eyes couldn't have been bigger. In my change room at the stadium, they took photographs and tried to convince me that I looked calm and collected, even though the swarm of butterflies in my stomach told me otherwise. But soon Gary and David were gone, leaving me to reflect on the long road I'd travelled to get this far and the enormity of the 80 minutes that lay ahead. This was it. This was my acid test. This was the reason why I had started out all those years ago.

I knew that, in addition to my brothers and the rest of my family, I had a lot of other mates and colleagues rooting for me on the day, and not only South Africans, but rugby people all around the world. Like head of Aussie refs Russell Trotter, who had emailed me words of encouragement before the game. He told me he knew just how much I had struggled to get where I was, but that I had beaten the system and got there on merit alone. "Well done," he said, and continued as follows:

> I am sure it is going to be a great day and you will enjoy the experience.
>
> Never have any self-doubt because all of your Aussie mates will be there to support you and we know you wouldn't be there if the Selectors didn't think you could do the job.
>
> Congratulations, Johnno, have a great day and go out there being confident that you will be the facilitator of a great match.
>
> All the best,
>
> RT

As I took my place for the anthems, my brothers saw my picture flash up on the big screen and heard the announcer introduce the referee as Jonathan Kaplan of South Africa. In a later email, this is what Gary said he felt at that moment:

> Very emotional, David and I watched as Jonathan stood between the two teams as the national anthems were played. I remembered going to watch Jonathan as a 4th-division ref many years ago. He travelled about an hour and a half to referee a bunch of casual players. With about three people in the stands, Jonathan reffed the match and, after sending a few players off the field who clearly thought they would be able to take advantage of this young and inexperienced official, we began the long trip home. Jonathan didn't need accolades and he didn't need crowds – in fact, he didn't need to be the centre of attention – he just loved the game and he wanted to do a great job. I knew back then that he had what it took and he was going straight to the top. And now the day had arrived ...

Down on the field, standing between the two teams for the anthems, I was oblivious to any of this. In fact, everything was a bit of a blur right up until I blew the whistle for the kick-off to the deafening roar of 36 000 spectators. Westpac, albeit slightly smaller than other renowned international stadiums, is known as a very noisy stadium. And then everything receded into a blur again. I have only patches of clear recollection, almost like a SuperSport highlights package.

The Wallabies went into an early lead and were up 12-0 after 16 minutes following a blistering Stirling Mortlock try and another by Joe Roff. Then the All Blacks roared back, with Christian Cullen bagging a brace of excellent tries that put the All Blacks in front.

At half-time, they were still ahead, 20-18, and they kept their noses in front in a desperately tight, fast-paced second half all the way into the last few minutes of injury time … momentous minutes that obliterated any of the other highlights of this frenetic game.

With the score locked at 23-21 and a New Zealand victory almost sealed, Todd Blackadder asked me about time. I looked at my watch and saw 2 minutes 45 seconds. At that stage, New Zealand, after a sustained attack in Australia's 22, had won a five-metre scrum. They attacked from the scrum, drove across the line, but were not able to ground the ball.

Instead, it shot out of the ruck like a pip and the All Blacks managed to attack again. It appeared to be all over for Australia when, unable to penetrate the defence, Christian Cullen audaciously chipped a ball in behind the Wallaby defenders. Westpac held its breath, but it bounced over behind the corner flag and I gave the Aussies a 22 drop-out.

Dramatically, they botched it, gifting the All Blacks a line-out on their 22. At the line-out, I looked at my watch. Still just over a minute to go. In another twist, Australia then stole the line-out off Mark Hammett's throw and flyhalf Stephen Larkham kicked hard and deep into touch all the way back to the All Blacks' 22. My watch showed just a few seconds remaining, and I decided this would be the final play.

Players trudged towards the line-out. All New Zealand had to do was win their line-out, kick it out and the match was theirs. But they cocked it up. The Aussies pilfered poor old Hammett's throw once again and kept it tight as they surged forward as if their lives depended on it. The All Blacks defended like men possessed. The relentless tension in the stadium ratcheted inconceivably higher.

Then the unthinkable happened. In their desperation to stall the Aussie onslaught, New Zealand's replacement prop, Craig Dowd, tried to secure possession from an offside position. It took me a few seconds before I blew his infringement, as I couldn't quite comprehend what I'd just seen. Digesting it all as players continued to join the ruck, I flashed a quick glance at the Aussie backline. Not to check anything, but just to give myself the moment I needed to compose myself for what must happen next.

There was no hesitation or indecision. I was just taking a few seconds to clear my mind and comprehend what a huge turning point this was, for both the teams and me.

Here I was in my seventh Test, in front of my biggest audience ever, reffing the two best teams in the world, being asked to make a huge decision. This was the moment where I had to hold my nerve and not look the other way. I could not even think what my decision would mean to this crowd, who were baying for the Bledisloe and Tri-Nations cups that depended on an All Black victory.

None of those implications impacted on my decision-making in those dramatic milliseconds. As I had done since I was 17, I simply took a moment to call what was in front of me. Then, with intent, I raised my arm and blew my whistle to award Australia a penalty 35 metres out, about 10 metres to the left of the upright.

I did it with impunity.

Without blinking.

I blew the penalty knowing that this was a career-defining moment for me. This was what I had been working towards for nearly two decades. Why I'd persevered when I injured my knee two years earlier and just got on with it. *This* was where I wanted to be.

Aussie captain John Eales picked up the ball and looked around for his kicker, Stirling Mortlock. But his try-scoring winger had been substituted. Turning up the tension yet another few notches, Eales indicated that *he* would go for poles. You could cut the air of disbelief and apprehension with a knife.

Unbeknown to me and, I'm sure, many of the spectators, Eales had unwittingly prepared for this moment during the preceding week when he had diligently worked on his kicking at practice. In fact, he revealed in later interviews that, as a kid, he won it for Australia in this way a hundred times over while practising last-minute penalty kicks in his backyard. But I don't think for one second that John Eales could ever have imagined how much would hinge on his rehearsals.

A picture of composure, he held his nerve and, without any fuss, kicked for poles. I saw the ball wobble a bit as it headed towards the right-hand upright before gently curving in and sailing over to make it 24-23 to the Wallabies.

Eales raised his arms in victory and turned to celebrate with his teammates, who swamped him soccer-style in a maul of sheer joy. It was a kick as dramatic as they come. It dazed the Kiwi crowd like a stun-grenade, retained for the Aussies the Bledisloe Cup they had held since 1998 and cemented their status as World Cup champions. And it stole a Tri-Nations victory right from under the All Blacks' noses – in New Zealand. If I had scripted a more dramatic ending, I couldn't have done any better. What unparalleled, exhausting, exhilarating rugby drama.

The All Blacks were shattered, but magnanimous in defeat. Along with the Wallaby players, each All Black shook my hand and thanked me for the game. I thanked my touch judges, especially the humble and supportive Ed, who had kept me calm and focused and had helped with some critical calls.

As I headed for the tunnel, a group of spectators started pelting me with plastic beer bottles. I saw them raining down around me, yet I didn't feel threatened. As far as I was concerned, it was just emotional fans letting off steam.

Then a bottle, filled with a bit of water to give it weight – I can't imagine a Kiwi throwing away his beer – hit me in the chest and exploded. Fortunately I was expecting it, so I trapped it like a soccer ball and it dropped harmlessly at my feet. I felt Ed pull me back to try to keep me out of range of other projectiles.

Unbeknown to me, up in the stands my brothers were almost in tears of outrage. Their impulse was to protect me, but they were powerless to reach me in time.

But All Black lock Norm Maxwell could. Already in the tunnel, he turned and saw the assault. And came back to fetch me. With his arm around my shoulders, he escorted me off the field while appealing to the bottle-throwers to stop. I was a bit taken aback at the level of the fans' aggression, but not much – by then, I'd been through the mill.

Afterwards, the press focused on the bottle-throwing and how I had played extra time. In reply to the latter, I gave them clear, concise, categoric replies. In a nutshell, how I'd seen it and how I'd called it.

Time had been added on for three instances, I explained. The first was for injuries (there had been three or four in the second half), the second was for substitutions, and the third was for time-wasting at line-outs, where I felt the New Zealanders were huddling and not getting on with the game.

Then, asked for my reaction to the bottle-throwing, I chose diplomacy over outrage. This is how Gary retold events in his email:

David and I made our way to the locker room, where we found Jonathan sitting on the concrete bench talking to his officials. As a hoard of reporters,

TV crew and photographers entered the change room to interview Jonathan, we stood aside as they began questioning him. All their questions focused on the "bottle-throwing incident", and at this time the police were involved and were looking to make some arrests. They were intent on making a big issue of this incident.

What Jonathan said, without preparation, without having had any time to think and having to respond to this intimidating crowd minutes after this humiliating incident, was dignified and under the circumstances quite remarkable. He said, "Gentlemen, let us focus on the real story here, since I never felt 'besieged' or under any real threat. This is a passionate crowd who love their rugby and they were very disappointed ... Surely the real story would be that an outstanding game of rugby was played, and if you can't make a story of that, then report on Norm Maxwell, the All Black lock who, at the final whistle, threw his scrum cap down in disgust, yet in the midst of his painful defeat, he had the good grace to see what was going on and come to my defence. That is the mark of a man, and Norm showed that there is more to life than just a game of rugby.

The next day, not all the headlines lived up to the spirit of a match that Kiwi coach Wayne Smith rated as better than the Match Played in Heaven. "The moment he broke our hearts" read one. "Bledisloe ref could have played on for another 30 seconds" claimed another.

I had been tested by the game. There is just no explaining what it took to keep pace with a Test match as intense and frenetic as that one. The first half just sped by – the match had been going for 34 minutes before I even had a chance to look at my watch for the first time. Bledisloe Cup rugby at its peak.

And despite all of that, I did not blink once. There may have been some grey areas, but I let the game roll as I had through the years in the countless games building up to that moment. I didn't let the huge occasion rattle me and get in the way of the game.

I could've reffed it tight and blown it to death, and in that way reduced the amount of time available to scrutinise my calls. When you ref like that, the less the ball is in play, the less risk for the ref to botch it. And the less there is to criticise.

Instead I let the Test unfold into a thrilling spectacle that had fans on the edges of their seats until the final whistle. I didn't think that the emotional rollercoaster could get any more extreme or intense.

In my heart of hearts I knew I had reffed the game of my life. I believed it would go down as a watershed match in my career that would propel me into the big league. My seventh Test would always be special, because it was one of those all-time epic rugby matches. My feelings were borne out by the feedback I got afterwards, which diluted any sensationalist headlines. I was impressed by the way All Back skipper Todd Blackadder, who in spite of his massive disappointment, found a way to congratulate me and add that he was looking forward to seeing me in the future.

It also meant a great deal that losing coach Wayne Smith publicly acknowledged the quality of the match and went on record to say that he had no complaints about me. The All Blacks had had opportunities, he said, they simply didn't nail them.

"Any complaints about time-keeping are excuses," he told reporters. Privately, in an email, Wayne paid me a great compliment: "Be assured that we recognise the fine game you had, particularly at the breakdown. All the best for the future."

I was also chuffed that my assessor, Jim Irvine, recorded that I had reffed exceptionally well in very difficult circumstances, in a very dramatic match. And I was grateful to Jim because his report officially rewarded the faith the IRB and SA Rugby had shown in me, and it set me up for a long time to come.

Emails of affirmation continued to flow in after the Test. "Kappers. Thanks for your kind message," wrote Ed Morrison in reply to my letter acknowledging his support. "For me the highlight of the trip was your modesty. So often talented referees let themselves down, their heads becoming too big. Not so with you. A long and successful career awaits you and I only hope I have the opportunity to work with you again."

It was reassuring to get a message from a Kiwi Test ref, my colleague and friend Paddy O'Brien, who was close to becoming New Zealand's most capped official:

Johnie, great to catch up with you again. You had a superb match, mate, and your future is assured. This was the big Test for you and you nailed it.

I will be in touch in the next few days after you get home. Put a smile on the dial all the way home and keep an eye out for those who will try and cut you down. You have clearly established yourself in world refereeing circles and there will be some who don't like that ... (you know the people I am talking about). Good luck for the next round of appointments.

That kiss … Honouring my mother 19 years after my promise to kiss her on the field at Twickenham, November 2002

With André Venter, my brother Gary and mate Sean Dunne in Dublin prior to the Six Nations Ireland vs England game in March 2003

England smashed Ireland 42-6 at Lansdowne Road to win the Grand Slam, 30 March 2003

The frozen South. Steam rises from the scrum during the All Blacks vs England Test at the House of Pain in Dunedin, New Zealand, 12 June 2004. The All Blacks won the game 36-3

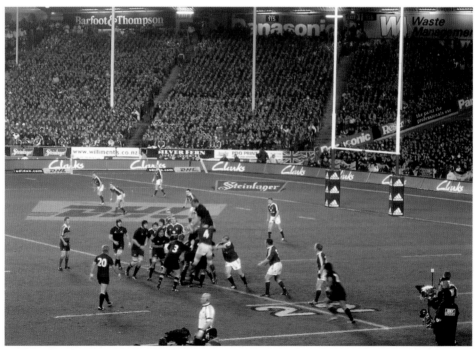

More than just a Test match: New Zealand vs the British & Irish Lions at Eden Park, 5 July 2005. The All Blacks scored five tries to one to obliterate their opponents

With Fijian Bill Cavubati, the biggest man to play international rugby, after Fiji beat Tonga 24-19, 16 July 2005

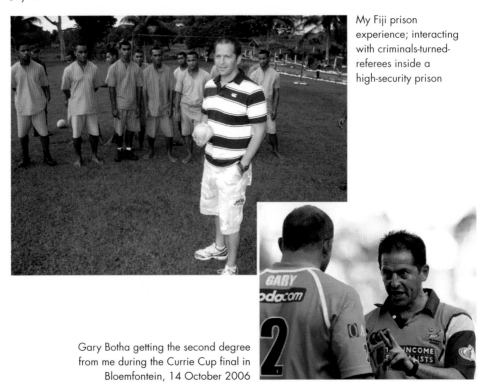

My Fiji prison experience; interacting with criminals-turned-referees inside a high-security prison

Gary Botha getting the second degree from me during the Currie Cup final in Bloemfontein, 14 October 2006

Downtime with Craig Joubert and Scott Young in Brisbane

With Marius Jonker in Canberra for a Super Rugby match

The South African contingent at the 2007 Rugby World Cup – Craig Joubert, Mark Lawrence, Marius Jonker, me and Tappe Henning. I'm struggling to hold up the big fella!

Enjoying a sing-song at the 2007 Rugby World Cup

Having a post-match beer with my team – Stuart Dickinson, Bryce Lawrence, Alan Lewis and Lyndon Bray – after Tonga vs Samoa in Montpellier, France

Doing duty as TMO at the 2007 Rugby World Cup

© Gallo Images/Getty Images

Me and Phil Vickery having a discussion during the Six Nations match between Scotland and England at Murrayfield, Edinburgh, on 8 March 2008

England strike early during their World Cup semi-final against France at the Stade de France in Saint-Denis, 13 October 2007

With John Smit and Os du Randt after South Africa beat England to win the 2007 Rugby World Cup final and lift the Webb Ellis Cup for the second time

Aussie colleague Stuart Dickinson was also full of praise:

> JK. I have only seen and read this rubbish about bottles etc. in the past 24 hours. What a crock of shit and I must say you have handled it all with aplomb. All the TV and press things I have seen are a credit to you, mate. You have well and truly risen above the rubbish and I can tell you those comments about Norm Maxwell were magnificent. That is a tribute to you, mate. You have shown grace and poise under fierce pressure. Well done. I hope the selectors and Steve Griffiths were there to watch.

One email from an unexpected quarter really did it for me. Stephen Bowness of the New Zealand Gridiron Officials Association wrote:

> I thought that you had a great game. Your calls were consistent, your management of the players was expert and your sense of judgement was great.
>
> However, one thing that stood out for me was that last call. The difference between a good official and a great official is that a great official will always make the tough call at the crucial moment without thinking about how it will affect the result of the game. That is exactly what you did. The fact that Australia won the game from that call does not detract from the quality of your officiating, but enhances it. A lesser man could easily have avoided the issue: you confronted it, and you should be congratulated for your strength of character.

The praise was *lekker*, but the best moment after the Test was a night on the town with my brothers. There was no way I was going to be intimidated by a handful of disappointed Kiwi fans and let them disrupt our family celebration in Wellington, which bubbled all night with talk of the Test. Gary and David had travelled my long road with me, and that night was our night.

Gary, a black belt in karate, shadowed me the whole evening. When I went to the bar for a drink, he was there, just to make sure no one messed with me. Nevertheless, one All Black supporter was so angry he told me to my face that I was a crap ref. He was not threatening, just full of blah blah.

Then, just before we packed it in at about 4.30 a.m., the same guy came to find me in my hotel bar. He apologised for his rudeness and added that I had reffed really well! He confessed that he had lashed out at me earlier because he was so gutted by his beloved All Blacks losing so dramatically.

What a perfect way to draw a line under a momentous day. Here was a fan living up to the spirit of the game by coming to shake hands, and in the process kind of atoning for his countrymen's earlier hooliganism.

Besides making good, that stranger's gesture also highlighted another huge responsibility that I would carry for as long as I reffed at this level. One that I hadn't thought about much until that night. A responsibility I dared never abuse. And that was the power, with just one blow of my whistle, to make a nation happy or sad.

16

Barking dogs

The year 2000 had been one of my most special years, and it was made even more memorable by a final magnificent Test in Marseille in November, where the French beat New Zealand 42-33 in front of a crowd of 60 000 at the Stade Vélodrome.

The Test turned out to be as much of an adrenaline rush as the weaving drive had been to the stadium from outside Marseille on the wrong side of the freeway with a police escort. I was in the vehicle with my assistants and good mates Tappe Henning and Scott Young from Australia, and we were so happy to make it to the ground alive, we hugged one another with relief.

The stadium bounced and heaved with an expectant crowd that was not used to rugby of this quality in their own backyard. The national anthems made the hairs on the back of my neck stand up, and the "Marseillaise" continued to ring out many times as the Test progressed and French national pride puffed out its chest.

France accelerated to a breathtaking 17-0 lead in just 10 minutes. From then on, it was helter-skelter as the All Blacks clawed their way back to within four points going into the final quarter. Ultimately, though, the golden boot of flyhalf and Man of the Match, Christophe Lamaison, tipped the scales for the French. It was heart-stopping rugby, but what really impressed me was how humble and gracious the defeated All Blacks were towards me after the final whistle.

Following a night on the town, at about 2 a.m. we went back to the dive where we were staying and cajoled the owner into giving us the keys to the bar. We made a huge racket and only stopped celebrating when Tappe's taxi arrived to take him to the airport at about 6 a.m. Boy, did we help him pack fast!

I don't like quitting. In my opinion, all it does is cut down on the opportunities life offers you. But sometimes sheer will is not enough. As in 2001, when I reffed an early-season Vodacom Cup game between the Cheetahs and the Lions in Bloemfontein. When I arrived in "Flower Fountain" the night before the Saturday game, I could feel the first signs of illness. My body just didn't feel right, but I had reffed with flu before.

So the next morning, I decided to grit my teeth and just get through the game. When a match is played in a less accessible centre like Bloem or Port Elizabeth, it becomes a logistical nightmare to find a replacement ref on the morning of a game.

But the closer I got to kick-off, the worse I felt. I went to the medical room to seek some relief, and the nurse suggested a Vitamin-B injection. It stung like hell, and it didn't make me feel any better. In fact, I felt progressively worse as the match dragged on. It was as if I was chasing the game the whole way through, and by half-time, my body was begging me to quit.

Back in the medical room I told the doc that I was feeling really shit. He told me to lie down and took my pulse. He asked how the game was going, and I told him I felt like I was playing catch-up all the time.

"Have you got a family?" the doc asked.

I was confused. "No," I said.

"Do you want a family?"

Given my condition, I found this line of questioning even more confusing. "Yes," I replied, "one day ..."

"Well, if that's what you want," he said, "you need to stop reffing right now. Because I can't feel your pulse."

The doc had made his point and I retired from the game. My touch judge, Marius Franken, took over, and I watched from the sidelines as the match finished without incident.

I was a bit embarrassed that I couldn't finish the job, but then again, my stats were not that bad – in 18 years, it was the only game I hadn't finished. Not too shabby. And, with any luck, I could still have a family one day ...

I got to ref another season of Super Rugby. Four games in total, plus my first semi-final, between the Brumbies and the Reds in Canberra. The Brumbies gave the Reds a hiding in a mismatch where George Gregan was on my case for large parts of the game. He never let up with his chirping, saying things like, "Are you not penalising Eales because he is captain of the Wallabies?" They were throwaway lines designed to sow doubt in the ref's mind. Gregan was very good at that. Mostly he was quite funny, but as much as I warmed to that part of his character, and as much as I admired him as a captain and a player, he could really get on my nerves after a while.

In April, while I was still reffing Super Rugby, I was informed that I'd been selected, along with Paddy O'Brien and André Watson, to ref the British & Irish Lions on their July tour of Australia. It was a massive honour. Every South African international referee wants to be able to look back and say he's reffed at least one Lions Test. I couldn't have asked for more. It was one of the pinnacles of this career I had chosen. But strangely, instead of feeling elated, I was overwhelmed by an incredible melancholy. There was so much more to life ... was this so special? That feeling of climbing the ladder, getting to the top, and then the realisation kicking in that this could all just be a rat race.

I couldn't put my finger on the cause, but the big changes I was making in my life might have had something to do with it. I'd just broken up with my girlfriend of about nine months. She was a special person, but our relationship had run its course. I'd also been thinking about beginning a new chapter of my life in Cape Town. With both my brothers now in Canada, there was nothing to keep me in Durban, and with my family split once again, it was time to start a new life.

Cape Town was also a more logical home base, as I could cut down on some travelling, which was taking more and more of a toll. For the past few years I'd been flying to Cape Town about 15 times every season for ref meetings or fitness tests. Sometimes those trips involved an overnight stay, which meant the additional hassle of finding someone to dog-sit my Staffie, Maisie. If I lived in Cape Town, I could simplify my life significantly, and besides, after varsity I had promised myself that one day I would live in the greatest city on the planet.

But I couldn't understand why I wasn't jumping up and down like I should have over one of the great appointments of my career. My despondency lasted for about six weeks, which was totally foreign to me. Instead of the usual joy I felt when I was given a big game with a special group of players, I felt oddly numb. Somewhere in the back of my mind it was beginning to dawn on me that there were pieces missing in the jigsaw of my life. A sort of mid-life crisis perhaps, who knows?

But the bleakness finally lifted and by June I was back to being my normal, positive self. It was a relief, but I was still unsure what it had all been about or what had brought it on. Perhaps it was all just a part of being a professional referee who travelled a lot and did not have a family to come home to. And perhaps it wasn't made any easier by the lack of support structures to help professional referees get through the tough times.

It was just as well that I was feeling mentally strong again, as more or less at that time Freek summoned me and my fellow professional refs to a Super Rugby "wash-up". Once I was in the meeting, however, another agenda unfolded. To my disgust, Freek and Steve Strydom started attacking me about an email I had sent Freek in the strictest of confidence.

I had written the email at the end of the Super Rugby season, after much deliberation, setting out why I was battling to get on with André Watson off the pitch. I considered him to be domineering and inflexible. There was nothing disrespectful in my email, but there I was, at this supposed Super Rugby post-mortem attended by Freek, Steve, André, Tappe Henning and Mark Lawrence, and Freek attacks me about the email in front of everyone present. He did this without warning me beforehand or having the decency to tell me that it was on the agenda for the meeting.

Both Freek and Steve asked me how I could send such a negative email about a colleague, making it clear that I was not a team player for doing so. It was unbelievable. It was an ambush designed to embarrass me and force me to apologise. It was way out of line. My email had been confidential, and I had by no means said that André was a bad person, just that I was battling to travel with him and suggested that if it was logistically possible, it might be best if we could be kept apart on future tours.

I asked Freek whether he had not read that I had sent him a *confidential* email, and how dare he raise the subject without consulting me about it. He then had another go at me, at which stage I decided to close up shop. I just sat back and listened to Freek and Steve rant on.

To his credit, Tappe eventually intervened, saying, "Guys, maybe Jonathan doesn't want to talk about this now. Perhaps this is the wrong forum." Freek then suggested that perhaps Steve and I should have a moment alone. That suggestion confirmed what I had suspected all along – that Steve was the driver behind this process. Everyone left the room, and just Steve and I remained behind. And we went at each other. I told him flat out that he had always supported me only reluctantly and had on occasion tried to undermine my progress. That made Steve defensive, and he said that he had always supported my career.

"How?" I asked. I told him that from the moment we had first started working together, he had disliked me. He had made it clear that I was too cocky for his liking. He had given me the Currie Cup semi-final only to inexplicably take it away. He had also criticised me as a person in the past and now he was doing it again in absolutely unprofessional circumstances. I underscored that by demanding to know whether he understood what a *confidential* email was.

Steve's defence was that once you pressed "send", an email was available to everyone. "Bullshit!" I said. "This was confidential. Do you as senior management not understand the concept?"

I might as well have been talking to a brick wall. It was pointless. I left angry and disillusioned. I had no idea how we would resolve the issue. Steve carried massive clout. He had played rugby for Free State and had even run their union at one stage. He was SA ref manager and was now chairman of refs. Overall, he was a significant contributor to South African rugby. It was a bit like pissing against the wind.

But I wasn't going to let it deter me. I had felt all along that they had tolerated me, even respected my ability, but, crucially, they did not respect and value my character and what I represented. They were not bad people. We had shared some good times, but I always sensed that they were suspicious of my independent thinking, my penchant to question the status quo and my resistance to blindly toe the line.

My work was not a mechanical process or a matter of just going through the motions; I was not just a number. My work was about me developing into a well-rounded, fulfilled human being. I wanted to be appreciated for more than just my work, and the only way that was going to happen was to be true to myself.

I was a square peg they were trying to fit into a round hole – it simply wasn't going to work. And I would not be distracted by sideshows. As Winston Churchill once said: "If I had to stop and throw a stone at every dog that barked at me, I would never reach my destination."

I was spitting mad, but after some thought I made a very important decision: I would never give up on my dream, no matter how hard the struggle. I did not care how rocky the road lying ahead might be – I would not deviate from my goal. Each hurdle that was placed in my path just made me more determined to succeed.

17

The 2001
British & Irish Lions

July arrived and I was raring to ref in my first British & Irish Lions series, which in my opinion is almost as good as a World Cup final.

It was hard to imagine a more mouth-watering contest. Not only would I be reffing the cream of the crop from England, Scotland, Ireland and Wales, but I'd be reffing them against the World and Tri-Nations champions, who boasted some of the best rugby players on the planet.

And here I was, one of two South African officials of the three selected for the series. That made me feel massively proud! I was still the new kid on the block, especially compared to my colleagues in the series, André Watson and Paddy O'Brien.

Both were well established on the international circuit. The selectors could have played it safe and selected another seasoned ref – from the north, to balance the panel – rather than put their faith in a young upstart. That alone made me hugely conscious of my responsibility to reward their trust in me.

I started off the series by running touch for André, who was reffing the opener at The Gabba in Brisbane. It was a sensible move by the selectors. As the least experienced of the trio, it gave me a chance to get a feel for the blistering intensity of a Lions Test match, which I soon discovered to be unlike anything I'd ever experienced. It was even more of a blockbuster event than a Test match, as here you had four countries combining into one mega team, supported by thousands of their fans, against the best team in world rugby.

The Lions walloped Australia 29-13 in that game, so the Wallabies found themselves under a lot of pressure going into the second Test, which was my baby. In order to ratchet up the public's interest, the organisers spared nothing in the pre-match razzmatazz, which included a full-on rock concert that really got the crowd at the Colonial Stadium in Melbourne pumping.

When I stuck my head out of the tunnel to a get a feel for what it was like under the stadium's closed roof, I was quite taken aback by the thunderous spectacle that was more American Super Bowl than rugby union. I'd experienced some booming stadiums in the past, but nothing compared to this.

The show didn't stop there. Showers of golden foil later cascaded down over the crowd, while images of Olympic champion sprinter Cathy Freeman flashed across the big screen. The Australian Rugby Union (ARU) had even roped in Aussie Wimbledon finalist Pat Rafter, who rallied the troops with a good-luck message. By anthem time, the Aussie chests could not have been pumped any bigger.

Of course the Lions fans, who were as passionate as the Aussies, were having none of it. In spite of the ARU handing out free flags, scarves and baseball caps, the sea of red and white was awe-inspiring. As was the rousing singing and chanting.

It was also typically cheeky. I couldn't help smiling – inwardly, of course – every time I heard the Lions fans break out in a subversive rendition of Australia's unofficial national anthem, which they renamed "Waltzing O'Driscoll".

The kaleidoscope of sights and sounds beautifully set the scene for me to blow the start to the second Test, which was greeted with a roar that almost lifted the roof. The loudest Test match crowd I'd experienced thus far had been my Bledisloe 2000 Test, but this was on another level altogether. Little did I know then that it would get a lot louder in the second half ...

Picking up where they'd left off in Brisbane, the Lions were all over the Wallabies. But they were their own worst enemy, as their finishing let them down. When we went back into the shed at half-time, it was 11-6 to the tourists, but I was baffled why they were not 20 points ahead instead.

The drama happened early in the second half when, to the delight of the home crowd, the Wallabies turned the match, and the series, on its head. It started minutes after the break. There was a messy phase, followed by a careless lob pass by Jonny Wilkinson that was snapped up by Aussie wing Joe Roff, who touched down. Matt Burke missed the conversion, and the Test was on a knife-edge at 11-all.

About five minutes later, Roff scored again, and from then on it was the Wallabies on a rampage, all the way to a 35-14 victory, with the Lions never looking like they could bounce back. It turned out to be the heaviest Lions defeat on Aussie soil, surpassing their 12-30 drubbing in the first Test in 1989.

I left the field as bewildered as the rest of the visitors by the Wallabies' second-half dominance. Quite how the world champs had engineered that dramatic turnaround was beyond me. It was most certainly a Test I would not forget in a hurry. And it set up a humdinger of a series decider in Sydney the next weekend, where the game went down to the wire, with Australia winning by the narrowest of margins.

Navigating my way through such a massive Test was a baptism of fire for an inexperienced international ref like me, one that would leave a lasting impression. What would also linger were two big moments that are still imprinted in my head like snapshots in an album.

One happened just before half-time, when centre Nathan Grey shoulder-charged flanker Richard Hill, catching him nastily in the face. Video replays later revealed it as a late hit, which my assistants and I had missed. The significance was that it took a bloodied Hill out of the game and later put him in hospital for X-rays, along with teammates Brian O'Driscoll, halfback Rob Howley and Wilkinson, who was stretchered off the field in the 69th minute. Hill was one of the Lions' most effective back-rowers and they missed his defensive presence.

The other indelible moment also involved Grey, who lined up O'Driscoll and smoked him with a beast of a tackle. The dazed Irishman bounced back onto his feet and acknowledged Nathan. "Great hit, mate," he said, before running back to his place.

Such classy sportsmanship in the heat of a supercharged Test battle spoke volumes for O'Driscoll, who by then had all the makings of a legendary player. Moments like that made me feel so privileged to have a front-row seat at the game, because you never got to experience them as a fan, no matter how close to the field you were.

A month after my unforgettable British & Irish Lions Test, my plans to leave Durban were about to kick in. But not before an incredible family celebration. It was my brother Gary's wedding to Lisa, his long-time girl-friend, who also hailed from Durban. He had flown back from Canada for the wedding and it was awesome to see him and David again and to be sharing such a special event with family and friends from all over the country. We all made sure that it was a beautiful day to remember, not just because of the occasion, but also because Gary was the first Kaplan brother to get married.

His wedding also marked the beginning of a new chapter in my life. Just two days later, on 14 August 2001, I packed all my worldly possessions into my Alfa 156 and waved goodbye to Durban, which had been my home for the past seven years.

I was planning on taking a road trip through the Transkei and along the Garden Route to Cape Town, where my only certainty was a flat in Higgovale that a mate said I could rent for a nominal fee.

Relocating to Cape Town was a challenging prospect, as this was the first time that I would be setting up a new home without my family, who by now was scattered around the world. That said, cutting ties to start again was the right life change for me. And what better place to do that than Cape Town, the city to which I always knew I'd return.

On the road, I had plenty of time to reflect on my experiences of the past year. The ending of a relationship, the conflicting emotions about my British Lions appointment, saying goodbye to my brothers again, leaving Durban and some good friends behind and a new beginning that lay ahead.

On the road between Port Elizabeth and Humansdorp, a massive shooting star flew across the sky from east to west. I thought it might be nature's way of saying I was headed in the right direction. So I pushed on to Cape Town, imagining the massive career opportunities that still awaited me in international rugby.

One was my third Six Nations Test match, Wales against Ireland at Cardiff's Millennium Stadium, which was supposed to take place on 3 March. But the Monday before the match, while I was sitting in the first-class lounge at Johannesburg International Airport, I suddenly found out on the internet that my game had been called off. The UK government had cancelled all public gatherings in an attempt to curb the spread of a disastrous foot-and-mouth outbreak.

After checking in with my ref manager, Steve Griffiths, there was a mad scramble to get my luggage off the flight, which was due to depart in 30 minutes, and to board another back home. I was disappointed about missing out on a Six Nations game, but not nearly as peeved as I would have been had I flown all the way to the UK for nothing.

As it turned out, however, all good things come to those who wait. In October, one of my first international flights out of my new home, Cape Town, was to Heathrow for my reinstated Wales versus Ireland clash.

It was a special game for me, as this would be my reffing debut at one of my favourite venues, Millennium Stadium, where I ran touch in the 1999 World Cup. All the signs were there that it would be a hell of a game. Ireland had been dismal against Scotland, so they would be revved up. Likewise Wales, who would be going all out to break their almost two-decade-long hoodoo of not beating Ireland at home.

Personally, I wanted to sign off the 2001 season with a top Test performance. I was well prepared after reffing some Currie Cup encounters that had been tightly contested affairs. And generally I was happy with my form and fitness.

However, the game didn't live up to its billing. Largely it was a scrappy affair with a litany of handling errors and a lack of cohesion from both sides. Until Ireland, 15-6 ahead with just seven minutes of normal time left on the clock, turned on the magic with a three-try blitzkrieg. Their 36-6 victory was historic, topping their previous best score of 19-3 against Wales in Belfast way, way back in 1925.

I was disappointed that it hadn't been a better game, as my brothers and a long-time friend from Durban, André Barnard, who now played for Swansea, were in the stands.

André's reputation preceded him, as he was one of the central characters in the Battle of Brive, which goes something like this. When he was playing for Pontypridd in 1997, André was involved in the infamous 30-man, all-in brawl that erupted on the pitch during an away match against the French club Brive.

Unable to leave it on the field after the match, the French came into the bar where the Ponty players were drinking, apparently all cocky about their win and demeaning of their opposition. Then all hell broke loose. André, Phil John and Ponty's Kiwi forward Dale McIntosh, widely known as The Chief, ended up going toe to toe with virtually the whole Brive team. Legend has it that they smashed them up and put a few of the Brive players in hospital. It got so hectic that the cops had to use pepper spray to break up the fight.

After the Test match, while waiting for me to wrap up some formalities, David and André found a bar to have a few drinks. Later the two of them went for a leak and overheard a drunk Welsh fan mouthing off at the urinal about how shit the ref had been.

"Fuck you," David told the drunk, "the ref's my brother." The Welshman, who was built like a coal miner, came right up to David, towered over him and told him that he didn't give a shit who the ref was related to, he was still crap. So David countered, "Well, you better start giving a shit." André said he thought another Brive was about to erupt. He was steeling himself for the worst, because he thought the drunk was about to headbutt David.

Luckily it fizzled out. But it yet again highlighted the inherent danger when you invite family and friends to share a big match. A lot of people talk *kak* after the game, some of it true and some not. Whatever the case may be, you have to let it go.

But it was difficult for family members when they were part of the crowd. They were much closer to the abuse, which I was largely oblivious to down on the pitch. They heard it all. And sometimes it got to a point where it was hard for them to tolerate any longer.

My concern was that it would get out of hand one day. The last thing I needed was anyone getting hurt defending my honour, because as far as I was concerned, I didn't need any defending. By now I'd learnt that I was not involved in a popularity contest. I would be judged on my merits between the four white lines. And that was where it should stay.

Fortunately no one got hurt in Cardiff, but sadly, about a month later, in mid-November, I heard the shocking news that my friend and colleague, Carl Spannenberg, had drowned while boating with friends at Zeekoevlei near Muizenberg.

His death was a tragic loss all round, and not just for his devastated loved ones. Yet again, rugby had lost another ref in his prime. Carl, who was just 33, had a bright future ahead of him.

I met Carl in the early 90s, after the unification of the non-racial South African Rugby Union and the whites-only South African Rugby Board. And I recall the camaraderie we had both felt then at finally being able to work together for the game we were equally passionate about.

Carl was a friendly bloke you couldn't help but like. He had an easy-going way about him and a reputation as a bit of a practical joker. I never saw him without a smile on his friendly face and a twinkle in his eye. Carl only reffed for a decade, but in that time he moved swiftly up the ladder to become a Super Rugby and Test referee. Along with me, he was also one of the original South African Rugby Football Union's first four professional refs. Yet in spite of Carl's quick elevation through the ranks – and this is what I really liked about him – he never lost sight of his Cape Flats roots. He was always willing to go out of his way to help upcoming refs from disadvantaged communities.

But all that had been snuffed out by an accident that is still shrouded in mystery today. So, for the second time in three years, I ended off a season burying a friend with whom I had a lot in common. Obviously it was distressing. And like colleague Neville Heilbron pointed out, not one of us wanted to believe that we would never see Carl's mischievous smile again.

But I tried to balance the pain of loss with the memory I had of waking up after my 1998 knee op and slowly realising, in my anaesthetic fog, that the man coming round two beds away was Carl Spannenberg. Neither of us had had any idea that we were both down for surgery, with the same doctor on the same day, me for my knee and he for his compartment-syndrome problem (a painful condition that occurs when pressure within the muscles builds to dangerous levels, which can lead to muscle and nerve damage and problems with blood flow). Seeing a friendly face post-op was both a pleasant surprise and a good boost for morale.

As we lay there, we chatted about the roads we had travelled and whether we would heal well enough to realise our dreams. It was a wonderful moment of camaraderie and recalling it lifted my spirits after his passing.

Once again, the loss of a friend was a reminder that I was still blessed with the opportunity to live my dreams.

18

"Omkeer!"

Early in 2002, I reffed the Leopards against the Eagles in Potchefstroom in an uneventful Vodacom Cup match. Afterwards I was getting ready to drive back to my Johannesburg hotel when touch judges Marius Jonker and Gareth Lloyd-Jones twisted my arm to stay for just "one" drink.

Gareth suggested that we go to a bar called Bourbon Street. Up to that point, my plan had been to have an early night, but from the moment we walked in and found everyone dancing on the tables, I realised I was being hopelessly optimistic.

One drink led to another, and soon it was after midnight. I was talking to the DJ, who was playing some amazing metal music, when I spotted a pretty young student dancing on a table. We caught each other's eye across the crowded room, I walked over to her, put my arms around her legs and gently pulled her off the table … She didn't resist, but she did put me in my place.

"I know who you are," she said, "and I'm not that easy."

We started chatting and eventually ended up kissing and having a cuddle. Then the Eagles players arrived and I got caught up in their partying. At about 2.30 a.m. I looked around for my new best friend, but couldn't find her anywhere. Marius was also nowhere to be seen.

Gareth informed me that Marius had wanted us to wait for him while he walked a student back to her digs. So we hung around until about 4 a.m., when Bourbon Street started to close, but there was still no sign of Marius.

At that point Gareth was confronted by four *skollies* who were clearly looking for trouble. I was wearing a golf shirt with an SA Rugby ref logo on it, so I couldn't afford to get caught up in a brawl; besides, fighting was not really my game. I asked one of the blokes what was going on, and he said he was going to *klap* Gareth for being rude to his friend.

"No worries," I said. "I'll talk to Gareth and get him to apologise. You go back to your mates and calm things down."

By then we'd been drinking for hours and Gareth was not thinking like a match official. So when I suggested that he apologise to the guys, he leant in closer and mischievously whispered in my ear: "I think we can take them ..."

Amused, I turned to the instigator and asked him if I could buy him a schwarma. He was hungry. The next thing we were all mates, eating our schwarmas.

When Marius finally appeared, we left in his car. We were about 40 kilometres out of Potch when I told Marius about the pretty student I'd met, but that she had just disappeared. What a coincidence – it turned out that the student Marius had walked home was 'my' student's friend. Even better, he had her number, so I grabbed Marius's phone, called the friend, introduced myself and asked her to get her housemate on the phone.

"*Sy slaap,*" the friend told me.

"Well, *maak haar wakker,*" I ordered jovially.

She took the phone to her friend, who told me she was about to go to sleep. Chancing my arm, I asked if I could pop in.

"Cool," she replied. I put the phone down before she could change her mind.

Suddenly, I was wide awake.

"*Omkeer!*" I ordered Marius, who moaned like an old granny. He was running touch in the afternoon and desperately needed his bed.

"Come on, Marius, just this once ..."

It took a bit of persuading, but eventually we were on our way back to the digs, with Marius grumbling how I owed him big time. As soon as we arrived, I went straight to the girl's room. My Afrikaans was atrocious and she couldn't cough in English, but that didn't matter. One thing led to another. And this time it was Marius's turn to wait. After several failed attempts to get me out of the sack, Marius's patience finally ran out at about 8 a.m., when he barged into the room to find me stark naked on the bed.

Almost 12 hours after "just one drink ..." we were back on the road to Joburg. From that day on, Marius called me "Omkeer". And he would think twice before suggesting a quick one for the road again.

The pretty student was not my only surprise of 2002. At the end of March, about a month into Super Rugby, I was dispatched from Brisbane, where the Reds had gone down to the Crusaders, to ref the Hong Kong Sevens. Brilliant!

Hong Kong was the one tournament I'd always wanted to ref, and all the other top South African refs had been, so I truly thought my chance had come and gone.

And the event lived up to every expectation. It was an amazing experience. I thoroughly enjoyed the rugby, the blokes I was reffing with and the carnival atmosphere that kept the crowds coming back. To cap this amazing experience, I got to ref a scintillating final in which England scored five tries to four to beat favourites Fiji 33-20.

From there I hot-footed it back down to Christchurch to ref one of my most memorable Super Rugby matches, between the Crusaders and the Brumbies at Jade Stadium. These were the two best teams in the competition, and both teams were chock-a-block with Wallabies and All Blacks, so the game was a cracker.

At one stage the Crusaders were 30-18 up. Then the Brumbies conjured up two brilliant tries and converted both to grab the lead. But the Brumbies knocked on after a Crusaders' kick-off, which gave the hosts a scrum. We were into the final minutes, and from that scrum the Crusaders launched one of their typical passages of play, taking the ball through a number of phases that thrilled the crowd.

Dramatically, Aaron Mauger slotted a drop kick in the final seconds to sneak the game 33-32. You couldn't ask for more from two of Super Rugby's superpowers, who would go on to contest the final.

Super Rugby continued to dish up more surprises that year, with one of the best being the mid-May, top-of-the-table clash between log leaders Crusaders and the second-placed Waratahs.

Again I was back at Jade Stadium, this time expecting, like everyone else, a close encounter between two of that season's most closely matched sides. But instead the Crusaders surprised all and sundry with a blistering first half of pure rugby perfection.

Playing the ultimate brand of rock-star rugby, they didn't put a foot wrong. Every time they kicked, it was perfect. When they went for the "no-look" pass, someone was always there. Every time they touched the ball, it all just fell into place. Sublime passes, great chips, absolute synchronicity between the players. The result, after 40 minutes of mesmerising rugby, was nine sublime tries from all over the place.

When I blew the half-time whistle with the score at 63-0, the big crowd rose as one in a resounding standing ovation. In that moment, there was no need for words. Everyone in that stadium knew they had witnessed something unique. Instead of the close clash expected, they had witnessed a bit of rugby nirvana – something they were unlikely to experience again in a lifetime of watching the game. It was the greatest half of rugby I had ever been a part of.

The Waratahs put up a better showing in the second half, scoring three tries, but the Crusaders had the last laugh, scoring the final five-pointer. Andrew Mehrtens, who up till that point had had a perfect day with the boot, missed the final conversion, which hit the right upright and bounced out. This final act of the game reminded the local faithful that they were not in heaven. But that little imperfection was somehow the perfect way to end what had been a flawless game of rugby.

A few months later I was back in Christchurch, which was turning out to be my favourite rugby city of 2002. This time it was for a Bledisloe Cup Test in extremely cold conditions. It didn't really bother me much at first because I've always been able to handle the cold. As my mates back in Cape Town will tell you, I keep the doors of my house open all through winter. I like it crisp!

So shorts and slops it was when I walked the half a kilometre from my hotel to the TAB to play the horses before getting ready for the Test. I'd discovered over the years that punting on horses and gambling in casinos – where I had enjoyed a couple of enormous wins – was a great way of relieving the boredom on the road. I mean, how much TV, computer games and reading in a hotel room can a bloke take?

After a few hours at the TAB in Christchurch, I packed it in and stepped outside to head back to my hotel. Bloody hell! The city had been hit by a blizzard, and it was now cold enough to make me call for a taxi. But there was none available, so I was forced to walk back to the hotel in the freezing cold or I wouldn't make it to the stadium in time for the kick-off. It was sheer madness – in near Arctic conditions, sleet slicing down, there I was, walking in shorts and slops. Anyone who saw me must have thought I'd lost the plot.

Back in my hotel room, it took a long, hot shower to warm me up, which made me wonder just how much colder the playing conditions were going to get. Of course we play rugby come hail or snow, but by the time I walked out onto the pitch, conditions were beyond atrocious. But the show had to go on, and the entire game was played in sleet and appalling visibility. And just to make things even more interesting, a storm erupted during the match.

The game turned out to be my first try-less Test – actually one of the few I would ever ref – with the All Blacks managing to grind out a 12-6 win. The remarkable stat from this Test was the kicks out of hand. The average that year was about 66 per match. That day, there were a whopping 183 kicks out of hand. The conditions were so bad that neither team wanted the ball, preferring to play aerial ping-pong instead.

By the time I hit the showers again, I was so cold I couldn't feel my toes. I spent a few painful minutes under the hot water before my circulation got going again. Later I heard that most of the game was played at –2 °C. It didn't surprise me. At half-time, one of my touch judges, Andy Turner, had shown me a white dot on the end of his nose, where he had lost all feeling. Later a doctor's examination revealed that he was showing the first signs of frostbite.

My work took me to another freezing-cold arena that year for a World Cup qualifier between Russia and Spain in Krasnodar in southern Russia, near the Black Sea.

The Test had already been called off once because the field in Moscow was too icy. And, while the ref, Nigel Whitehouse, was hanging around waiting for the Test to be rescheduled, he slipped and broke his leg. That was how the offer to ref the Test came my way.

Figuring it was one of those once-in-a-lifetime experiences, and knowing I would be the first South African to ref a Test in Russia, I grabbed the opportunity with both hands. And I was not disappointed, even though it required three long-haul flights to get to Krasnodar. In fact, it turned out to be one of the best rugby travel experiences I would ever have.

It all unfolded a bit like a Quentin Tarantino movie. I was offered the game before I'd even unpacked my bags from my last international appointment, England versus New Zealand at Twickenham. My visa was rushed through and a couple of days later I was on a flight back to London, where I met one of my touch judges, Simon McDowell, an impeccably dressed, well-mannered man, in the business-class lounge.

My other touch judge was Wayne Barnes, a guy with no dress sense, like me. But he had missed his flight, so Simon and I flew out of Heathrow six hours later and landed in Moscow, which was *much* colder than Christchurch.

Weirdly, Simon and I were booked into different hotels at opposite ends of Moscow, which is a monster city. So we told our driver to take us to the same hotel. By then we had already stood in a queue at the airport that was 20 tourists long and took an hour and a half to process. It took an hour to check into the hotel – even though there were only about five people in front of us at reception. But we didn't complain. When in Russia, do as the Russians do ...

The hotel was massive, 60 storeys high, and we were on the 40th floor. And, oddly, we had to find the cleaning lady to obtain our room keys. They do things a bit differently in Russia ... Weirdly, the bed in my room was the size of a cot. I am only five foot eight, but it was so tiny, my legs hung over the edge. I couldn't complain, though – six-foot-two Simon had an even more uncomfortable night ahead of him.

After a fitful night, I woke up feeling a bit groggy. Opening a window to shake off the cobwebs, I nearly seared my nostrils as I breathed in. It was -10! Now I knew exactly why this game had already been called off once. I made a mental note to watch my step when I left the hotel.

A few hours later Simon and I boarded a very noisy Tupolev for Krasnodar. Wayne was still playing catch-up, but we had been joined by our match commissioner, Kees Blaas, a man surely destined to be a referee (for those of you unfamiliar with the language, "blaas" means "blow" in Afrikaans). When I say the aircraft was noisy, I mean you couldn't hear yourself think, let alone speak. After it took off, I detected the smell of cigarette smoke. When I pointed it out to the flight attendant, she said, yes, the passengers were smoking in the toilets. They did it all the time ... Interesting.

Coming in to land, you couldn't help but notice that the ban on smoking on board was not the only airline regulation being flouted. There they were, all the locals, cellphones out, merrily texting and calling their mates. If this was the Russian way, I thought, were the pilots flying this noisy tin can of a similar mindset?

Those were not the only air-travel oddities in that part of the world. After landing in Krasnodar, at what appeared to be an air-force base with plenty of parking space around the terminal, we taxied for ages, for what seemed like a kilometre, down the runway and then waited for some time for a bus to arrive to take us to the deserted terminal. Then we waited nearly an hour for a tractor to load our luggage off the plane and deliver it to us ...

As I'd discover over the coming days, such quirks were very much part of the tourist experience. There was always a fascinating cultural reality check around the next corner. A good example is when we arrived at the Test-match welcoming dinner that evening with Wayne, who had finally caught up with us. I had to pinch myself when the Russian coach started talking to me in Afrikaans! It was what you'd expect from a James Stofberg from Potch, but out here, in a remote Russian city?

I was trying to get my head around this when our hosts announced that we must drink a toast before supper. Out came the shooter glasses, which looked more like close cousins of draft beer glasses. And they were filled to the brim with vodka.

Alarmed, I requested a snack to line my stomach and was met with a hearty laugh that indicated how much the hosts appreciated my unintentional joke. So much so that they drank another toast. And another. Eight toasts later, and we, the Russians and the Spanish were all rat-arsed before supper had even started. And this on the eve of a World Cup–qualifying Test!

As you'd expect, supper had its little surprises too. Not that I can remember many of them. I do recall, however, one booze-fuelled moment of hilarity when we asked our young Russian liaison officer, who looked more like a robust tighthead than a chaperone, whether he played rugby. Because you should, we suggested with the best intentions. He did, he told us in broken English. Until the previous week's game, when he took exception to the touch judge's decision, headbutted him and got banned from playing. "That's how I got *this* job," he said, grinning from ear to ear and raising his vodka glass to the heavens.

When we got back to our hotel, the surprises assumed a surreal quality. Off our heads, our hosts guided us to the fourth floor, which we were told was a "special" floor. We walked in and found the place wall to wall with the Spanish players and dozens of scantily clad women. It was clearly the hotel brothel. Wayne and I walked to the bar and ordered two double espressos and, while waiting, Wayne walked up to a woman in tiny hot pants, boobs falling out all over the place, legs splayed, and asked her, with a dead-pan expression, what she did for a living. "You don't know?" she asked with a pout that left nothing to the imagination.

The next morning we tried to smooth out the night's rough edges with more espressos and a tour of the local market, where our minder, a bloke who looked like he could be quite at home in the underworld, with hundreds of bank notes bulging from his blazer pockets, helped us buy the finest Russian vodka at one dollar a bottle. The market itself was rather sad, revealing the meagre existence these people eked out selling nuts, root vegetables and other bits and bobs just to stay alive. It made me feel very grateful for the life I had.

Eventually it was game time, and we headed for the local stadium. But just before we got there, our driver turned off and stopped at a hotel … We got out, followed him up two flights of stairs, along a corridor and into a room. Bizarrely, this was the referees' change room and, looking through the window,

I realised it was a significant distance to the pitch, as the half a kilometre walk through the town in our boots proved. At the stadium we were greeted by four army tanks parked around the ground ... turrets facing the field! "What the hell," I thought, "are these blokes expecting trouble or what?"

While inspecting the ground, we couldn't help but notice a huge pipeline running around the entire perimeter, dangerously close to the touchline. Kees and I felt this was of huge concern, but we were reluctant to call off the Test again, especially after flying halfway round the world.

So we discussed it with the Spanish players, who said, "Yes, we've also flown far and had all these delays. Damn sure we're playing." After agreeing that they would treat tackling over the touchline with caution, we headed over to the Russian change room where, unbelievably, I was greeted by Tenk Hendriks and Bloues Volschenk!

Despite their South African imports, however, Russia found themselves on the back foot. They countered by sending on super-subs Tenk and Bloues, and they ended up scoring a few tries, but Spain were too good, winning 38-22. However, Russia qualified for the World Cup on points difference, but were later disqualified for fielding ineligible players. Who do you think they were?

The crowd of about 500 didn't seem particularly fazed by the loss. Yet we were escorted from the field back to the hotel change room by these Dolph Lundgren lookalikes with guns inside their jackets. It was quite funny, to say the least. Was this perhaps a part of the world where they bumped off refs when they didn't get a result?

That evening Bloues took us out for a night on the town and the vodka flowed again. It felt really weird being there with a bunch of countrymen who, I learnt, played their rugby for a club called Nordjavestk in Siberia.

The next day we were back at the airport feeling a tad ragged on a bus that trundled on for miles before reaching our plane, which was waiting down the runway. At check-in, a blonde bombshell Simon had been chatting to earlier came up to me and eventually asked if she could sit next to me on the flight. I liked her thinking ...

Once on board, Anastasia was very affectionate, holding hands with me and being quite suggestive. I thought the mile-high club could not be far off. When we landed, she asked if I would like to spend a few days hanging out with her in Moscow. I was tempted. Marius was a million miles away, so there would be no interruptions. But sanity prevailed and I politely declined the offer.

19

"Ek het die ref ..."

Several months before I flew to Moscow, an incident occurred that shocked the rugby world and brought shame upon South African rugby in particular. It was 10 August 2002, and no one who had gathered at Kings Park to watch the Springboks take on the All Blacks that day could have suspected how events would unfold. Least of all me, sitting on the sidelines as the fourth match official.

But I'm jumping ahead. The Wednesday before the Kings Park Test, I had a massive night out with my mates in Cape Town, which ended at 4 a.m. when my friend Gary Normand and I left a Green Point bar. That was the start of what turned out to be the biggest "weekend" of my life.

Come Thursday morning, after just two hours of sleep, I hopped on a flight to Durban, where I crashed for the rest of the day. Well rested, I hooked up with some old Durban mates, including Greg Bruwer, James Moss and Kevin Schraader, as well as others who had flown down from Joburg for a long-overdue reunion involving rugby and a lot of revelry. We ended up at the Skybar, where we partied through the night until 6.30 a.m. And that was only because the cleaners jokingly threatened to sweep us up with the trash unless we hauled our asses out of our bar stools.

All of us slept through the day until Friday evening, when my mates from Joburg, who couldn't get off work on the Thursday, arrived. It was supposed to be a recovery pasta night at Primi Piatti in Umhlanga's Gateway Centre, until the latecomers heard that they'd missed out on the previous night's party and insisted on making up for it by ordering tequilas for dinner.

Yet again, one thing led to another, and it wasn't long before our incorrigible group found ourselves a fireman's pole in the restaurant and were all sliding down it – upside down – from the next floor up. Again and again and again, we all jostled to outdo one another. Plain bloody ridiculous. Just how no one fell or broke something was an absolute miracle.

By 4 a.m., no one in the group felt left out of anything any more, and we merrily trundled back to our hotels. I only woke at about 11.30 on the Saturday, just in time for a coffee with referee Dave McHugh. And then I squeezed in a quick, late breakfast with plenty of orange juice so that I could leave for Kings Park at 1.30 p.m.

By the time the Test kicked off, I was still feeling ragged – and ever so grateful that I was only holding the boards and pushing a pen for the match as the number-four official. Delivering the occasional drink of water to McHugh was as much running as I was prepared for on the day.

Enter stage right, this beer-boep figure in a Bok supporter's jersey, lumbering onto the field. I thought he was some drunk idiot trying to show off in front of his mates. Not for one minute did it cross my mind that he was targeting McHugh, who was focused on a scrum he had called.

Piet van Zyl's tackle on McHugh was a despicable act. Fortunately it was nipped in the bud by a quick-acting Richie McCaw and A.J. Venter, who punched him. Van Zyl then disappeared beneath a combined Bok and All Black maul from which he emerged with a bloody nose. That moment of madness highlighted how vulnerable match officials are to thuggery, but what made me as angry as the next guy was that a clown had disgraced my country and my code.

I was also irritated because suddenly I was promoted to touch judge, replacing Chris White, who took over McHugh's whistle. Later, my mate James told me that from up in the stands he started laughing uncontrollably when he saw me gingerly preparing to run. He knew it was the last thing I needed that day. But in reality, it was no laughing matter. My head ached and every time I looked up into the afternoon sun from the open-side touchline, it fried my brain.

In the end, the Springboks lost narrowly to the All Blacks, but I would certainly not remember that game for the final score (30-23). The following day, while reflecting on this incident, I felt embarrassed when the vast majority of people who called in to a TV rugby show justified Van Zyl's behaviour. Their rationale was that McHugh was having a poor day at the office and deserved what he got. What utter rubbish! No amount of bad decisions on a rugby field deserves retribution of any kind.

That August afternoon was an aberration for me, because Kings Park had always been a hallowed ground, where the seeds of my rugby ambitions were sown. As a kid growing up in Durban, my dream had been to play in a Currie Cup final. And then, once I'd started reffing, to ref one.

For many years I had felt that I was more than capable of doing a Currie Cup final. But I never cracked the nod. Even though I had risen quickly through the international refereeing ranks and had performed really well in some of the biggest arenas of world rugby.

That said, I hadn't lost sight of the bigger picture. I may have had a burning obsession to ref a Currie Cup final, but it seemed as if I was getting a lot more support from the international community, so that was where I focused. I was more than happy with my job. I loved the challenge of Test refereeing and the honour of representing my country, and I knew I was really growing as a ref.

My goal was to be the best I could be, not only for the sake of personal ambition, but in the best interests of Rugby Union. To win the respect and buy-in from coaches and players until, eventually, the weight of their opinion would hold sway. I knew that if I delivered excellence to those I served on the field, eventually it would be rewarded. I knew that if I did this, while remaining steadfast in my burning desire to ref a Currie Cup final, success *would* follow.

Along the way I got the inside track from SARU CEO Rian Oberholzer, who took me aside one day and confirmed what I had suspected all along. "Look, Kappie," he told me. "They're not going to give you a Currie Cup final. They keep putting André's name forward." Of course Rian didn't want to be seen taking sides, but he gave me invaluable advice: "Since Freek and company keep saying that you can't ref the final because you're a Western Province referee, my suggestion is, join Boland refs."

That was at a time when Province had made the finals two years in a row, in 2000 and 2001. I was astounded at what Rian had said. But then I recalled that when I lived in KwaZulu-Natal in the late 1990s, I was told that the reason I wasn't chosen to referee a semi-final was because the Sharks were playing in the other semi. The implication was that I would be biased and facilitate an "easier" opponent.

In this day and age of professionalism, how could you base a selection policy on a perceived provincial bias? What did that say about my integrity? And what did it say about the men for whom I worked? I found the whole thing preposterous. Bizarre, actually.

But it was not within my power to control what people thought of me. So I followed Rian's advice and joined Boland. I was now playing the system. André lived in Benoni, had joined the Falcons and reffed the Lions. I lived in Cape Town, joined Boland and was able to ref WP. (Years later, I would ref my sixth Currie Cup final living in Cape Town, a WP ref reffing WP in the final.) And so I have Rian to thank for cleverly opening the door to my first Currie Cup final. The disappointments notwithstanding, I was still enjoying myself, living my dream and refereeing in the best domestic competition in the world, the Currie Cup.

Come October 2002, the Lions whacked Province 50-13 at Ellis Park in front of 50 000 spectators in a game I reffed. Then the Lions went on to make the finals the following weekend by beating the Cheetahs 43-29 in Bloem, and that same weekend the Bulls beat the Sharks 22-19 in Durban.

In the days that followed the semis, I tried not to think about the fact that I might have a shot at reffing the final, although it lurked around in the back of my mind. Then the call came while I was relaxing at home on the couch with my laptop.

It was a short, to-the-point exchange. No fanfare. In fact, my appointment for Saturday 26 October at Ellis Park was conveyed with no mention of the elephant in the room.

After I hung up, I had every reason to leap up and down and go beserk. Instead, I sank back into the couch as an incredible wave of relief flooded through my body, followed by a massive rush. Woohoo!

There, alone in my house, with just my fat dog Ruby looking on knowingly, I wanted to raise my arms in the air like a heavyweight boxer who has gone the distance and finally won the title on a unanimous points decision. After all those years of trying and trying, I'd finally made it. I let it sink in for a while and then reached for my cell to spread the good news. My phenomenal news. I phoned everyone who knew what this meant to me. My family first, and then my friends, like Phil Botha, who had always told me I was a star, and Paul Dobson, my best friend in rugby.

For the next hour, as the congratulations poured in, I rode a wave of euphoria. Then, as things quietened down, I began to think about the responsibility of the immense privilege that lay ahead. I couldn't take anything for granted. This could be the only Currie Cup final I ever got, so I needed to ref it as if it were my last. I needed to make this one count.

My only regret was that my uncle Mendel Musiker was not around to share this moment with me. My uncle on my mother's side – my granny Sonja's brother – Mendel had been a massive Bulls fan who got a big kick whenever I gave him comps to come and watch me ref a game at Loftus. Nothing would have made him prouder than watching me ref his beloved Bulls in a final.

But sadly Mendel had fallen ill earlier in 2002 and died a while later. His funeral was one I would never forget. As I and the other mourners walked away from his graveside at the end of the service, I turned and saw the solitary figure of my cousin Steven – Mendel's youngest – lingering at the open grave. Then, as I watched, he reached for a shovel planted in the mound of earth nearby and slowly covered his dad's resting place, one shovelful at a time.

It was one of the saddest moments I ever witnessed, and it absolutely broke me. So it would be hard not to think of Mendel when I ran onto Ellis Park on match day. It would be one of those private thoughts I would carry into the game.

As it turned out, I was almost late for my big day. I normally cut things very fine going into a match. I knew just how to time it so that I arrived at the ground psyched and ready to roll. I hated hanging around kicking my heels, waiting for kick-off time to arrive. But that Saturday I hadn't bargained on the traffic jam that was going nowhere fast.

Crawling towards Ellis Park along Harrow Road, it got to the point where I had to admit I was not going to make it on time. I couldn't believe it. One of the biggest days in my rugby career and I was trapped in the traffic jam from hell.

Time for plan B. I called in the cavalry, and they arrived from the opposite direction in a traffic-police car containing Officer Soekie and my refereeing friend James Sheriff. Relieved beyond measure, I swapped places with James and roared off with Soekie in the opposite direction, siren blaring and lights flashing, approaching Ellis Park from the south. There I was, racing along at 160 kilometres an hour, with Soekie radioing ahead to colleagues: "*Ek het die ref*! *Maak oop die pad*!" (I have the ref! Clear the road!)

In between all this, she was composed enough to notice that I wasn't wearing my seat belt. "I suggest you buckle up, ref," she advised.

"No worries," I replied. "I'm safe with you."

Nothing could wipe the schoolboy grin off my face as we flew past Bulls and Lions fans who didn't have a clue just how important it was for them to give way. We arrived at the ground with 25 minutes to spare.

For most, that would be cutting it fine. But the speed of my change-room protocol was legend. I'd got it down to such a fine art that it literally took me three minutes to be completely kitted up. And I didn't do a warm-up – I never did. Other refs had warm-up clothes, warm-up shoes, a whole routine. By the time they got to the game, they'd blown a gasket. Me, I liked to hit the ground running.

The toss was over in a blur. As I made my way out of the tunnel, the crowd roaring in my ears, I had a lump in my throat and I felt as proud as I had ever been in my life.

Out in the middle there was a moment to reflect on the hard work and sacrifices it had taken to realise my childhood dream, as well as the debilitating injuries and some discord with my bosses. But finally, here I was, about to blow for the start of the 2002 Currie Cup final. Hooohaa!

It was one of those games where everything flashed by in a blur. All I recalled afterwards was the Bulls being at their rampant, brutal best. And the Lions being their own worst enemy, making error after error.

The hero of the day was flyhalf Derick Hougaard, who could not put a foot wrong. He slotted five penalties from all over the place, as well as a pair of deadly drops, *and* went over for a try. Scoring 26 points in the Bulls' 31-7 goring of the Lions, he wrote himself into the history books by toppling Naas Botha's 15-year record for the most points scored by a single player in a Currie Cup final. Soon after this, Hougaard would be dubbed "*die liefling van Loftus*", and Gé Korsten's "Liefling" would ring out every time he put one over the poles.

Up in the referee suite after the game, colleagues were shaking my hand and slapping my back. It felt good to get their affirmation for reffing a long-overdue final. Like me, they hoped it was the first of many. I still could not believe that I had realised my childhood dream, but it felt awesome nevertheless.

When the time came to say a few words, I had nothing prepared. So I thanked my family and my friends and SA Rugby. I also paid tribute to the teams for making my job easier on the day. Then suddenly it came to me ...

"I would like to dedicate this final to Ian Anderson, who would have reffed a final. Carl Spannenberg, who could have. And Ian Rogers, who should have."

Afterwards, my colleague Craig Joubert, who had become a friend, strolled over for a word.

"Those are such powerful sentiments, Jakes," he said. "Well said." I thanked him for the compliment, but I knew I should have added: "And Craig Joubert, who will."

20

Twickenham ... at last

For months now I had been planning a big party in London for family and close friends to celebrate my 36th birthday ... and my first Twickenham Test.

On its own, England versus the All Blacks is always a big moment in any ref's career. But the added significance was that the appointment coincided with a watershed moment in my career. Almost two decades ago, in February 1984, when I'd started reffing as a 17-year-old schoolboy, my mom had predicted that I would ref a Twickenham Test one day.

At the time, I thought it was all pie in the sky. Nevertheless I promised her if it happened, I'd kiss her on the Twickenham pitch in front of the crowd. Now that moment was only two weeks away, and to cap it all, it was a moment made all the sweeter by my first Currie Cup final. So, quite unexpectedly, I'd now be celebrating my 36th birthday and my Twickenham Test with all my career goals achieved.

It turned out to be an amazing weekend, one I would never forget. A total of 36 of my friends flew into London from all over the world. And family, too: my dad and his wife Terry, as well as my mom and my brothers.

Even my gran Sonja made the trip, from Israel. It was a huge effort for her, as she was on a portable oxygen tank and could only get around in a wheelchair. But she was living with us when I had made my Twickenham promise and, having driven me to as many games as my mom did before I got my licence, she deserved to be there. The flight from Israel was a big risk for her, but she wasn't going to miss this game for anything.

The five-day-long "weekend" started on the Wednesday. But I paced myself in the days leading up to the Test, making sure I got some sleep. Especially on the Friday night, when everyone partied well into the night.

That evening, my girlfriend Nicky made an excuse to leave early. She later called me and asked me to come back to our Hyde Park Intercontinental hotel room. When I walked in, she'd prepared another kind of surprise. There was a "Happy Birthday!" banner on the wall and presents and shiny moons and stars scattered over the bed. I was touched that she'd made such an effort, although I nearly had a heart attack the next morning when she took the banner down and the Prestik didn't release.

There was a deadly silence when she ripped off a section of the wallpaper in our £320-a-night room. Fortunately, and with a little ingenuity, we managed to patch it up and no one was any the wiser.

And then it was the big day. The buzz around the ground was everything I expected it to be, and more. Twickenham is not just hallowed turf. It's one of those grounds that has both history and prestige. And what added to those factors on the day was that I got to soak it all up before the game in a walk-about with my mom, my dad and Terry, and my brothers, who were so full of *nachas* (pride) that I could actually physically feel their support.

The day had finally come …

While we were strolling along, I tried to find a way to surreptitiously sneak my mom onto the field, but couldn't find a way through. I wasn't that disappointed. Although I'm all for marking big occasions, I wanted to keep this moment out of the limelight. So we found a gate as close as possible to the pitch and my mom and I posed for an iconic photograph that would take pride of place on both our mantelpieces and would spark many a conversation with visitors who saw it for the first time.

My mom was very emotional. There was no escaping just how momentous this occasion was for her, just as it was for me. For a while during our stroll I reflected on the 19-year journey I had travelled with the incredible, unstinting support of all my family. On the fortitude that was required and the enjoyment it produced. My own sense of pride was as intense as my family's *nachas*.

But before we could complete our pilgrimage around Twickenham, I could already feel myself slipping into game mode. You could see it in my eyes by the time I posed for another memorable photo, this time with my brothers. I was physically present but already starting to zoom in on the responsibility and job that awaited me. Ahead of me lay one of the biggest Test matches of my life, and it was time to leave sentiment behind and focus.

The Test turned out to be a ripper and hung in the balance until I blew the final whistle. England were in the process of building that magnificent

RWC-winning team of 2003, and they wanted to prove to themselves that they could beat the best team in the world. And they went on to play one of their most accomplished Test matches that day, inspired and led by Wilkinson's tactical excellence and goal-kicking skills, Martin Johnson's leadership abilities, a dominating pack of forwards and a stellar performance by the back row.

But still New Zealand, coached by John Mitchell at that point, managed to stay in the game, scoring four tries, two of them by the incomparable Jonah Lomu. With Andrew Mehrtens running the show, they pressed England really hard in the closing stages, and only a desperate corner-flag tackle by Ben Cohen and a crucial line-out steal by Ben Kay denied them victory.

A magnificent game of pure rugby theatre, it kept the 81 000-strong crowd on the edges of their seats until England held on to win it 31-28. Everyone, that is, except my mom's gay fashion-designer friend, Steven Rich. He had been with us in the car when I made my Twickenham-kiss promise, and he would often keep my mom company while she patiently waited for me to finish reffing a game.

Steven still knew nothing about rugby, but he insisted that he would not miss this occasion for the world. He even got into the spirit of the moment by dolling himself up for the Test in All Blacks gear. But then, I heard later, he fell asleep on my mom's shoulder 15 minutes before full time. Bored out of his tits, he told me afterwards.

English fans, however, were ecstatic. And who could blame them? It was only the fifth time in the history of the game that they had beaten the All Blacks. What's more, it was a significant victory, as they would go on to beat the Boks and the Wallabies as well in their build-up to their 2003 World Cup triumph.

I was also on a high. The feedback was that I'd reffed a good Test and had enhanced my 2003 World Cup prospects. There was a lot to celebrate that evening as I headed off with Nicky and our huge entourage of family and friends to the Eclipse nightclub in South Kensington, where I'd booked us a space for the night.

At that moment, I could not have been more grateful or more content. It felt like I was closing a chapter. In fact, if my career had ended right there, I would have been able to look at myself in the mirror with no regrets. Because right there, right then, that, for me, was as good as it gets.

21

The 2003 Rugby World Cup

I came down with a fever on the Wednesday before my first big appointment of 2003, but there was no way I was bailing. I loved reffing the Six Nations, which was a very special tournament for me. And this season I would do the last match of the championship, which might as well have been a Cup final.

It was England versus Ireland at Lansdowne Road, one of those massive, winner-takes-all Tests with history thrown in for good measure. Unbeaten that season, England were poised for a Six Nations Grand Slam, but had stumbled several times at this final hurdle in previous quests. Ireland were also unbeaten in the competition and had not won a Slam in 55 years. It was also only the sixth time in Five and Six Nations history that two teams faced up to each other in the championship's final week with an undefeated record.

Fortunately Ireland's manager of refs, Owen Doyle, a respected former international ref, grasped the significance of a Test like this with the World Cup looming. He was unbelievably good to me and, with his Irish connections, discreetly arranged for a doctor's appointment. I did not want to risk news of my illness leaking out and getting yanked from a fixture that meant so much to me.

It was touch and go. On the Saturday I was still feeling bleak, but thanks to the meds, I was well enough to go ahead with the game. But only just. Once I arrived at Lansdowne Road, though, the electric atmosphere was like a miracle cure.

Out in the stands, the crowd was buzzing with anticipation. They were expecting something massive, as was evident when two tickets on the halfway line were auctioned off for charity in the week leading up to the match. Two minutes before the end of the radio auction a friend of mine bid €7 000 for them, but even that was not enough.

Meanwhile, down in the changing rooms the tension between England and Ireland was palpable. And it reached near boiling point before I even blew my whistle for the kick-off. Martin Johnson led his team out of the tunnel and turned right instead of lining up his men on the left-hand side of the red carpet, as match protocol apparently dictated. It was a seemingly innocuous mistake, except, as some of the Irish lads pointed out to their captain, Brian O'Driscoll, England were standing on Ireland's "lucky" side.

So, instead of lining up along the vacant left-hand side of the red carpet, O'Driscoll led his team behind the England players so that they could still line up on the right-hand side. Even though this meant that Irish president Mary McAleese and the other dignitaries would now have to muddy their heels in the grass to shake hands with the Irish players.

I could see that Martin Johnson was irked from the moment he became aware of the Irish filing past him behind his back. And steam was close to spurting out of his ears when one of the stewards asked, and then insisted, that he shuffle his team to the left. The steward wanted both sides positioned as planned, along the edge of the red carpet.

The steward asked for my assistance, but Martin told me that he wasn't moving. I let it be. Pre-match formalities were not a ref's responsibility, and I always tried to go into a match as calm as possible. The last thing I wanted was to get caught up in a brewing hurricane.

The more the steward demanded, the more defiant Johnson became. He was moving for no one. Not for the steward, not for the Irish president, and, least of all, not for his superstitious opponents. Right then and there he drew a line in the sand, sending a very clear message to everyone of what was in store in this match: England would *not* be dominated.

It was a fantastic mind game that upset everyone but only fuelled Johnson and his team, who I could see were super-psyched to take this match by the scruff of the neck. As one journalist later put it, it was like shitting on someone's doorstep and then standing there and saying, "Yes, we did it. Now what are you going to do about it?" In that cameo, which I'd never see repeated, England were saying they were there for the Grand Slam.

The match itself was tight and ferocious for the first hour, but then, after a three-try rout in the last 15 minutes, England claimed the Grand Slam and made no bones about their World Cup intentions.

Like England, I, too, felt on track for the World Cup when I reffed my next big game of 2003. This time it was the final match in the Tri-Nations tournament. I knew Test matches like this one only got awarded to refs at the top of their game, particularly when they involved nations as evenly balanced as Australia and New Zealand were that year. This hinted at me being groomed for big Tests at the back end of tournaments, which was excellent news going into the World Cup, just two months away.

The Test at Eden Park was a nail-biter. Dominated by the All Blacks, it was nearly snatched away by the Wallabies in the dying minutes of the game when their centre, Elton Flatley, made a brilliant break. With the try line beckoning, his inside pass was knocked on and, with no time left for a scrum, I blew the final whistle at 21-17 to the All Blacks.

In early October, I flew into Sydney in a confident mood for my first World Cup as a referee. So long as I delivered good performances in my pool matches, I thought I might be in contention at the business end of the competition.

A good omen was that I not only passed the pre-tournament fitness test, but managed to make it through unscathed. By the end of testing, six out of our group of 15 were injured. It would have gutted me to be one of them.

As far as I was concerned, the testing was poorly conceived. First, we were asked to perform demanding endurance and speed tests just days after most of us had flown across the world from another time zone. Second, the venue was appalling. We did the 40-metre sprint tests diagonally across a sports hall that was too small to have a run-off area. So at the end of the sprint we had to swerve sharply to avoid running into a wall and a vending machine. To make matters worse, the running surface was also quite slippery.

The sprint test alone took out several refs, including Australian Scott Young and my compatriot Mark Lawrence, who tore both his hamstrings trying to run the fastest time. I felt gutted for Mark, and my heart went out to Scottie, who completed the sprint but then pulled a hamstring just as he was trying to execute his swerve. Poor management cost Scottie a dream opportunity to perform in front of his home crowd and his family.

Several days later, at the welcoming cocktail party at the Sydney Opera House, I spotted Rian Oberholzer among the dignitaries milling around. I strolled over to say howzit, and we chatted. Then he told me: "Keep your head down, Kappie ... Do your work ... You're in a strong position for the final ..."

Rian was involved at the highest level in the IRB, so this was good motivation for my pool matches. I felt confident and unfazed by the pressures of these big occasions. At the same time, I had no idea how my games would pan out. I still had a lot of hard work ahead of me before I could start getting excited.

My opening game was Ireland against Romania, which turned out to be an easy one to ref. My second appointment was Scotland versus the US, a tough, testy encounter in which I was forced to be punitive in order to get my message across.

I then reffed England for the third time in 11 months, this time in Melbourne against Samoa, who should have been easy prey, given the way Martin Johnson and his lads were dominating Pool C. But Samoa were ferocious. They went toe to toe with the heavyweights until the 62nd minute, when England's superior fitness turned the tide on the Islanders' slender 22-20 lead. Even though the Samoans lost 22-35, they won a lot of respect from everyone in the stadium, including their opponents.

I was chuffed with the way I'd handled that Test. In fact, it was one of the standout games of the tournament, which so far had produced pretty sterile results. The crowd had certainly been entertained by a match that for a long time simply didn't go according to script. I had to penalise England 15 times before they got their act together in the last 20 minutes. However, I later realised that perhaps management did not agree with my assessment.

After the pool stages, ref manager Steve Griffiths (a bloke I'd always found to be polite, an absolute gentleman and a great facilitator) pulled me aside and stunned me with the news that I'd been given the France/Ireland quarter-final – but it would be the *last* game I reffed at this World Cup. It hit me like a truck hurtling out of my blind spot – I did not see it coming at all.

Dumbfounded, I asked Griffiths for management's reasoning behind this decision, which didn't make sense, given the big Tests I'd successfully reffed in the three years leading up to the World Cup. He told me that management was of the opinion that I was "front-running" a lot and, as a result, could miss something significant.

I found this explanation hard to swallow. What Griffiths was saying was that instead of me staying in line with play, I was tracking ahead in anticipation of the next move in the game. While it is true that front-running can result in missing the odd forward pass, staying in line with play also has its issues. If the player in possession is quicker than you, he's going to raise the odds of your missing an infringement as he runs away from you. For me, good reffing was neither one nor the other. Rather it's about striking a balance between the two strategies.

In two decades of reffing, my style of officiating had never been an issue. In that time, front-running had not been raised in one single report covering approximately 150 first-class games. I was approaching my 20th international and front-running had never been mentioned *once* by any referee selector, or assessor, or by any country under my whistle. Nor had it been raised after any of my World Cup pool matches.

I told Griffiths this. In addition, the assessment system was very much a work in progress. No matter how we reffed a pool match, most refs at this World Cup were scoring between 87 and 92 per cent. Personally, I was scoring higher marks in the World Cup Tests than I had in any of the Tests I'd reffed prior to the tournament. And none of my pool-match reports pointed out significant reffing errors. It is possible, and plausible, that my inexperience played a significant role here, but that was never brought to my attention.

The whole thing smelt like bullshit to me. Nevertheless, the fact remained that I had an important World Cup quarter-final ahead of me. No matter how gutted I was, I had to pick myself up and make sure that I reffed a blinder. And here's the thing: despite my disappointment that this would be the last game I reffed at the 2003 Rugby World Cup, I was absolutely thrilled to be in charge of a play-off game.

Incidentally, in the lead-up to the France/Ireland quarter-final, and at the toss specifically, it became apparent to me that this would be the last match for the losing captain of this fixture. Both Fabien Galthié and Keith Wood knew this at the toss and had a laugh about it. As it turned out, Galthié retired the following week after his team's loss to England, while this would be Wood's last Test. They were both great rugby players, great leaders and wonderful people.

The match itself went off without major incident. France surged ahead 37-0 after 48 minutes with tries by Olivier Magne, Christophe Dominici, Imanol Harinordoquy and Jean-Jacques Crenca, and then took their foot off the pedal. It allowed Ireland's Kevin Maggs and Brian O'Driscoll (two) to score a few consolation tries, but the truth was that their World Cup was as over as mine. France won 43-21.

It was not a difficult Test to ref and I was proud of the way I'd gone about my business. This was reflected in the mark I got from my assessor, Kiwi Stu Beissel. But to my astonishment I also read in his assessment that I had missed initial infringements because of my front-running and had only picked up on second or third infringements.

It really got my back up. I watched a video replay of the match just to make sure I was not deluding myself, and then I approached Beissel in his hotel room and asked him to give me the time lines of the infringements that I had missed because of my "front-running". I also made sure that I backed up my objection in writing.

Beissel told me that he would get back to me on the matter, and he later sent me a written apology. In black and white he said that he could not find any of the incidents he'd mentioned and promised to retract their mention from the report.

I had no complaints about Beissel. I'd always found him to be a really decent bloke, so I could move on from this incident. And I'm not one to hold a grudge. But I was bitterly disappointed. World Cups only come around every four years, and this one was already over from a reffing perspective.

For the rest of the tournament, especially in social settings, I battled to keep my head up. In fact, I disappointed myself by wearing my heart on my sleeve. England's Tony Spreadbury, ever cheerful and mindful of others, helped me through that difficult time.

But it was time to move on. Personal ambition needed to be put on the back burner as I switched to auxiliary team man to assist my very deserving colleagues so that they could enjoy their special moments. My next appointment was as television match official (TMO) for Australia's semi-final clash against New Zealand in Sydney. My job was to support England's Chris White, who had been having the tournament of his life. New Zealand's Paddy O'Brien was awarded the other semi, between England and France. I was so pleased that he had been given a chance to redeem his highly criticised performance in the 1999 World Cup, which infamously denied Fiji a victory over France.

I was also chuffed as a South African when André Watson was appointed to ref the 2003 World Cup final, between England and Australia, as at least *one* South African would be on the field that day – excluding Mike Catt, of course! That said, there was no denying the fact that I would have loved the challenge down there in the middle on the big day. The occasion would not have intimidated me one bit. I would have relished the opportunity to prove that I had all the attributes to perform on rugby's biggest stage. But it was not to be. Life doesn't always give you what you want, and that's okay.

I didn't have to make any decisions during the final, but down on the field, André had his hands full. Although he didn't ref badly, he upset England by repeatedly penalising their dominant scrum, which hadn't been the case all through the tournament. Courting controversy, André boldly penalised the England front row again in the 79th minute with the score at 14-11 in England's favour. Elton Flatley converted and took the match into extra time.

England then snatched the lead in extra time with a Jonny Wilkinson penalty, but with two and half minutes remaining on the clock, André penalised them yet again. Flatley's kick went over and a packed Telstra Stadium teetered on a knife-edge. Until Wilkinson released the tension with a dramatic drop goal with just 20 seconds to spare.

As I left the box, I crossed paths with an English reporter, who felt obliged to tell me that if it weren't for Wilkinson's heroics, my colleague would be facing an inquisition. I was poker-faced. Even if I was sure of the reporter's motives, André was a colleague of mine. He may not have got all the scrums right, but on the whole I felt he had a very balanced game. Besides, the reporter was wrong. Despite England's 20-17 victory, the press inquisition the following day was widespread and intense.

I could not have scripted a more dramatic ending to this World Cup if I'd tried. And I was honoured to have been involved right until the end, albeit on a minor level. But it nevertheless took me a good few weeks before I started letting go of my disappointment and arrived at a point where I realised that what defined me as a ref was not a single Test, but my ability to *consistently* deliver a spectacle. This was the single biggest revelation I took away with me from the 2003 Rugby World Cup.

But I was still disappointed in myself. I had come this far and, while many things didn't quite add up, I hadn't quite nailed what I'd set out to do. Obviously I needed to acknowledge that for some reason my performance had not been what they were looking for, and I accepted that, but it was hard to swallow.

22

Shifting blame

I was invited to go to Singapore for a Sevens tournament in April. I never baulked at the chance to experience a place in the world I had never visited before, and the tournament itself did not disappoint. Neither did the flight over. I travelled with the Harlequins team from Durban, and sat next to one of my favourite reprobates, Trevor Wright, a seasoned campaigner who knew how to let his hair down. We started off with a serious chat about how to fix the game, always one of my favourite topics, and then switched from coffee to alcohol, which dramatically changed the landscape of the tiring flight in economy, squashed in like sardines.

A few of us started off having screwdrivers, and by the time we were five to six hours into the long haul, we had polished off all of the aircraft's stock. Legends in our own time. Boisterous was a mild understatement, and we were frequently warned about keeping the volume down.

Amazingly, it seemed more important to kick back and enjoy the flight rather than get some sleep; our minds were far too overactive for that, and the jokes that were flowing were far too funny. I must admit that I did manage some shut-eye, but even so, I only just made it through the first day's activities. Reffing with a blinding headache that no amount of water could dull and getting a nasty dose of sunstroke into the bargain, I was happy to retire to my hotel room after the match for a serious session of rest and recuperation. I got through the tournament pretty well after that, even refereeing the final.

Afterwards I had a memorable run-in with Pat Phibbs, who would later go on to play for the Brumbies. We exchanged some pretty strong words, though I can't actually remember what it was about – probably some kind of pissing contest, as usual, and we laughed about it later, when he had carved out a very successful career for himself at the Brumbies.

I reffed a full season of Super Rugby before getting my first Test of the year, in June down in Dunedin, where the All Blacks were gearing up to host world champs England.

Even though the visitors were without almost a dozen players from their World Cup squad, I was expecting one of those tight, hard-fought encounters. But new coach Graham Henry had prepared a ferocious All Black side who came out with guns blazing and crushed England 36-3. The visitors' biggest defeat since their 22-64 loss to New Zealand in 1998, it was a lesson at the House of Pain they would not forget in a hurry.

England captain Lawrence Dallaglio, never one to throw in the towel, hit the nail on the head afterwards when he openly admitted that England had been dead and buried by half-time. By then they were already down 3-30, courtesy of three killer tries converted by dead-eye Dan Carter, who also slotted two penalties.

My next Test match took place in early August at Sydney's Telstra Stadium. It was one of those tense, uncompromising Bledisloe Cup matches punctuated by niggle. Early on, Aussie flyhalf Stephen Larkham tried to stop counterpart Carlos Spencer from taking a quick throw-in and they ended up strong-arming each other over the advertising hoarding. Wanting to nip it in the bud, I vaulted over the hoarding to separate them. I then had a quick chat with the captains, telling them they wouldn't want their players to take an early shower because of bad discipline.

But frustrations continued to mount for the rest of the half, not least with the determined Australians, who felt they were not getting the rewards they deserved thanks to a Kiwi rush defence that flirted with the offside line.

Towards the end of the first half, the All Blacks lost a line-out, Australia bashed it up and Spencer, who had already been blown for going woefully offside, repeated the misdemeanour. I judged it not to be cynical but that he had just got his timing wrong in the rush defence and jumped the gun. So it was a penalty to Australia in front of the posts and time to lay down the law.

I was on my way to speak to captain Tana Umaga when Wallaby skipper George Gregan was in my ear, shouting, "Yellow card, mate! Yellow card! Offsides, mate! Yellow card!"

I turned and fixed him with one of my dispassionate stares.

"George, I've got it, but let me deal with it my way."

I went back to Umaga, but Gregan chose to ignore the line I had just drawn. "Yellow card, ref! Yellow card!"

For the second time I warned Gregan and told him that I was dealing with it. I was trying hard not to spoil his 101st Test appearance, which equalled David Campese's record as Australia's most capped player. But Gregan continued chirping me. So I reversed the penalty. And New Zealand kicked it out for a line-out.

It generally didn't bother me when players challenged me, but they had to do it in the right manner. It was a pity Gregan was so persistent, because I wanted Australia to get their three points and their reward in a match where both teams were finding very little space. But I had to get a hold of him there and then or else lose him and his side for the rest of the game.

It was a tense moment, but I had to assert my authority. My body language after the reversal was as important as the punitive sanction itself. So I walked my talk towards the line-out. And, as I did, Gregan was in my ear again. But this time the penny had dropped.

"Okay, Jonathan. I'm calm and rational now."

It took discipline to keep a straight face. It was vintage Gregan, who was never short of a chirp or a wisecrack. And the natural reaction would have been a hearty laugh. But the most I could afford right then was a big inward grin. Of course, that moment was the subject of much mirth afterwards. It was also why I loved my job, as spectators, and indeed even many players, never have the privilege of experiencing those moments.

Even better was that the reversal didn't dictate the final result. Not long afterwards, I sent All Black lock Ali Williams to the bin for repeated team offsides. And during his absence, winger Lote Tuqiri crossed for a try that ultimately sealed the match in Australia's favour.

There wasn't much more to write home about in 2004 except a memorable schools game between Hugenote and Swartland that only went ahead because the boys were so insistent that they play despite the terrible conditions. There was so much mud and water around that they needed water wings. It wasn't surprising, therefore, that after a couple of missed kicks for poles and much thrashing about, the match ended in a 0-0 draw. A throwback to the blank sheets of the early 1900s, it was my first and only 0-0 experience.

I wrapped up my year with another special occasion when I reffed a heroic Argentine side who mauled France 24-14 at Stade Vélodrome. It was a proud and passionate win that the Los Pumas players, not least those plying their trade at French clubs, would cherish for a long time to come.

But what made this Test special for me was that both my brothers and a couple of friends had responded to my open invitation to Marseille, which is such a special city. We partied massively after the game and enjoyed some rather hung-over sightseeing the next day.

I found these spontaneous gatherings such a joy because they broke the monotony of travel, and it was great to have some company. It sometimes got very lonely on the road, having no one to share things with. It was a great way to unwind and made up for the social life I missed out on back home.

Without a doubt that was a great weekend, but it paled in comparison to the blast that heralded my 2005 season. I was at a loose end in Dublin a week ahead of Ireland playing England, my first Six Nations appointment since 2003, so I called my mega-wealthy mate, Sean Dunne, to make arrangements to hook up. He asked me whether I liked football, which I do.

"Then be ready at 12. We're going to watch Manchester United play AC Milan ..."

"But that's at Old Trafford?"

"Yes, so don't forget your passport. My chauffeur will be there soon."

Sure enough, the chauffeur arrived and whisked me off to a private airfield, where I met a bunch of high rollers in the VIP lounge. The next thing the eight of us were in the air, being pampered by a flight attendant who politely informed me that the one thing she *didn't* serve was coffee.

Several Johnnie Walker Blues later we touched down in Manchester, where a minibus whisked us to a posh seafood restaurant. As we took our seats in the private dining room, pre-briefed waiters delivered steaming-hot seafood to our table.

Twenty minutes later, one of the blokes announced that we had three minutes to finish our food. I didn't pay serious attention, but the rest of Sean's mates had done this before. Rising as one exactly three minutes later, they boarded a private bus for Old Trafford, me trailing in their wake (which wasn't that unusual).

I was amazed by the timing, as we took our seats just as the teams were about to kick off. Two minutes before half-time, Sean said, "Okay, let's go." This time I paid attention and followed the group into a VIP room, where all the drinks were on the house.

We headed back to our seats in time for the start of the second half. Then, two minutes before the final whistle, with Man U 0-1 down, Sean and his mates swung into action again. We piled into our bus, which was waiting downstairs in a no-parking zone right outside the exit, and the next thing I knew I was back in the air getting high on more Blue.

So this was how the big hitters rolled, I thought as I leant back in my seat and surveyed the cabin. It was seamless. No hanging around. No time-wasting. Maximum enjoyment. It was foreign to me, but I knew I could get used to this regimented indulgence without much practise.

Halfway back to Dublin, I had to take a breather. So I joined the pilot just in time to see Dublin's lights twinkling in the distance across the Irish Sea. Alcohol or not, it was a special moment that I would not forget in a hurry.

Back on the ground, we headed to Dublin's famous O'Donoghue's bar in another minibus. By now it was after midnight, well past closing time. But not for us. By now there were just six of us, and we drank into the wee hours, shooting the breeze and cracking jokes. The next morning I woke up, my head a little fuzzy, and for a minute or two I wasn't quite sure whether I'd dreamt it all.

A few days later I was back at work at Lansdowne Road in a seesaw Test where the lead changed seven times. An inspired Ireland eventually deservedly clinched the match 19-13. It was the world champions' third Six Nations loss that year and their second in a row to Ireland, who remained on course for their first Grand Slam since 1948.

I didn't sense the slightest controversy in the match – not even when Clive Woodward's successor, Andy Robinson, came to me at half-time and challenged me about my decision to blow winger Mark Cueto for being offside. I had judged Cueto to be ahead of flyhalf Charlie Hodgson's high diagonal kick cross-field, which Cueto gathered to dot down in the right-hand corner.

I politely explained that Cueto had been offside. In my opinion.

"Ooooohah! That's a big call!" exclaimed Robinson.

Okay, I thought, without saying a word. And I headed into the shed, not giving it another thought.

But after the game I heard that Robinson had had a go at me in a post-match TV interview. I was quite surprised, because I didn't think there had been anything untoward or unusual about the Test. It had been one of those close games that could have gone either way. So, I was even more taken aback when I heard what Robinson had said.

"I'm absolutely spitting. I'm livid," he told reporters. "There are two tries we've been cost. I think Mark Cueto scored a perfectly legal try – and I think he should have gone to the video referee on Josh Lewsey.

"It is how we use the technology. It is there, and it should be used. I am still trying to work out the Cueto try. I have looked at both, and they both looked like tries.

"We are very disappointed, and this will hurt, there is no doubt about that. We are upset now, but the referee is in charge and he has called it his way and we have got to be able to cope with that."

As far as I was concerned, Robinson was barking up the wrong tree. Blowing Cueto offside, way before he dotted down, was a judgement call I had made to the best of my ability. And nothing after the match challenged my decision. There was no TV evidence to suggest I'd got it wrong, because Cueto was outside the frame. So referring the matter to the TMO would not have proved anything – even if protocol had allowed me to go upstairs, which it didn't.

I was just as certain about the other contentious incident, which involved England winger Josh Lewsey, in the closing minutes. When the England maul surged over the Irish line with Lewsey in possession, I was standing right there. My view was unobstructed. I could clearly see that the ball was held up and then carried back into the field of play when flanker Johnny O'Connor, hooker Shane Byrne and flyhalf Ronan O'Gara rebuffed the maul.

I was so sure that I blew my whistle. I did not need to check. IRB protocol required me to adjudicate, and that's what I did. And even if I hadn't, going upstairs would not have helped. TMO Hugh Watkins later reported that he couldn't see the ball being grounded. So once again there was no evidence to suggest that my decision had been incorrect. And, quite frankly, I didn't see how Robinson could have been in a better position than me to prove differently.

If there had been evidence to show that I had made the wrong decision, I would have put up my hand. I had regularly displayed the ability to take ownership of mistakes I had made, so this time would have been no different.

The controversy escalated. When I collected my match tie at the post-match presentation, some of the English coaching staff were quite rude to me, which was unnecessary. I knew when I'd made a mistake, and on that day, I definitely had not.

I didn't need any more confirmation that I'd made the right calls, but I nevertheless got it when I asked O'Connor, Byrne and O'Gara if they thought I'd got it wrong. "Nonsense," they told me. "It was never a try."

"Look," I said, "you have the result; you've got nothing to lose. Just be straight up and tell me if I got it wrong."

All three Irishmen gave me an absolute, categorical thumbs-up.

I didn't confront Andy about it. I let it ride. I knew he was under pressure, and so was his squad. Since winning the World Cup, England had underperformed. Andy had lost eight out of 12 games and was desperate for a result going into this Test, which England most certainly could have won.

Unfortunately, it didn't end there. The following day, Colin High, the Rugby Football Union (RFU) referee manager and an IRB selector, fuelled Andy's blame game by having a full go at me in the *Daily Mail*.

"The International Rugby Board will be disappointed. Jonathan Kaplan is in the top 20 in the world but that wasn't an international performance. It would not have been acceptable in the Zurich Premiership. If one of my referees had done that, I would have had my backside kicked for making the appointment. If any English referee refereed like that in a European match, there would be an inquest. No question about that. If someone had performed like that, he would have been pulled from the next game."

I didn't want to get personal – and not because it was against IRB protocol, but because it is just not my style. If I have a problem with a coach or a player, I deal with them face to face, in private – not in the press. Nevertheless, there comes a time when you have to put the record straight. On my return to Cape Town, and with SA Rugby's blessing, I told the Press Association that, on a personal level, I was very disappointed with Robinson's remarks.

"I don't feel it is going anywhere when a coach publicly criticises a referee," I said in my statement. "There were two matters which he believes were critical, and I am quite certain I made the correct decision in both of them."

Sanity began to be restored when the RFU denied reports that they were lodging an official complaint with the IRB. And Josh Lewsey showed the kind of composure I'd have expected of Andy, who by that stage should have known that he was not only wrong, but out of line.

"All players have bad days and rugby referees are only human," Lewsey told reporters. "Sometimes players can cost you Test matches and referees can as well. But I have no issue with [Kaplan]. That is Test-match rugby. You have got to take it on the chin. Sometimes you get the rub of the green, sometimes you don't. The sign to me of a world-class team is being able to close that game even when you haven't got it [decisions] on your side. We still had an opportunity to do that and we didn't.

"It's very easy to blame other factors, but I think on a playing level we will certainly look within and pick out areas where we can develop and improve."

I later received an apology from Colin High after my manager, André Watson, wrote to him expressing concern over the public nature of his criticism and its contents, given his position at the RFU and IRB.

To his credit, High apologised unconditionally for both the contents of his criticism and going public with it. He also added that he continued to hold me in high regard. I knocked the matter on the head there and then and accepted his apology. I also tried not to dwell on Andy's silence, even after he got a mere slap on the wrist following his RFU disciplinary hearing. He showed poor form, but I understood that he was both a passionate, committed rugby man and a coach under pressure.

What did, however, leave a bad taste in my mouth was why the RFU had been so lenient with Andy. Their reason? Apparently he did not actually mention my name when he publicly had a go at me ...

23

A Super season

Two weeks later I was back in the UK, this time to ref Scotland at home to Wales. No one except my family and closest friends knew this, but my return to Murrayfield was a very emotional moment, for 13 March 2005 was the day I finally got to honour the memory of my friend and mentor Ian Anderson.

One of Ian's dreams had been to honour his Scottish roots with a Murrayfield Test. He came close when he was given the cherished appointment, only to have the Test match cruelly snatched from under his nose. For some reason, the powers that be had decided that Ian didn't have enough experience to ref a top-tier Test match. Instead they gave the Test to Freek Burger, and Ian never got another opportunity to fulfil his dream before his life was tragically snuffed out in a car accident.

In the months before his death, while I was touring the UK and Europe trying to gain more reffing experience off my own bat, I bought Ian an Anderson-clan scarf. But I never got to give it to him. Now, after over a decade in my cupboard, it was back on the road. I would wear the scarf on my journey from the hotel to my dressing room. Ian would get his Scotland Test, if only in spirit.

The Andy Robinson hullabaloo was still on my mind. The Test had happened two weeks ago, but it seemed as if more media space was being devoted to the manufactured controversy than to Prince Charles's upcoming wedding to Camilla.

I decided that there was no better way to deal with the fallout than to ref this Test out of my skin. And it turned out better than I could ever have imagined. Playing their sexy brand of rugby in overdrive, Wales scored five sensational tries to end the first half 39-3 up. It included one of the best counter-attacking tries I'd seen in years.

Just four minutes into the game, burly flanker Ryan Jones burst straight through the Scottish locks and passed. Four pairs of dazzling hands later, the ball came back to Jones, who went over to give Wales the perfect start and himself the best possible 24th birthday present.

Scotland never gave up until the final whistle, but it was to no avail. Unbeaten Wales stayed in the hunt for a Grand Slam with a thoroughly magnificent 46-22 victory that would be talked about in the valleys for years. One of the match stats worth mentioning was that the ball was in play in excess of 43 minutes, which is enormous for a Test match. I had let it all hang out with as brave a performance as I could muster. The players were out on their feet. Even coach Warren Gatland remarked after the game how much ball had been thrown around and how much it had taken out of his troops. I even got a cramp in my calf with a few minutes left on the clock, normally the reserve of those a lot more athletic than me.

Hugely relieved that I had been able to ref such a great game of rugby after a challenging few weeks, and having finally honoured Ian's memory, I celebrated in an Irish bar in Edinburgh. The pub was wall to wall with Welsh fans singing "Wales! Wales! Wales!" like there was no tomorrow. In between spinning a few tracks, the DJ would stop and ask the crowd, "So, who won today?"

"Wales! Wales! Wales!" the crowd would respond, and so loudly that it would drown out the next track. And so it went on like a stuck record that, strangely, got more and more entertaining as the night wore on. What a way to knock an eventful Six Nations on the head.

A fortnight later I was back in Super Rugby mode, this time with my friend Tappe, for whom I was running touch in Dunedin for the Highlanders versus the Brumbies. When we checked into our hotel on the outskirts of town, I was in a cheeky, frisky mood. So while Tappe was checking in, I entertained the receptionist with the pile of hotel business cards stacked neatly on the counter. I shuffled them and then announced that I was going to predict the next day's score.

I drew a random number of cards from the deck and counted them. Nineteen in all. "This is how much the Highlanders will score tomorrow," I declared.

Then I drew another random number of cards from the deck and counted them … 18 in total. "And this is what the Brumbies will score. That's it, 19-18," I told the receptionist.

The following day the Highlanders were leading 19 – yes, 19 – to 13 with

20 minutes to go. Now I was starting to think that this could get weird. The Brumbies then scored a try and Stirling Mortlock missed a difficult conversion. Now it was 19-18 – freaky! But we were into the last quarter with plenty to play for, so I reckoned the score would not stay that way for much longer.

The score on the board didn't go unnoticed. As Tappe ran past me after Mortlock's missed conversion on his way back to the halfway line, he shot me a wide-eyed, quizzical look that said, "You are kidding me."

From then until the close, Tappe rightfully awarded a couple of kickable penalties to both teams. But, unbelievably, not one of them found their mark. So by the time Tappe blew the final whistle, the score was still locked at ... 19-18! I'd never experienced anything like it on a rugby field before, and I reckoned I never would again.

The following week Tappe and I headed over to Wellington, where I was reffing the Waratahs against the Hurricanes. On the morning of the match, my new Italian girlfriend, Alessia, called me. It was early days in our relationship and we hadn't had much time to talk about the nuts and bolts of my job. She had a rudimentary grasp of the basics and was keen to learn more.

We chatted and she asked what I did on match day. I told her I usually relaxed, walked around town, maybe grabbed a coffee, met up with friends if I had any in the match city ... Then I would drift down to the local tote and play the horses, maybe go back to the hotel and have a snooze, and then be ready for my lift to the stadium, which generally arrived an hour and a half before kick-off.

Once at the ground, I would drop my kit in my change room and then go and speak to the teams, their captains and the coaches. We'd discuss our expectations and any issues that needed airing, and then we'd go outside for the toss ...

"Wait, wait! I know! I know!"

Up till then, she had been quiet and all ears. But now she broke her silence with the enthusiasm of a novice eager to please.

"I know exactly what the toss is," she said.

"What?" I asked, really curious about what she'd say next.

"That's when all the forwards get together and bump into each other!"

At the end of that season's Super Rugby tournament, I was over the moon when I was awarded the final between the Crusaders and the Waratahs. In fact, the Crusaders' 35-25 victory at Jade Stadium was a watershed moment in my career. There was no greater honour than to ref a final in a major tournament like the Super 12.

It was also a great confidence-booster for the Lions Test I had been appointed to ref, which dished up a surprise in the form of an apology from Andy Robinson, who was Sir Clive Woodward's forwards coach.

Before the pre-match discussions got under way, he drew me to one side and apologised for criticising me in the press. Even though I sensed that privately he was still angry about losing that Test, Andy's apology was sincere. I accepted it without reservation. I'd always enjoyed my pre-match interactions with Andy, who, like me, was passionate about his rugby and always had something positive to contribute. And Andy's gesture on that particular day helped keep that tradition intact.

This third British & Irish Lions Test against the All Blacks unfolded without incident and according to script, with the latter comprehensively outclassing the Lions yet again with a five-try, 39-19 romp that gave them a series whitewash.

After the game, Clive Woodward approached me on the field and said, "Thanks, Jonathan. You were the best ref on this tour by a country mile."

I didn't generally get too carried away by one man's opinion, but I had a lot of respect for Woodward, who had achieved what no other English coach ever had when his team won the World Cup in 2003. On top of that he was congratulating me as a losing coach, which said a lot about the man's character. It was a meaningful compliment, one that didn't come around that often, and it was also the perfect book-end to that season's unpleasant start at Lansdowne Road in February.

Controversy, major Test matches, a British & Irish Lions clash, my first Super Rugby final and a few surprises in between ... the year had had it all. But there was more to come. At the end of October, I returned to Loftus for my second Currie Cup final, between the Bulls and the Cheetahs. And I was licking my lips, because the match had "humdinger" written all over it.

24

David and Goliath

It was one of those David and Goliath games, with the Free Staters out to avenge their demoralising 33-42 defeat the previous year and determined to secure their first Currie Cup in 29 years. I had run touch in the previous year's dramatic match, so I had a good idea of what to expect that afternoon.

I also knew that the Cheetahs, under the helm of new coach Rassie Erasmus, had arrived at Loftus resolute that this time they would not be bullied by the Bulls, who, with all their Boks, looked to be unbeatable on paper.

The Bulls had become near invincible under Heyneke Meyer, who had utilised their traditional strengths and given them a new sense of pride in the jersey. He had paid his dues as a coach and was now on his way to greatness. Meyer was assisted by high-performance manager Ian Schwartz, and their recruitment was the best in the country. They either had the best players or players who would eventually be the best in their positions.

In Bakkies Botha and Victor Matfield they had the best locks in world rugby, and they were complemented by a very strong leadership group that included Anton Leonard, Fourie du Preez, Bryan Habana and Gary Botha. They also had at their disposal the metronomic boot of Morné Steyn and a massive pack of forwards. Plus, they were also the three-times defending champions and had beaten Free State twice already that season, by four and 10 points respectively (although one of those games involved Free State playing the majority of the game with 14 players after Ollie le Roux was sent off).

Free State were the Bulls' little *boeties*. No less proud a union, though, and perhaps more of a family, Free State had improved their structure and tactics consistently over the past few years. Now they approached play-off matches with far more intent than in previous years. They chose a massive front row for the final, sending out a clear message to their counterparts that they would not be bullied.

I thought Free State won the front-row battle on the day, but the Bulls won most of the other battles. Their tactics, their line-outs, their physical backs, especially J.P. Nel and Wynand Olivier, their huge kicking game and their pack were paving the inevitable path to success … or so it seemed. Free State were only hanging on by a thread, but, crucially, were not taking a step back.

But the Bulls were confident. They had the ascendency and it showed on the scoreboard. They were executing their game plan with precision and were slowly strangling their opponents, who were relying on guts and heart. Sometimes, that is not enough at this level. Young Juan Smith, Barry Goodes, Hendro Scholtz and little Ryno van der Merwe were working their arses off on defence.

Inevitably, there was a lot of argy-bargy in the game, with players squaring up to each other, snorting, pushing, pulling, shoving. And I was thoroughly enjoying the challenge of keeping this cauldron under control, letting the players know in no uncertain terms that they had better get a grip.

At one stage that involved sending both Victor Matfield and Os du Randt to the cooler for the obligatory 10 after an unacceptable altercation. I had a lot of respect for both men, who normally displayed admirable restraint, but that day's brutal collisions were turning the two Jekylls into Hydes.

Eventually the cauldron boiled over and exploded into a tornado that even sucked in personnel off the bench, including Basil Carzis, the Bulls' strength and conditioning coach. It was time to read the captains the riot act.

"Listen, gents," I said with my steeliest glare. "I understand that this is a contact sport. But this is a Currie Cup final and you guys are forcing my hand. I've allowed you your moments, but your moments are gone now. So the next player who transgresses will be gone. Do you both understand?"

I had to be firm – after all, this was the showpiece of the South African rugby calendar. It was the right time to rein them in. Anton Leonard and Naka Drotské assured me that they understood. But talk is cheap. In the last quarter the Bulls launched a high up-and-under and a charging Bryan Habana nearly throttled receiver Bevin Fortuin in his follow-up. Loftus was distinctly unimpressed when I gave Habana his marching orders, but if I didn't follow through on my earlier threat right then and there, the final could have ended up being a disgrace.

With the Bulls one man short and the score 25-15 in their favour, the final entered the last quarter. The Free State revival may have been sparked by touch judge J.C. Fortuin, when he intervened after Free State's attack broke down. It resulted in a penalty and led to three points for them. Or perhaps the turning point occurred when TMO Craig Joubert disallowed a try by J.P. Nel – Joubert ruled that the ball had been lost forward, which was questionable, as the ball had rolled under Nel's body. Tough call.

But the fact is that the game took an unexpected turn when Free State took the ball through multiple phases and Bevin Fortuin went over for a try. Willem de Waal converted, and all of a sudden it was game on at 25-22.

The next play would live with me forever. The Bulls kicked off, Free State gathered and mauled up-field for about 30 metres, and then Falie Oelschig launched a seemingly innocuous up-and-under.

Waiting for it in their 22 as Loftus held its breath were two of that season's most reliable players, fullback Johan Roets and scrumhalf Fourie du Preez. It should have been a doddle, but somehow neither of them gathered and marked the ball. Instead, it bounced between them.

Enter 19-year-old rookie Meyer Bosman, a recent acquisition from South Western Districts, who was playing off the bench. Innocuous or not, he was chasing down the kick. And it paid off, as the ball bounced straight into his hands.

Bosman scored under the sticks, De Waal converted and it was as good as game over. After awarding the try, I glanced up into the stands, which, moments earlier, had been a sea of Loftus blue. Now it was a swell of ecstatic white. The transformation was quite astounding. I hadn't realised that Free State had quite that amount of support at Loftus on the day.

Down on the field there was all the joy and swagger you'd expect from a team that had just pulled off one of the greatest giant-killing acts in domestic rugby. No question, it was one of the Top 10 greatest games I ever reffed.

The Free Staters had every reason to back-slap and hug one another. They had arrived at Loftus as rank underdogs and had not given an inch in the bruising battle to end their almost three-decade-long Currie Cup drought. It was such a massive achievement that I could completely understand the incredulous looks on *all* the players' faces.

It was an incredible achievement for the eternal bridesmaids, and especially for Rassie, who, with Free State's first ever Currie Cup final victory over the Bulls, had emphatically announced his arrival on the coaching scene. It was a proud moment for Free State. The kind of moment befitting the smoking of a big, fat, triumphant cigar. Which was exactly what Ollie le Roux did, right there on the field, for all to see.

25

The Waratah story

For two decades I had taken a long, hot shower after every match that I'd reffed. But on this day, like Scotland surprising France in the game I had just reffed, I, too, deviated from the script. Like a Scottish lord I was soaking in the biggest bath I'd ever encountered in one of the most spacious change rooms on the world rugby circuit. It was just what the doctor ordered after a freezing 90 minutes at Murrayfield.

Judging by the celebrations that echoed down the corridor from the Scots' change room, they were in high spirits. Much to the delight of their roaring fans, they had just ripped up the 2006 Six Nations form book by beating championship favourites France 20-16.

I was happy for them, because they thoroughly deserved their hard-fought victory, thanks to two converted tries by winger Sean Lamont – one of them untypically from the back of a rolling maul – and some typical Scottish courage that suffocated a valiant French second-half fight-back.

I was particularly pleased for coach Frank Hadden, a decent man who deserved more days like this one. The way he wore his pride on his sleeve after the match resonated with me.

"The only thing that really makes you proud is when you do something special for your country and you can get a bit more success in the professional era than we have had for a wee while," he told reporters. "So obviously I was massively proud of the lads' performance today. I said during the week that we would play well and we did play well … I thought in terms of guts and determination and commitment to the cause it was absolutely outstanding."

Nothing could compare to the pride flowing through Scottish veins on that day, but I, too, was proud of my contribution. The Test had gone off without controversy and, in contrast to the criticism I had faced after the England Test,

Bernard Laporte was a gracious losing coach who was genuinely grateful for the officials' efforts. And that definitely made my bath more enjoyable.

Normally I'd go through the match in my head while I showered, but today my touch judge, Steve Walsh, was in the *other* bath running through the post-mortem with me. Walsh didn't have much to add to my wash-up, calling it pretty much like I did. So instead we chatted about Scotland's remarkable giant-slaying, which we didn't see that often in the Test arena.

With us in the change room was Scottish ref manager Iain Goodall, who suggested that we capture the moment for posterity. To look respectable, I grabbed the bottle of Famous Grouse the hosts had presented to me after the match as a thank you. You can't see it clearly in the photo, but the bottle had a customised label that read "The Famous Jonathan". I want to make it clear at this point that the label refers only to my rugby exploits.

Scotland's victory, celebrated well into the wee hours, was a memorable ending to a great week in Edinburgh. By the time I boarded a flight home, my head was clear, thanks to a six-hour walk in the biting cold around the castle and up and down Rose and Princess streets.

At that point in my career, I felt I had not yet achieved all my career goals. I had unfinished business with the Rugby World Cup, for instance, where I felt I was capable of much more.

My main goal was to improve my game, to become more versatile and to limit my deficiencies; to forgive myself for moments where I had not been at my best, because my work was more than just the accumulation of facts and figures. It was about my evolution as a person via the vehicle of refereeing.

I'd managed to pass huge tests of character in my career so far, sometimes through periods of intense loneliness while living out of a suitcase in empty hotel rooms, and I was proud of that. I felt encouraged when I heard through the grapevine that I was considered to be at the top of the refereeing tree and had been for some time. But I knew this could change in the blink of an eye if I did not remain humble and continue to work hard. You could never rest on your laurels as an international referee – you were only as good as your last game.

This was borne out when I was appointed to ref the Super Rugby semi-final between the Hurricanes and the Waratahs in Wellington. I was always a bit obsessive in my habit of keeping match stats, so I'd been aware for a few years of the unusual relationship I had with the Tahs. They almost never won when I was the ref. By the end of the previous Super Rugby season, they had only managed one win in 12 matches that I'd reffed, and the win dated way back to 1998, against the Hurricanes in Sydney.

I found that intriguing, as the Tahs were one of the better teams in the Super Rugby competition. They'd certainly been good enough to make the final the previous year, which was played against the Crusaders in Christchurch, and which they lost by 10 points. Not a bad result, considering how dominant the Kiwi outfit had been throughout the 2005 season and in the final. And the Tahs were good enough to start the 2006 season as third favourites in the newly expanded tournament now known as the Super 14.

At the start of that year's Super Rugby season, I decided to keep a watchful eye on how I reffed them in case I was missing something. I knew that this trend, if you could call it that, had nothing to do with how I felt about Sydney or the Waratahs. Sydney is a great place to visit, and I certainly held nothing against the franchise or the personnel. I'd always got on with the players and whoever coached them.

But I did start wondering whether there was something about their style of play I did not grasp. Did I perhaps judge them with a jaundiced eye when I reffed them in New Zealand? Was I subconsciously biased, or perhaps overcritical? Whatever lay behind the stats, I decided to take a closer look. I wanted to understand what was going on.

The first time I reffed the Tahs that season was in Round 9 in early April, against the Crusaders in Christchurch, when they were on track for the semifinals. They lost 11-17 in a match where I had penalised them only once.

Then I reffed them a second time, at the back end of the competition in early May, when they narrowly lost 33-37 to the Chiefs in Hamilton. On that occasion, I penalised them four times.

However, I was still none the wiser as to the cause of their losses when I arrived in Wellington two weeks later for the Tahs' semi-final clash against the Hurricanes. So I was somewhat taken aback by the breathtaking insight of the Sydney newspapers.

A statistician had indicated that the Tahs' overall 53 per cent winning rate in the competition plummeted whenever I reffed them. The insinuation was that I could cost the Waratahs a final. The newspapers alerted readers to the fact that in the 14 games I had reffed, their side had only won once. And they stressed that the Tahs always lost away from home when I was in charge.

The sensationalised stats might have made compelling reading for Waratahs fans ahead of a crucial away semi, especially when former Australian and

Waratahs coach Bob Dwyer weighed in. He claimed to be aware of the stats and urged the team to "have a chat" with me.

If someone had bothered to ask me for my input, I would have told them that the stats were not unusual at all. The Tahs lost against New Zealand's best teams when they played away in New Zealand no matter who the ref was. I hardly ever refereed them when they played at home. Considering that Kiwi teams were the perennial winners of the competition, you would think that their top sides would win the vast majority of their home fixtures, or at least 80 per cent of them.

I wasn't too put out by the media's lack of insight, but I nevertheless chatted to IRB referee manager, Paddy O'Brien, who was aware of the stats and how they had been sensationalised. He reassured me that there was nothing wrong with my approach or the way I'd reffed my Waratah games and that I shouldn't pay any attention to the media.

Revealingly, Waratahs coach Ewen McKenzie poured cold water on the media spin when he told a journalist in a pre-match interview that he had no concerns about my reffing and that the stats were "of little significance".

What happened next was unbelievable, but possibly inevitable. In one of those very close, 50/50 Super Rugby games played with passion, energy and intensity, the Tahs went down 14-16 to the Canes. In my opinion, the match could have gone either way, as it had been an attritional game in which defence took centre stage and suffocated the super skill sets of both teams.

But instead of seeing it like that, McKenzie spat out his dummy. And he didn't do so face to face with me after the game, when he had the opportunity, but in a newspaper interview. According to the report, Ewen had a long list of my decisions that he found perplexing. His biggest beef, to cut a long story short, was when I penalised Al Baxter for collapsing a scrum, which resulted in Jimmy Gopperth's match-winning penalty.

According to reports, Ewen was seething and planned to lay an official complaint with SANZAR, the Super 14 competition's ruling body.

I was not happy to be in the media spotlight again, but I recognised it for what it was: a moment of extreme discontent. When a coach is frustrated with a result, he occasionally vents in the media. I'd learnt that the hard way. This case was no different. I could handle it, as long as it didn't cross the line and get personal.

That said, Ewen and the papers got it totally wrong when they claimed that by penalising Baxter, I had cost them the match. Ewen is an ex-prop, so he should have known better than to contest the scrum penalty.

Here's what really happened. After the scrum had collapsed for the second time, Tappe told me through his mike to come round to his side to check the binding of the Hurricanes' No. 1. But the Tahs' defensive coach, Les Kiss, incorrectly interpreted it as Tappe telling me to penalise the Hurricanes.

What players, coaches and fans don't always realise is that sometimes the ref only receives information from the touch judges for future flagging. That means that the information is for consideration in the next phase. Tappe had flagged something he wanted me to be aware of at the next scrum. That's how it actually works, but, unfortunately, in this case it wasn't sexy enough to make the papers.

So after Tappe's comment I went round and reset the scrum. And I watched Al Baxter take the arm of the loosehead and drill it towards the centre of the scrum. He had quite obviously collapsed the scrum, and I penalised him for it.

That decision was perceived as a major injustice, but it was a clear and obvious infringement. And it was corroborated by Tappe, who was on the same side as me when I blew the penalty, and by the camera evidence that I later reviewed.

Quite frankly, I would rather not have penalised the Waratahs at that stage of the game, given the stats saga and the months of self-assessment I had gone through prior to the match. If anything, I was being extremely cautious in how I refereed that game. As it turned out, the penalty count in this game was quite balanced at seven apiece.

Of course, I also had a duty to be fair to the Hurricanes. I could not manufacture results or overlook transgressions simply because the Waratahs had poor results with me. My job was to ensure that both teams got a fair crack at the game.

As far as I was concerned, I had to view the situation holistically, not in the simplistic way the media sensationalised it. As much as it sometimes hurt, I had to learn to transcend the emotion attached to media reports. My job was to be clinical on the field and never stray from my vision of how a match should be reffed.

I could never lose sight of the fact that my job as a ref was not to make everyone happy. My job was to apply a standard. And as long as that standard was applied consistently, and players and coaches were aware of the standards that I aimed to apply, that was all that counted.

What some rugby journalist thought or said was not what was important. The journalist was not selecting me, nor was he qualified to select me. He was a parochial penman who used a shotgun rather than a subtle paintbrush to peddle sensationalism, because in this world, cold, hard facts don't sell newspapers.

Despite all the off-the-field brouhaha, not one Waratah player was ever rude to me or displayed any bad manners towards me, which said a lot about their character in particular and the wonderful spirit of rugby union in general. In fact, years later, just before I retired, I called Phil Waugh, the most capped Waratah player of all time, to request an autographed Tah jersey to add to my memorabilia collection, and he magnanimously agreed.

Instead of just dropping the jersey off at the hotel, he suggested that I join him and a bunch of his Tah mates for a few beers at the Sydney University–Randwick club match. It was a really enjoyable afternoon and far removed from the story being told in the papers.

This was further borne out by a later conversation I had with the former Waratah team psychologist Warren Kennaugh, who was a presenter at our annual Super Rugby course. He assured me that during his term with the franchise, my name had never been raised in anger, and there had never been so much as a whisper of bias. Having said that, I do acknowledge that it must have been increasingly difficult for some of the players and coaching staff to be able to relax when I was appointed to one of their games, and that for some of them I was pure bad luck!

The Waratahs story has a happy ending. When I reffed them for the last time in 2013, they finally won an away game when they beat the Kings in PE by a record score of 72-10 (the highest away win in Super Rugby history).

26

Vrystaaaaat!

I was simply thrilled when I was appointed to ref the Super 14 final in Christchurch between the Crusaders and the Hurricanes. However, this game was also not without its pre-match drama. Except this time it was about the quality of the playing conditions.

As I was driving to the stadium, it was obvious that the heavy fog that had rolled in over the city was going to make the match very challenging. In fact, it might even ruin the big day. From the outside it certainly didn't look good. Draped in mist, the stadium itself looked eerie, like a ship in a dockyard with only bits and pieces showing.

But out on the playing area, which was cocooned in fog, it was not as bad as expected. From about 20 metres up in the stands you could see nothing, which was not going to please the spectators. But I thought there was enough visibility on the playing surface for a game to take place safely.

So I consulted the players and the coaches, and to a man they wanted the game to go ahead. So, too, did the broadcasters, who had to adapt by taking their cameras off their mounts so that their roving cameramen could get decent pictures from ground level. It was not perfect, but it worked.

Plan B was to see how it went in the first half and, if continuing was not viable, I still had the option of calling off the game. It was only once we started the second half that the result would stand, no matter what hell broke loose on the field.

What became known as the Final in the Fog turned into a beautiful game. Not because it was a great rugby spectacle, but because both teams resolved to make the best of a bad situation. They rolled up their sleeves and got stuck in. As in the old amateur days, both teams played in the spirit of rugby union and left the result to the universe.

Fortunately the game unfolded without any controversy or injuries. The only problem was that the weather was not conducive to precision up-and-unders, which turned out to be a bit of a lottery. It was anyone's guess when and where the ball was going to exit from the solid ceiling of fog 20 metres up.

Casey Laulala scored the winning try for the Crusaders to deservedly win the championship yet again. But on the day, the public clearly felt robbed of an opportunity to enjoy a much-anticipated final. I was just glad that the players and officials had made the decision together to go ahead with the game. Subsequently, when people asked me how I felt about this particular final, I would always respond, "I don't have a fogging clue."

One occasion I really enjoyed occurred in June 2006, when I was given the opportunity to run touch for my friend Tappe at Ellis Park, when the Boks went head to head with a World XV in his last major fixture before his retirement. Understandably, after nearly two decades in the saddle, it was a very emotional day for him, and I was happy to celebrate this occasion with him.

Tappe and I had watched each other's backs throughout our careers, in the process building a friendship based on mutual respect. Despite coming from very different cultural backgrounds, we shared a passion for rugby and respected each other's abilities. And we could count on each other's support in trying situations. With Tappe, I always got the impression that he was interested in me not only as a fellow referee, but also as a person.

Tappe was also a great travelling companion and I enjoyed being on the road with him. He has a great sense of humour, which was invaluable on those lonely, desolate days when you wondered what the hell you were doing so far from home.

But Tappe's farewell and the Final in the Fog turned out to be brief respites from May's Wellington hysteria. I was back at Christchurch's Jade Stadium, this time for a Tri-Nations opener between the All Blacks and the Wallabies, and this time I really did have a bad day at the office.

Destroying the Wallabies in the front row, the second row and the back row, the All Blacks were deserved 32-12 victors, but there was no denying that I had delivered a sub-standard performance. My overall impression after the Test was that my decision-making had not been accurate enough, and that the Wallabies had inadvertently borne the brunt of this. But my decision to sin-bin Aussie Rocky Elsom after three infringements in a row at the tackle was the correct decision. The All Blacks scored two tries during the 10 minutes he was off the pitch.

After the game, Wallaby coach John Connolly said that I should have penalised All Black wing Joe Rokocoko for falling on Wallaby flyhalf Stephen Larkham near the Australian try line as he went back to cover the ball. It enabled Richie McCaw to score his team's third try.

Even though I was a lot closer to the action than Connolly, I still couldn't be sure whether Rokocoko had dived on Larkham or not. I also couldn't be sure that Rokocoko had prevented Larkham from getting up. But I did feel that I got the balance of that decision wrong and should have awarded a penalty to the Wallabies.

I had other problems on the pitch too, applying advantage inconsistently at times and not awarding clear and obvious penalties. On one occasion I didn't allow Australia enough advantage and the All Blacks broke out a couple of phases later and scored a try. It was a bad day at the office, for sure, and I was very disappointed that I had let people down.

I was always harsher on myself than anyone else could ever be. After that Test, I had to tell myself that that had not been a typical Jonathan Kaplan performance. However, I also had to remind myself of the bigger picture, which was that my career could not be judged on one Test alone, and that I would continue to strive to improve in my job. I hoped to demonstrate as much in my next Test match.

But the disappointment dogged me for weeks. I beat myself up about it. After a sub-par performance such as that one, I felt as if I didn't really deserve to be in the privileged position I was. But I resolved to stay confident in my abilities and committed to refining my performance.

At that stage of my career I'd also come to realise that, despite my best efforts and intentions, despite my best preparation, despite being considered one of the best refs in the world, I would never get everything right. There would always be a couple of key moments in a match when I did not make the right calls, and they would affect the outcome of the game.

By then I was convinced that it didn't matter how good a ref you were or how much you tinkered with the nuances of the laws, the bottom line was that rugby was too complicated for one man to referee. The way rugby is administered and officiated needs to change dramatically in order for officials to make fewer mistakes on the pitch and eliminate those off-days.

Fortunately, a good day at the office is never far off. As when I reffed my third Currie Cup final, in Bloemfontein in October 2006. I got a taste of what was in store for the match when André, who was already in the City of Roses, called me shortly before I boarded my flight to Bloem.

"Kappers, what's the greatest atmosphere we've experienced together?" he asked on speakerphone.

"Well, we've been to a few Wold Cups, but there's no doubt my best rugby atmosphere was Dunedin."

"Absolutely! One hundred per cent. Do you remember what Dunedin was like?"

"Of course. I'll never forget it. It was the most awesome rugby occasion I've ever experienced."

Back in 1999, when I'd run touch for André in the Super 12 Highlanders/ Crusaders final, the whole of Dunedin had come to a grinding halt. Everything was put on hold for the rugby. That's how much that final meant to the locals.

"Well, Kappers," André said, "you may have to rethink that after this weekend, because Bloem is twice what Dunedin was. It's hard to believe, but I'm not joking."

André was bang on the money. From the moment I landed, it was clear as a whistle that Bloem had raised the bar on Dunedin. The atmosphere was bigger, crazier. Which was understandable. Bloemfontein had not hosted a Currie Cup final in a long time. Plus, they now had a team capable of repeating their giant-slaying act of the previous year. You could feel everyone in Free State colours believed that.

Bloem was living, breathing, seething rugby. Virtually every single person I encountered was wearing either a Bulls or Free State jersey, from the newspaper vendors and the petrol attendants to office workers and people in coffee shops. And all the talk was about the game. Who was the best. Who was the greatest. And who was going to teach who a rugby lesson.

In a nutshell, Bloem was rugby *befok* on a level that I had never experienced in two decades of reffing around the world. And it was so chock a block with rugby fans, I had to book into a bed and breakfast instead of my usual hotel.

The game itself lived up to expectations. Played in typical Currie Cup fashion, it was high intensity. Little brother pitted against bigger brother. And, unlike the year before, there were no niggles or off-the-ball nonsense. This was a contest to behold, more flowing, more pleasing to the eye, cut and thrust, both teams giving it horns.

Free State were rampant at the beginning, with early tries by Philip Burger (who had had a sensational season, scoring 15 tries with some supreme side-stepping skills) and Kabamba Floors. This shocked the Bulls and gave Free State some breathing space before the inevitable heavyweight onslaught that would come towards the end.

The Bulls' Marius Delport had also scored a couple of long-range tries and they were by no means out of the game. It was seesaw until the closing stages, when it seemed as if the home team would hold on. But the Bulls were applying tremendous pressure, camping out on the Free State try line, and a succession of penalties in their favour was rewarded when J.P. Nel crashed over to set up a difficult conversion for Morné Steyn. But Steyn converted the try to level the scores and take the final into extra time, pushing the supporters a little bit further towards the edges of their seats.

In the first 10 minutes of extra time I awarded a penalty against a youthful Heinrich Brüssow right under the poles, much to the consternation of the home faithful. And much to their relief, in the second half Meyer Bosman converted a penalty to level the score yet again. And that was how it ended – a draw after extra time for the first time in the 127-year history of the Currie Cup.

This time there was no big, fat, gloating cigar. Just a sharing of the trophy. Of course everyone prefers a winner. No doubt the home crowd felt a little robbed. But I couldn't help thinking that with the passage of time, there would be no regrets. There was no shame in sharing the spoils with this great Bulls team, which had far more resources at their disposal than the home team. While for the Bulls, coming back from the dead the way they did showed championship mentality. Besides, drawing in the Cheetahs' den was not to be scoffed at.

For me, there was something poetic about the trilogy of finals between the two teams ending in a draw, especially since it was unlikely that the sequence would occur again for a long, long time.

Getting smashed and tearing ligaments in my elbow during a Test in Christchurch on 21 June 2008. New Zealand beat England 44-12

Yellow-carding Mike Tindall of England during the same Test – no laughing matter

The men … The three brothers Kaplan with our dad at Nicky's wedding in 2007

On 22 November 2008, at the Millennium Stadium in Cardiff, I set a new benchmark by becoming the most capped international referee in rugby history. My brothers, David and Gary, celebrated with me

My family getting ready for the Twickenham experience in 2009: my brothers Gary and David, our mother Tikvah, and Gary's two oldest sons, Benjamin and Daniël

Pounding the road on the Atlantic Seaboard

"What shampoo do you use? My hair is really thinning…"

Always proud to be wearing the blazer! With Richie McCaw and Steve Borthwick before England vs New Zealand, 21 November 2009

Mils Muliaina makes a break as I fall backwards during the Test match between the All Blacks and Wales in Hamilton, New Zealand, 26 June 2010

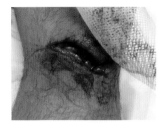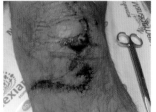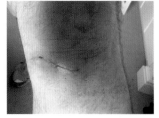

The wound. My knee directly after my scooter accident on 19 July 2011, and then about 10 days later. The last pic is what my knee looked like at the start of the 2011 RWC

Warily eyeing the streaker who ran onto the field during the 2011 Rugby World Cup pool match between Tonga and Canada in Whangarei, New Zealand

A Japan player gestures to me as his teammate burrows over the line to score a try during their 2011 Rugby World Cup pool match against Canada in Napier, New Zealand

The moment I dislocated my shoulder and tore a bicep tendon during Ireland vs Italy in the pool stages of the 2011 Rugby World Cup in Dunedin

My champ Ruby sitting at the Sand Bar in Camps Bay having a birthday breakfast

Me and my Lola

Love the expression on the faces of Lola and Dexter, 2013

My 1 000th fixture. The Leopards and Griffons give me a guard of honour, 2012

A *Volksblad* cartoon depicting my achievement of becoming the first referee to ref 100 Super Rugby games, 23 February 2013

In 2013 I reffed the biggest schools game on the South African calendar: Paarl Boys vs Paarl Gym. Just before the kick-off, the respective headmasters gave me this award in honour of my service to SA rugby

With the Du Plessis brothers, Bismarck and Jannie, after the 2013 Currie Cup final between WP and the Sharks at Newlands. My eyes are still red from all the emotion

With the legendary Paul Dobson, the father figure in my rugby career, and WP referee manager Ben Theron, after the Currie Cup final

A post-match jersey swap with the "Incredible Schalk"

27

Preparing for the 2007 Rugby World Cup

As I lay waiting to go into surgery at the end of my 2006 season, there was no escaping it: for the past eight years I had been reffing on borrowed time. After my 1998 knee operation to repair my split articular cartilage, there had been no guarantees how long I could continue reffing. It was always in the back of my mind that the terminal nature of my injury could end my career in a heartbeat. I'd seen enough collateral damage on a rugby field to know that.

That's why I embraced every day, every year, every big game, every final, every tournament as if it were my last, and squeezed every last drop of enjoyment from each.

Sure, I had to make difficult choices in the process. Putting that long-dreamt-of ski holiday on hold because the risk of injury was simply too great. Stopping my road running, because my surgeon believed that my cartilages would not cope with the battering.

And giving up my passion, touch rugby.

I still missed those days a decade ago when I could accept a mate's invitation to play touch. Once, just before the 2003 World Cup, I thought, to hell with it! I threw caution to the wind and played a game of touch. And got hurt so badly that I had to stop training for six weeks. Luckily no permanent damage was done, but it was a wake-up call. I realised that if I took the second chance that surgery had given me for granted, I might live to regret it.

So from that day on, I religiously followed doctor's orders. I adjusted my training to avoid anything that required sudden lateral movement or sudden sprinting. Being the carthorse that I am, I had to find a more gentle way of picking up speed before I "accelerated".

Swimming lengths was one way of keeping fit, but I didn't enjoy the pool. So I chose the treadmill, which, although boring, worked well enough for me to remain one of the fitter refs on the park. Not the fastest, but right up there with the fittest.

Challenges bring out the best in me. Often what appears to be a problem or obstacle in life's journey is really a blessing in disguise. By the time they wheeled me into surgery in December 2006, I had been blessed with a run approaching 200 first-class games, including three treasured Currie Cup finals and a raft of truly memorable Test matches. By January 2007, when I got the green light that the straightforward clearout operation on my knee had been successful, life presented me with another fantastic opportunity: a shot at RWC redemption.

Buoyed by the good news and in a very positive mindset, I refereed a stunner, a Six Nations Test match where underdogs England beat France 26-18 at Twickenham.

On the final weekend of the tournament, Ireland needed to beat Italy in Rome by quite a significant points margin to clinch the trophy. Ireland were masters at percentage rugby, so I had my doubts whether they could turn it on. But they surprised me and scored eight fantastic tries to win the Test 51-24.

Ireland's magic set up the Six Nations for a thrilling climax at Stade de France, where the home side now knew by how much they needed to beat Scotland to trump Ireland's bid for Six Nations glory. As it turned out, the Test went right down to the wire and the whole tournament was eventually decided on the back of a bold call by my friend and colleague Craig Joubert.

It was one of those tense Tests, with France battling to get over the line to score the points they so desperately sought. They eventually did it, but in a very messy way in the closing minutes. Craig had to go upstairs to make sure that there was no reason why he should not award a try to French No. 8, Elvis Vermeulen. However, the outcome of the 2007 Six Nations would be decided not by how the TMO responded, but by the question Craig asked of him.

I was watching the match on TV and, knowing Craig, could see that he thought he'd seen the ball being grounded, but knew how important it was to ask the TMO the right question. It was a tense few seconds before he made the call. Craig could have gone upstairs and asked, "Is this a try, yes or no?" I was pretty sure if he did that, the answer would be something along the lines of, "I can't see the ball being grounded, so five-metre scrum, attack ball." In that case, Ireland would win the Six Nations.

Instead, Craig asked the TMO to give him a reason why he *couldn't* award the try. Basically he was saying, "I'm almost sure that a try has been scored here, so you need to find a reason why I can't award it. And if you can't, then I'm awarding the try."

The replay footage was so bad that the TMO couldn't help out. So he told Craig, "I can't give you a reason why you shouldn't award a try, therefore you can award it ..."

What a way to end the championship! It just illustrated on what small margins this glorious game could be decided. A different question would have resulted in a different result, and a different winner of that year's Six Nations.

I wasn't given many high-profile Test matches on which to stake my World Cup aspirations, but the selectors knew what I was capable of and I was happy with my form leading up to the 2007 tournament. I was also reassured by the well-informed grapevine, which told me that if I wasn't the top-ranked ref in the world, then I was pretty close to the top of the pile and had been for a good few years.

I nevertheless had some special moments on the pitch, most notably when Bishops beat Boland Landbou 36-33 in Wellington. Some schools games are better than others, and this one was stellar, a superb contest between the power and brute force of the farm boys versus the skills and acumen of the city kids.

And it yielded one of the most memorable schoolboy tries of my career. It will certainly be remembered by the 120-kilogram Landbou prop who was still breathing heavily long after rumbling his way through all his opponents from the halfway line. And he didn't just bulldoze his way down the field – he displayed some deft touches along the way: a bit of a dummy here, a break through a tackle there, and then a hand-off before powering over the line prop-style. I swear, you could almost hear the mountains rumbling their approval behind the raptures of the local crowd.

I loved reffing schools rugby. It is the purest form of the game. These amateur matches gave me the opportunity to give something back to the game with the skills I had at my disposal. Having a top ref allowed the schoolboys to focus on the game instead of the refereeing. And because of their naivety, I could invariably push the right buttons that allowed them to play a beautiful game. This was the artist in me. Rugby was my passion, not just a career and a cheque at the end of the month. This was the part of the game that was food for my soul.

Which was just as well, because games like that were a foil for the unpleasantness that occasionally reared its head. A good example was when I flew Down Under to run touch for Marius Jonker in his debut Bledisloe Cup Test. On the way, we had a conversation during which Marius asked me for some guidance. I was happy to give it. Like I always did when colleagues asked me for advice, I gave him my take on how to be successful in international games played on the world stage. I mentioned a particular Currie Cup game he had reffed at Loftus where he blew about 10 penalties for players arriving at the tackle and sealing off.*

In that season's Currie Cup, André Watson had had a bee in his bonnet about sealing off. He'd made it clear from the start that he wanted it punished. And I had already told him that I didn't agree with his philosophy of penalising one thing at the expense of other important factors at the tackle area.

I told Marius, "If you ref your Test match like that, [the IRB] will never give you another Bledisloe again. Blow 10 penalties for sealing off and you're gone. They won't even look at you again."

I explained to him that you had to have a more holistic view of the tackle. You couldn't just be vigilant about sealing-off players and miss everything else. "I'm not telling you not to watch sealing-off players," I added. "But just be aware that it's André's bugbear in this season's Currie Cup and the rest of the rugby world is less interested in what he thinks."

It was a decent exchange. I was quite proud to be with Marius for this very significant milestone in his career. Once again, here was another South African ref being exposed to the Bledisloe Cup, which I considered to be the best-quality rugby played at Test-match level. I was very chuffed to assist. And Marius seemed pleased that I had shown an interest. He seemed to understand that I was not instructing him on what to do, but that he could use the advice any way he saw fit. The buck stopped with him, so he had to do what he thought was best.

Marius must have told André what I'd said, because André later called me and accused me of "poisoning Marius's mind". It was an unfair accusation and it made my blood boil.

"Marius asked for my opinion and I gave it," I told André. "I didn't go

---

* Sealing off occurs after a ball-carrier has been tackled and a support player or players fall onto the tackled player to ensure that their side retains possession.

to him and instruct him on what to do. He's an adult, not a two-year-old. He can work things out for himself."

André might not have agreed with me on what I'd said, but that should not have come as a surprise to him – he knew me to be a person who spoke his mind. This incident was a further illustration of the sometimes tetchy and difficult relationship I had with my bosses. As I would never compromise my integrity and was not afraid to stand my ground and confront those more powerful, it was inevitable that we would sometimes lock horns.

Back on the field, I got an unexpected surprise. Okay, so it was nothing more than a dress rehearsal for the Boks, a chance to get their players and systems in place. For me, however, it was as prestigious as it was for Namibia to play at Newlands against one of the world's top Test sides. This game would make me the only South African referee in the modern era to ref his country of birth. And that, for me, was a huge source of pride.

The Test itself was pretty one-sided, with the Boks quite predictably thumping Namibia 105-13. The professional make-up of the two teams could not have been more different, nor could the resources at their disposal, the level of conditioning, and the difference between a world-class outfit striving to win tournaments and another just there to compete.

It was my last warm-up before the World Cup, but I did ref a couple more Currie Cup and schools games. Then I boarded my flight for France, excited at what lay ahead. I was feeling fit, my knee was strong, I was mentally focused and I was ready to deliver my best.

28

World Cup redemption

I arrived in France very excited to once again be a part of the greatest show on the rugby calendar. I was one of the senior referees of the tournament, along with Alain Rolland, Tony Spreadbury and Chris White. We had a good mix of experience and youth, and I thought that by and large, the best refs were chosen (although Craig could consider himself desperately unlucky to have missed the cut).

We had our usual team-building exercise, this time up in the Alps, at a resort called Tignes, where we got to know one another better with a few drinking games and fun activities. It was the perfect venue to unwind away from the public eye and the glare of the media.

From the outset, the tournament far exceeded my expectations – it was exceptionally well organised, often with an abundance of volunteers helping out. The majority of the fixtures were well supported, with the locals really warming to all the underdogs.

My first assignment was in Lens, a town in the north of France, more famous for its football team's exploits than rugby. England had kicked off their World Cup defence with an anticipated victory over the United States (28-10), but thanks to a spirited Eagles performance, England left Stade Félix-Bollaert in Lens without sending shivers down any other team's spine.

I, too, left Lens feeling I hadn't hit all the right notes. Although I had reffed fairly well, I'd not effectively dealt with a couple of foul-play incidents. One of those was a trip in the 13th minute by England captain Phil Vickery that quite possibly prevented the Eagles from taking an early lead. It was also missed by my two assistants, Bryce Lawrence and Lyndon Bray.

In addition, towards the end of the game flyhalf Olly Barkley was spear-tackled by centre Paul Emerick. I issued a yellow card on the basis that the player had not been driven into the ground, and that Emerick had merely lost control of the tackle once Barkley was airborne. In those days, intent to drive the opponent into the ground was the threshold for a red card.

At the disciplinary hearing, I explained my reasoning, but it did not find favour with the judicial officer, who kept trying to get me to change my story. I refused. After nearly two hours, he gave up. I left, but later I was surprised to hear that Emerick had received a seven-week ban, which ended his tournament. Both Nigel Melville, the American coach, and Emerick told me afterwards that they were grateful I had stuck to my guns.

Years later, just before my retirement, Emerick sent me a special message to congratulate me on my career. More importantly, he thanked me for the stand I had taken.

"In the judicial hearing, your statement for the defence of the player really stuck out in my memory. I vividly remember the judicial officer almost badgering you to get the answer he wanted, but you stood your ground and defended your decision and the player. Always love a player's ref, and you've demonstrated that on many occasions."

That simple acknowledgement meant the world to me.

But back to the 2007 World Cup. I was also just okay in Montpellier the next week, when Tonga beat Samoa 19-15 in stifling heat.

And then, when I least expected it, I got a game that I really enjoyed. Japan and Canada, two minnows of world rugby, dished up a nail-biting contest in Bordeaux that required as much skill as patience from my side, but delivered a memorable ending. Trailing 5-12 going into injury time, Koji Taira of Japan crossed the line, and then Shotaro Onishi, who couldn't hit a cow's arse with a banjo throughout the match, nervously slotted the conversion to scenes of sheer jubilation.

The Canadians were gutted. For the first time in their World Cup history they would return home without a single win. But the Japanese, and the locals who had adopted them for the day, were absolutely ecstatic. Witnessing the scenes of pride and joy in the stands, you'd never have thought that this was the end of Japan's World Cup.

Emotions on the field spilt over when the Japanese players, many of them unashamedly crying tears of pride and joy, hauled out a national flag as big as a double garage that each one of them had signed and written a special message on. They then paraded it around the ground in a lap of honour. That moment of national pride was out of the top drawer and will stay with me forever. Even in defeat … what a triumph.

Four days later I ran out at Saint-Étienne's Stade Geoffroy-Guichard feeling that I had to deliver a strong performance if I wanted to feature at the back end of the tournament. It was not going to be easy. I normally hit my stride when I was able to free up a game, but this fixture was unlikely to deliver that possibility.

The stakes were high. Italy were desperate to secure their first quarter-final ever. And Scotland, who had never missed the quarters, were equally determined to keep their World Cup track record intact. It was going to be a very physical, closely contested Test match.

I wasn't wrong. Played in awful wet weather, it was one of those nervous, frenetic battles that involved a lot of up-and-unders, very little space, pick-and-goes and hard-nosed contests at the breakdown. And to make matters even more unpleasant, I again felt a bit off the mark. I missed a couple of infringements, in particular a trip on a Scottish player. It happened behind my back and I only picked it up on the big-screen replay. Not as obvious a trip as in the England game, but a trip nevertheless. And unfortunately my touch judges Wayne Barnes and Dave Pearson also missed it.

Come half-time, with Scotland hanging on to a narrow 12-10 lead, I walked back into the shed bitterly disappointed in myself and battling, uncharacteristically, to control my emotions. I was convinced that I'd blown any opportunity at a World Cup redemption with my poor performance. And I felt gutted at the prospect of going home from yet another World Cup with broken dreams.

I asked my assistants to give me a moment and headed for the showers, where I smashed the wall a few times with my fist. It was the only time I ever lost my cool during or after a match. At least I managed not to express this gross outpouring of emotion in front of the players or anyone else.

Although I'd calmed down considerably by the time I returned to the change room, Wayne picked up on my mood and asked what was wrong. He listened as I explained how disappointed I was in my performance.

"Okay, so you missed a trip," he responded. "It's one of those things that can happen to anyone. I don't think your game is as bad as you think. Pull yourself together. There's 40 minutes of rugby left for you to focus on getting a good game going."

By the time I started the second half, I was still not convinced, but nevertheless determined to do justice to the Test and not worry about the future.

The result was that I reffed a much better second half, which went right down to the wire. Trailing 16-18, Italy got an opportunity to make history in the closing minutes when I awarded them a penalty. But they missed it, and Scotland went through to the next round on the back of six penalties, courtesy of Chris Paterson's unerring boot. On these small margins are the fates of players and coaches decided. Despite Italy's loss, their coach, Pierre Berbizier, was gracious about my performance after the game.

Once the dust had settled, my New Zealand assessor Bob Francis and I discussed the errors I had made, but he felt that by and large I had controlled the game well, and with the firm hand it had needed. I was still not happy with my performance, though. I didn't think it was my best, but I was more than relieved that Bob didn't view it as a disaster.

After the pool stages, the appointments were announced for the quarter-finals, and Wayne Barnes, who had done particularly well in his first World Cup, was entrusted with France and New Zealand in Cardiff.

Before the game, IRB referee manager Paddy O'Brien told me to look after Wayne while I was running touch for him. He'd got this appointment on merit, but Paddy was mindful that Wayne was a relative rookie and that the quarter-final would be a big step up. Wayne might need a wingman.

Paddy's words kept milling around in my head throughout the game. And I did the best I could. But all the best intentions in the world were of no use to Wayne when he missed a forward pass on my side of the field that led to Frenchman Yannick Jauzion's match-winning try – a try that would play a significant role in New Zealand's World Cup demise. I wanted to call it, but because of player movement I couldn't detect where the pass had come from, so I hesitated. We were under instructions to only call the clear and obvious.

Afterwards Wayne copped a lot of flak, not just for the missed forward pass, but for his general handling of France's shock 20-18 victory over the tournament favourites. I felt for him. I knew what it was like. And even though I wasn't in a position to make a call about the forward pass, in my mind I had let him down at a moment when I could have saved him a lot of grief. On review, it was obvious that it had been forward.

I'd also let Paddy down. Back in the change room, I talked about it with him and he confirmed that the pass had been forward. But to his credit, Paddy wasn't angry or complaining. Instead of making a big song and dance about Wayne's mistake, he praised him for undergoing a baptism of fire and kept reiterating what a great game of rugby it had been.

Paddy saw the bigger picture and recognised that refereeing careers could be made or broken in moments like that – which was why he backed Wayne in the press.

"New Zealand losing that game was not all about the forward pass," he said to the media. "The pass was forward, but that's rugby refereeing. I thought the referee actually had a decent game. Hindsight is a wonderful thing, but you can't turn back the clock. He's a superb referee and we have a lot of confidence in him, that's why we gave him the quarter-final."

However, the truth was that we had *all* made a critical error. And it didn't matter who you were or where you came from or how much preparation you did, these types of errors will continue to plague rugby union until administrators make some big decisions about the appropriate use of technology by match officials. I will discuss this in much more detail later.

Thankfully my selectors didn't hold any of that against me. I'd been told in confidence that I was in the frame for a semi-final, so I wasn't too surprised when they announced that I'd been selected to ref France versus England in Paris.

My selectors were straight with me, which I appreciated. They told me that they didn't think I was the form ref of the tournament, which was a fair assessment, but they felt that I was their "big-game" referee. I had big-match temperament and could ref the major Test matches with the right mix of composure, accuracy and flair, so I was their logical choice for that game. They encouraged me to go out and prove that their faith was not misplaced.

I felt that my consistency in big games over a long period of time was being acknowledged. Super-excited about reffing the semi, I felt as if a weight had been lifted off my shoulders.

Fortunately there was time for some light relief before my big day. One evening a few friends and I went out for drinks. At some stage during the long evening, we reluctantly decided it was time to get something other than alcohol into our stomachs. About 12 of us sat down and I ordered a few bottles of red wine and some beers for the boys. Then my mate Dan Swanepoel decided he needed a Fanta Orange. Which the waitress brought to the table as she was about to take the food order. Dan promptly opened the can and poured the Fanta straight into the glass of red wine. The look of horror on the waitress's face as she tried to stop him was only made more comical when he tried to down the drink. Klerksdorp had come to Paris!

On match day, there was no denying that I felt nervous, which was unusual for me. I'd only felt like that about a handful of games. And I knew why. Unlike the Six Nations, or the Bledisloe Cup or the Tri-Nations, I knew I would never have this opportunity again. I might ref at another World Cup, but I was pretty certain 2007 would be my biggest. So I couldn't afford to make any mistakes. I had to make it count. Not just for myself, but to justify the selectors' faith in me.

Aside from the nerves, though, I arrived at Stade de France feeling that I was in a good space. I was completely focused and ready for whatever the game was going to throw at me. And most importantly, I was physically the strongest I'd been for a while.

A Josh Lewsey try within 80 seconds got England off to a spectacular start. But France quickly established dominance and, despite fierce English resistance, were able to hang on to a narrow lead for much of the game thanks to three penalties by flyhalf Lionel Beauxis.

But much like he broke Australian hearts at the 2003 World Cup, Jonny Wilkinson then stunned the host nation. First with a penalty awarded against Dimitri Szarzewski, the French hooker, for a high tackle, which put England into the lead. And then with a trademark drop that sealed the deal at 14-9.

It had not been a pretty game, but it had been tight, gripping and entertaining. It was a bruising, uncompromising and tactical affair that could have presented me with some tough moments, but I managed to fly under the radar and make the important decisions when they counted. I was proud of the way I managed this and how I let the players decide the outcome. I felt I'd delivered my best performance at the tournament when people were counting on me the most. I must say, I felt a great deal of relief and satisfaction as I walked off the field.

From that moment on, I was in a positive head space. I might not have got to referee the final, but South Africa got to play in it. I was pretty chuffed for Jake White, a good friend of mine. Like me, he'd also had a lot of ups and downs on his way to World Cup glory.

South Africa deservedly beat England 15-6 in a dour, tightly contested match, thanks mainly to Victor Matfield's superhuman line-out exploits, as well as some brutal defence, a decent kicking game and superior teamwork.

The same peer support was sadly absent among the referees after the game, however. After watching the final with Tappe, we returned to the team room at our hotel and found Stuart Dickinson struggling to regain the world-class composure he had shown when making a tough TMO decision at a critical moment in a very tense final.

This was due to the fact that, back in the change room after the Test, Steve Walsh, the fifth official, had attacked him in front of all the other match officials for his decision to disallow a try by England winger Mark Cueto.

As he dived for the try line early in the second half, Cueto was tackled into touch by Bok No. 8 Danie Rossouw. Quite rightly, Alain Rolland, who was reffing the game, asked Stuey to determine whether Cueto was in touch before grounding the ball. Stuey looked at it from every angle and correctly ruled Cueto's foot to have been on the touchline before he dotted down. So Alain took play back to a previous penalty infringement, which Jonny Wilkinson then converted to reduce South Africa's lead to 9-6.

Stuey was aggrieved that Walsh had criticised his decision, even though it had been absolutely correct. On top of that, instead of taking Stuey aside and talking to him in private, Walsh had belittled him in front of his colleagues. It was poor form. No one needed that kind of nonsense at the end of a World Cup. None of us wanted to leave with a bad taste in our mouth. And by and large, the camaraderie among the refs was usually excellent. We were, for the most part, genuinely supportive of one another, though we may on occasion have disagreed about selection issues.

I watched footage of the incident while reviewing match reports on the computer in the team room, and there, as clear as daylight, was a freeze frame of Cueto's foot touching the line. As painful as it was for the English, Stuart had made a very ballsy, and correct, decision under a lot of pressure.

Tappe, who was watching the footage over my shoulder, shouted jokingly across the room at Walsh, "Do you want to apologise to Dickinson now?" There was a pregnant pause. What was required was a humble apology as public as the earlier humiliation. Instead, there was just silence.

But I didn't allow the incident to colour my World Cup experience.

I savoured the farewell parties and in my mind relived every moment of a fantastic tournament. And on the final day, when all the officials were saying goodbye to one another, I went over to chat with Paddy, who was sitting with some of the selectors.

As I walked over, he spotted me and stood up.

"Well done, Kappers," he said, as we hugged each other goodbye. "You were outstanding in this tournament."

My response was straight from the heart. "Thanks, Paddy. You will never know how important that semi-final selection was for me. It was my redemption."

But I think he knew. In World Cup 1999, he had infamously denied Fiji a victory over France in a pool game that basically put paid to his dream of reffing the final. And then, in 2003, he had redeemed himself at the same stage of the tournament, ironically also in an England/France semi-final.

"I *do*," he replied.

We left it there. There was no need for further explanation. I could see from the tears in his eyes that he knew exactly where I was coming from.

29

Slaying the Bledisloe dragon

It was ostensibly a "warm-up" club game to prepare myself for my first 2008 Test, between Scotland and England, but Glasgow Warriors versus the Opsreys at the end of February turned out to be one of the coldest matches I would ever ref.

As I ran onto the pitch, icy rain pelted down and then, just before blowing the whistle for the start of the game, the temperature plummeted even further below zero as a monster hail storm swept the field. The hail was so thick that I lost sight of the players taking up their positions for the kick-off. And as I stood there like a drowned rat for a few minutes, I wondered whether it would be the first match of my career I'd call off.

Justin Marshall and a few of the other Ospreys players were about to leave the field when it cleared enough for play to go ahead, albeit in weather conditions fit only for the insane – and rugby fanatics. I was so cold by the time I blew the final whistle that I knew I could expect a very painful hot shower afterwards.

The miserable weather reminded me of another trip to Scotland, when I accompanied Tappe and André. While there, we were asked whether we would like to play a round at St Andrews, the hallowed home of golf. It was a dream come true for André and Tappe, who were frothing at the mouth before the offer had even been extended.

I was happy to tag along and hack a few balls into the wind, but then it started raining and the wind was fierce by the time we got going. I remember thinking, "What the hell am I doing out here?" There was more play-and-miss than a Shane Warne/Daryll Cullinan innings. We lasted all of nine holes before returning to the very austere clubhouse with its ancient traditions and glorious splendour. Although I really enjoyed the experience, I must say that it felt a bit like feeding strawberries to pigs!

Fortunately it wasn't quite as cold or miserable when Scotland met England at Murrayfield the following weekend, but it was still chilly enough to ensure that my first Calcutta Cup fixture was one of the dullest Test matches I ever reffed. The foul weather ensured that both teams kicked the ball whenever they could and, when they did not, fumbled one pass after another. In the end, the Scots edged it 15-9, but it was, all in all, a forgettable game.

Disappointed, I returned to my hotel room wanting an early night, but my friend James Fleming, in Edinburgh on a bachelor's weekend, was insistent that I meet him for a drink. So I agreed to join him at Molly Malone's Irish Bar in Haymarket. "But just for two drinks," I told my touch judge, Marius Jonker, with a wink. He showed no sign that he had heard it all before. "Just two drinks," I said. "Twenty minutes max, and then we'll be out of there."

Quite a few hours later, after much pub crawling, I found myself walking back to my hotel arm in arm with a very attractive, young Irish lass. It was about a one-kilometre walk in sub-zero temperatures, but that didn't matter. Because back in my hotel room it got hot for the first time since I'd arrived in Edinburgh.

An hour or two later I was woken up by a cellphone ringing. I heard my date get up and bump into furniture, so I switched on the light so that she could find her way to the bathroom, which was situated right next to the hotel-room door. After hearing a door close, I switched the light off again and went straight back to sleep.

When I woke up properly the next morning, she was not in bed. I called out, but there was no reply. Thinking maybe she had done a runner, I checked my valuables. But nothing had been touched. Then I noticed that her bag and clothes were still lying where she had left them.

Because we were really drunk when we got into bed, I thought maybe she had fallen asleep in the bathroom. But she wasn't there. Next I searched the corridor and then the stairwell. But the girl was nowhere to be found.

By then I was starting to panic. I had slept with a woman I hardly knew and she had gone missing in freezing weather wearing nothing more than her skimpy G-string and clutching her cellphone. Had something bad happened to her? Had she perhaps been abducted? Or fallen off the balcony? Whatever the case, it would not look good if the cops came knocking and found all her stuff in my room.

I called Marius, who told me not to panic. He came over and searched the girl's belongings for her cellphone number, being careful not to leave any fingerprints, but unfortunately the search yielded nothing.

Stumped, Marius and I went down to breakfast to talk it through. We had to come up with a plan before we left at 10 a.m. to catch our flight to Wales. Marius calmed me down and told me that the only option was to think positively. So I returned to my room and packed all of the girl's stuff into two laundry bags, which I dropped off at reception when I checked out. With my heart in my mouth, I told the woman behind the desk that my friend would collect them in the next day or two.

The trip to Wales was not the most pleasant of my career. No matter how hard I tried, there was no getting rid of the foreboding that rattled around in my head. The whole episode was like a bad movie, and I just wanted the credits to roll.

A day later, still worried sick, I logged onto my Facebook page and found a message. It was her! She thanked me for a great evening and said she was grateful that I had left her things, including all the money in her wallet, at reception. It turned out that she had wanted to take the phone call in the bathroom but had mistaken my hotel-room door for the adjacent bathroom door and had wandered into the corridor by mistake. After a brief conversation with her friend, she turned around to go back to my room, but could not remember my room number. Not wanting to wake anyone up, she had called her friend to pick her up. "Thanks," her Facebook message concluded. "It was a fun night!"

A month later, in the middle of another Super 14 season, feeling that creep of long-distance loneliness that had become my all-too-familiar travelling companion Down Under, I found a wonderful moment of temporary respite that I will treasure forever.

Feeling peckish after reffing a remarkable game of 10 goals and no converted penalties in the Chiefs' 42-28 victory over the Brumbies, I went in search of food at my Canberra hotel and bumped into Chiefs coach Ian Foster. He invited me to the team dining room, where he said there was plenty of food left over.

Normally I would have declined. When you ref a team week in and week out, season after season, there's every chance that familiarity increases the likelihood of creating an expectation. I had never wanted to go there, so had always elected to remain detached from the players and coaches, even when staying at the same hotel.

Those boundaries remained intact as I served myself a plate of food and sat down alone at a table rather than join any of the players or coaching staff. For a while I was a silent spectator of a team winding down after a satisfying win. I was fascinated by the rare glimpse I was afforded into an inner sanctum, and drawn to the friendship and camaraderie in the room. *That* was what I missed on the road. That was what referees didn't have when they were far away from home. But as much as I was enjoying the moment, I knew I had to leave.

Then Mils Muliaina came over and extended an invitation. The team was about to start their fines meeting, he informed me. He'd understand if I had to leave, but I was also most welcome to stay and watch from a distance.

Normally fines meetings were very private affairs, so I was quite surprised by his invitation. But I also sensed that a moment like this would not repeat itself in a hurry. So I accepted the Chiefs' hospitality with gratitude and relief that I wouldn't, as usual, be returning to the solitude of my hotel room.

The fines meeting took the form of "boat races" and other drinking games, punctuated by a lot of joviality. What I found really interesting was that even though the beer was flowing, the players still respected those teammates who abstained. If you were fined and didn't drink alcohol, you still had to drink. But you could drink water, which looked as if it was just as bad to down as beer. The drinking was often accompanied by a boisterous countdown.

After the fines, the spotlight fell on the workmanlike prop Simms Davison, who had just played his 50th game. In addition to the obligatory down-down of three beers, Liam Messam and Mils Muliaina paid glowing tribute to their front-ranker's contribution. The bottom line was how much they respected him, and I could see the prop's already ample chest puff out a little more.

Then came the most special part of the evening. After presenting Davison with a memento marking the occasion, the team rose and gathered round in front of him. The room shook as they performed a type of haka I had never witnessed on the field in all my days of reffing the All Blacks.

It was so loud and pulsating with such raw energy that I was sure the guests on the seventh floor heard it. If they didn't, they must have taken a heavy dose of sleeping tablets, because every bloke in that room was as pumped and as passionate as he would have been in the throes of a Test-match haka. And although I did not understand a word of what was being chanted, there was absolutely no mistaking the all-round respect for Simms's contribution. What a privilege to have been there!

Now far less homesick than usual at that time of the year, I returned to South Africa to ref a couple of domestic matches to warm up for my All Blacks/ England Test in June. Again I was well into another season with no problems from my dodgy knee. Then, a week before the Test, during a friendly between

Free State and North West, a massive lock ran into me and hit me squarely in the middle of my right thigh with his leading knee.

I didn't often get injured by players. The last time was when I took that clearance kick in the nuts at Newlands in 1999. But every time I took a hit, it was extremely painful. In Potch, water, not tears, jumped out of my eyes and my thigh buckled as it went lame. The pain was excruciating and it took a whole lot of *vasbyt* to hobble through the remaining 15 minutes of the game.

Sore as it was, though, there was no way I was going to let the injury rob me of a Test that I had been eagerly anticipating. So I got one of the physios at the ground to treat me and took her deep-needle acupuncture like a man – not that I looked like one when she stuck the needles in.

She assured me that with anti-inflammatories and further treatment my injury should heal in time for the Test, but as I hobbled onto my Christchurch-bound flight a few days later, I felt that it would take a miracle for my dead leg to heal by Saturday.

My job was undoubtedly getting harder with age, but again my powers of recovery did not desert me. On Test day I was good to go at an eerie Christchurch stadium in the midst of a major refurbishment, which had left only the main grandstand intact. But just as I started to find my rhythm, and in the midst of following an All Black attack, I again got taken out by a player!

This time it was in spectacular fashion. I got totally upended, as if I had been spear-tackled. And with my feet pointed skywards, I crashed down on my left hand, which I had thrust out in front of me in an attempt to break my fall. As I hit the ground, my left elbow popped and the ligaments tore.

"What the hell is going on?" I thought as I gritted my teeth to finish another game in pain. Referees need to stand *somewhere*, and sometimes you are going to get it wrong. So I expected to be taken out now and again; it was an occupational hazard. But I found it quite weird that I had been hammered hard two Saturdays in a row. Ultimately, my elbow would take almost two years to heal completely.

Fortunately it was an injury I could work around, as my next assignment was in Nairobi to ref my first Elgin Cup Test between Kenya and Uganda. Although it might not sound like the most glamorous fixture, for me, reffing international rugby was not just about the big, prestigious Tests. What a lot of punters don't realise is that a Test match is still a Test match no matter who the protagonists are. There was always a lot of national pride at stake, so I approached Tests between minnows with a lot of respect.

What I also loved about the less glamorous fixtures was that they were more than just a rugby experience. You got to visit new countries, meet new people and experience different cultures. So after Kenya won a pretty decent game of rugby 39-20, I treated myself to a safari in the Maasai Mara, where I went on game drives and cruised silently in the breeze in a hot-air balloon looking down on thousands of wild animals. It was truly amazing.

In September I flew to Brisbane for an eagerly anticipated Bledisloe Cup appointment. Ever since my bad day at the office in Christchurch in 2006, I had wanted to prove to myself that I could ref another quality Bledisloe Test. And much to my delight, I did. Both teams attacked with intent and defended with courage right until the end, when the All Blacks squeaked home 28-24. And, as usual, the crowd at Suncorp Stadium was the best in Australia – loud, vociferous and passionate.

The All Blacks were down 7-17 at half-time, but in typical fashion they came back and outscored their opponents by four tries to three. In the process, they not only exposed Australia's defensive frailties, but also exhibited their own counter-attacking genius.

A bustling try by Ryan Cross after a sustained attack put the Wallabies back in the game, but in the end they simply ran out of puff and time. It was a fast-paced, free-flowing game in which the players ran themselves to a standstill. I, too, was exhausted by the time I blew the final whistle.

This time there was no carping and I pocketed my whistle feeling a satisfying sense of accomplishment. It was one of those rare Tests in which I'd reffed well and enjoyed the spectacle as much as the crowd. A mission accomplished, it banished the bad memories of 2006 for good.

30

A new benchmark

I thought I'd reffed my Currie Cup matches well enough in 2008 to believe that I might be called up to ref my fourth final. It was a final I really wanted, as it would be played at Kings Park, where the Sharks were hosting the Bulls. My rugby journey had started there when my dad and I used to watch the game every Saturday afternoon during the season.

But the call never came. Instead, someone on the selection panel told me that I had been overlooked in favour of a less experienced colleague. I couldn't believe it. Neither could the person who told me, who revealed that the vote had been really close.

Of course I didn't have a "right" to ref the final, but I did think that I had been the standout ref of the tournament that season and had earned the final fair and square.

Fortunately my informant on the selection panel felt as unhappy about the appointment as I did and was determined to do his best to try to rectify the situation. I was not privy to the finer details of what went down in the board-room, but I do know that another vote was taken because the panel was not in agreement about the initial selection.

I wasn't sure who tipped the new round of votes in my favour, although I believe that André backed me, which said a lot considering how many times in the past we had locked horns. Whatever the case, the selection was reversed on the Tuesday before the big day and I finally got the call to polish my boots for Kings Park.

It was a massive moment in both my career and on a personal level. But in spite of all that emotion and the clamour of the crowd on match day, I felt a deep-centred calmness inside of me. I stood quietly on the halfway line just before the start, looking up at seats T19 and T20 in Block D – the very same seats where I'd sat with my dad for so many Saturdays as a kid watching club rugby and the Toyota Club Champs.

I was switched on and ready to go, but in those moments just before kick-off a whole lot of childhood rugby memories came flooding back. For a few seconds time stood still as my past flashed by. And as I blew my whistle for the kick-off, I briefly reflected on how this very significant moment, which I will always treasure, had almost got away.

To add to the magic, the match turned out to be one of those really gripping, edge-of-your-seat Currie Cup finals that either team could have won. The game-changing moment probably occurred when François Steyn ankle-tapped Bryan Habana as he was heading for an early try.

Ultimately, though, it was a game summed up in the closing minutes when the Bulls turned over a Sharks scrum on the 10-metre line with the home side leading 14-9. Although the Bulls were better than any of their adversaries at making that kind of pressure count, the Sharks managed to secure another turnover in the closing seconds of the match and win the game. Kings Park was delirious with joy.

That game had meant so much to me. From the moment that I got selected, I was determined to make sure that my performance justified not only my selection, but proved what I had thought all along: I was the best man for the job. I wanted both teams to feel that. But the cherry on top was losing captain Victor Matfield running halfway across the field to congratulate me on the fair manner in which I had officiated. I loved that.

My season could have ended on a perfect note right there and then. But there was one more gift in store that year.

For some time the plan had been for my family to be present when I reffed my 47th Test match, which would make me the most capped international referee in rugby history. This huge milestone in my career would take place in Cardiff at the end of November, when Wales played the All Blacks at the Millennium Stadium.

I was looking forward to it tremendously – I had come a long way in 24 years. But at the eleventh hour I got a call to replace an injured Steve Walsh for France versus Argentina in Marseille. Unfortunately it was too late to change the family's travel plans, so I broke Phil Honiss's world record of 46 Test caps on 8 November 2008 without any fanfare. But the lack of a celebration didn't really bother me, because I knew there was a party waiting for me in Cardiff two weeks later.

I knew when I was approaching a significant milestone because it's been a hobby of mine since the start of my career to keep a spreadsheet with detailed statistics of every game I reffed. I used these stats to monitor and improve my performance and sometimes to identify any trends that might be developing with teams and which might warrant closer consideration.

However, some people in the rugby hierarchy may have misconstrued my motives and thought I was only chasing numbers instead of focusing on improving the quality of my refereeing. Mind-boggling! If I'd racked up the numbers, it was for no other reason than I was doing what I loved. It's a bit like going on a road trip and soaking up the sights, and then later looking down at the odometer and seeing just how much mileage you have managed to clock up.

I saw nothing wrong with acknowledging one's achievements or even using the lure of a new benchmark as a motivational tool. As I have always said, the benchmarks that sportspeople set on their respective journeys do not belong to them; they belong to the sport they are involved in. There is only transient glory in breaking new ground.

But back to the match in Cardiff and a Test that will long be remembered for Wales's defiance in the face of the haka. The whole idea behind the tradition is that the All Blacks stare down their opposition after their war dance; their opponents must be the first to look away. But Welsh coach Warren Gatland wasn't having his Six Nations Grand Slam champs backing down for anyone. So he had primed his charges to stay put, come what may.

Backed by a partisan crowd, who roared their approval as soon as they cottoned on to the drama, Wales stood their ground for about a minute before I decided to intervene. But the All Blacks refused to budge, saying that I should get the Welsh to disperse first. I said I was on my way to tell them that, but in the meantime they should take up their positions. Welsh captain Ryan Jones was equally defiant when I suggested his team get ready for the kick-off. He was following his coach's orders to the letter.

So I decided to return to the halfway line and let the players have their moment. Obviously by that stage the home crowd was roaring the roof off the stadium. It was pure theatre and the Welsh supporters were lapping it up.

Wales managed to carry their defiance into the first 40 minutes and went into the break leading 9-6. But as the second half wore on, the All Blacks' superior skills and conditioning began to dominate and they pulled ahead to win convincingly 29-9.

Although I'd set a new benchmark in Marseille, the Cardiff Test with its iconic preamble and my family in the stands will always remain the true marker of my proud achievement. By then I had pretty much resigned myself to the likelihood that I would never fulfil my dream of reffing a World Cup final. But this was one of the many other moments that made up for that.

To my delight and surprise, the moment was not lost on Welsh referee manager Bob Yeman, a former international ref who was also a good friend. He was probably more aware of my achievement and what it actually meant because of our friendship and the fact that fellow Welshman Derek Bevan had been the most capped ref for years before Paul Honiss bettered his 44 caps.

Whatever the reason, what counted was that an official from another country took the time and effort to mark the occasion. At the post-match cocktail party, Wales presented me with an inscribed glass paperweight that still has a special place among my memorabilia. It made me feel a part of the global rugby family, and that had always been my dream from the moment I embarked on my international Test career.

31

The art of refereeing

I am often asked how does one ref a big game and leave a stamp so indelible that rugby fans will remember the match forever and not the ref. A good understanding of the game, sufficient preparation and ample experience are very important, but there are certain personal traits and qualities a good ref should possess that are just as, if not more, important.

To start with, the following are what I consider to be a ref's defining responsibilities:

1. To make sure we officiate within the laws of the game.
2. To try to remain the 31st person on the field while the players take centre stage, almost acting as the conductor of an orchestra, only stepping in when we need to make big, bold calls.
3. To facilitate the best possible environment for the players to exhibit their skills for their own benefit and that of the public, and only penalise if there is an influence on the game.
4. To give the players our support by acting as a conduit to creating a great game.[*]

I have previously mentioned that I developed a simple philosophy on my role as a rugby referee early on in my career: flair, judgement and nerve.

In addition, a good ref obviously has to be fit. The fitter the better. But what enables a referee to elevate his performance beyond competent, and take his refereeing into the realm of art?

---

[*] For further reading, Robert S. Weinberg and Peggy A. Richardson's *Psychology of Officiating* (Human Kinetics Publishers) is very insightful on the role of the referee and the qualities he/she should possess.

The relationship between the physical and the psychological aspects of refereeing is more interconnected than people realise. Often, if the referee is uncomfortable, for whatever reason, his efforts will not be appreciated no matter how physically fit he may be. A great referee surveys the terrain like an eagle searching for prey, remains dispassionate from the outcome, shows very little emotion and gives the impression that everything is under control – all of which I prided myself on doing.

I can't remember ever putting too much thought into making this happen; it came naturally to me. I found that opposing gladiators prefer a calm, respectful presence to any other type of management. While administrators recognise that this quality is vitally important, I am not sure whether there has been much development of the psychological factors involved in refereeing; certainly it has never been a priority. Some of us are born with these innate skills, but that does not presuppose that they can't be developed.

As I have alluded to, good judgement and technical skills are the bedrock of what we do. But all those at the top end of the game will recognise that it is the art in our work that defines our performances. To achieve that, I developed an additional array of skills over time.

One of the most important skills is consistency, which is also the most common reply when we ask our stakeholders what they expect of us. I, however, would put competence first, as consistency can be achieved only after you know how to deliver a high-class performance.

In my experience, it is not only the main protagonists who demand consistency, but the rugby public too. What the players and coaches really want is some sort of reliable outcome so that it makes it easier for them to prepare. As long as they know what they are going to get, most players can adapt to individual referees and their eccentricities.

Sometimes, though, fair does not mean equal. It is not important to be giving similar penalty counts when one team is being wilful or desperate, but at the very least communicate your thoughts. Even if you are wrong, at least the players will know what you are on about. There will be no subterfuge and it goes a long way to improving your rapport with the players and can positively impact on the game.

The longevity of a ref's career is directly linked to what kind of on-field service he provides to the players. I personally don't believe that I was the most friendly ref around. But in my own inimitable way, which was sometimes a bit abrupt, I believe I always paid the players the courtesy of an explanation and, when they requested further information, some discussion time off the pitch.

I was firm on one thing, though – I would not allow gamesmanship to creep into the match in an attempt to corrupt my vision of the game or the basic ethos of rugby union, which was to provide a fair contest at all times.

Empathy with the charter of the game needs to be balanced with the needs of the players. I had weaknesses in my arsenal, just like everyone else, but this was not one of them. I strongly identified with the players and what they were trying to achieve, and I always tried to marry that with the laws and the charter of the game. If I erred, I would almost always err on the side of the player. Generally, if I wasn't sure, the player would get the benefit of the doubt. This empathetic approach won me many friends among the players, but surprisingly many more among the rugby public. Often, Joe Public would come up to me and say that I was their favourite ref (not the best – there is no such thing in any case). I can only deduce that they felt that way because of the empathy I showed the players.

For a referee to truly earn the respect of the rugby public, self-interest, ambition and ego must be relegated to the backroom. You do this by focusing on the game in front of you, by preparing well and delivering a performance that facilitates the best outcome for the game and the players. There is no room for self-interest or concern about what your manager or selector is going to say after the match.

Make no mistake, this did not mean that I wasn't tough or firm. I am very confident, some would say cocky, and I have a very *hardegat* side to my nature. I quickly realised that my involvement in the sport did not include making friends on the field. I could elicit respect, yes, but not cultivate friendships.

I may sometimes have made hugely unpopular decisions, but I never shied away from making bold calls because I feared the consequences. I was happy to let the players take responsibility and play to their game plan and skill sets, but when push came to shove, I was comfortable whenever I had to take over the reins and I could be very decisive in my thinking.

Another psychological aspect that is often given less attention than it deserves is motivation. Or rather, what motivates you as the ref. The outcome of the game could be compromised if the ref is not motivated. It's not about policing the laws of the game, but what makes each individual tick, i.e. why we are doing this job in the first place. For some refs, ego is a great driver, but it gets in the way. Most great referees find a way to keep their egos on the back burner so as to best serve the game. Those who don't have this skill get found out time and again. It takes clinical, intense concentration and the application of your ultimate vision of how a game should be refereed.

Something else that really motivated me was to always be my own man, despite having to operate within the corporate environment and the business that is sport. This I can categorically say was something I was never going to sacrifice. If I couldn't be myself, and do my job according to my personal values, then I was not going to hang around. If you ask anyone, anywhere, who came into contact with me, they will all tell you the same thing: he was his own man.

I challenged myself, all the time, with equal doses of humility and mongrel. I challenged my work environment in the same way, never being scared to broach difficult topics. Not at all anti-establishment, but very much transformational where necessary. I did not seek the resultant clashes I had with authority figures, but I did not fear them either. And this part of my character fed into my match performance.

At the same time, I never shied away from exhibiting a fair degree of vulnerability in admitting my less glorious moments. I don't see a hell of a lot of that around. My personal integrity has earned me the respect of the stakeholders I served. Sometimes that little acknowledgement goes a long way towards building one's career and leaving a lasting legacy.

And, lastly, I believe it is very important at the top tier for refs to show dignified and classy behaviour despite the pressures they are under. It is that extra little factor that allows the public to see your real persona, your true character. Sometimes it's not what you are saying, it's how you are saying it; sometimes it is just the tone in which something is conveyed that will be appreciated. Sure, everyone is striving for excellence, but often class defines those who succeed the most.

32

50 up!

In March 2009, in the week leading up to my second Six Nations Test of the season, between Scotland and Ireland at Murrayfield, I was about to become the first referee in rugby history to ref 50 Test matches. The media asked for comment from SA Rugby's manager of referees. Describing my achievement as "truly remarkable", André contextualised it in a way that pleasantly surprised me.

"This is equal to a player playing 100 Tests for his country," he said. "Players play on average 12 Test matches a year, whereas referees get on average four, maybe five appointments a year. This indicates how long Jonathan has been around on the world scene.

"I cannot think of a nicer and more humble guy to achieve this remarkable feat. He has always shown the potential to become a 'great', and he has achieved this status while he is still active, which makes him a living legend in my view. I trust the rugby world will join me in raising a glass to salute Jonny."

It had taken a lot of hard work to get to 50 Test caps, and being acknowledged by my own was the cherry on top. Unfortunately the Test itself did not live up to the press hype, but the fact that it coincided with Ireland's march to their first Grand Slam win in six decades made up for that.

Played in very cold conditions, it was a game of attrition. Both sides persistently stonewalled each other's attack, giving away the odd penalty in the process. Eventually the result was decided by the diminutive Irish scrumhalf Peter Stringer, who surprised everyone – including me – when he broke from a line-out through a gap too big to refuse and the move led to a try by their No. 8, Jamie Heaslip. It sealed a 22-15 victory that kept Ireland in the hunt for the Grand Slam.

I was really taken aback at the post-match celebrations when Scottish referee manager Roy McCombe paid me a memorable tribute that included both teams presenting me with autographed Irish and Scottish jerseys and the match ball signed by both captains.

In addition, Scotland presented me with their traditional navy-blue jersey, which had "Jonathan Kaplan 50th Test" and the date embroidered beneath the thistle. I was completely taken by surprise and humbled that they had made the effort to mark my milestone.

To crown it all, SA Rugby gave me a wooden plaque at their year-end function, where they normally acknowledge significant achievements. They also commissioned former professional cricketer and artist Richie Ryall to paint a caricature of me alongside a list of the 50 Tests I had reffed.

Over the years, I've accumulated a fair amount of memorabilia from the matches in which I've been involved. This remarkable collection of autographed jerseys, team ties, blazers and framed photographs provides me with incredible memories of the happy days I spent on the rugby fields of the world.

Way back in the mid-2000s, Crusaders coach Robbie Deans said that he would rather have me reffing a Super Rugby play-off game involving a South African team than a neutral referee who was not considered in the elite top few. This led to a serious discussion on the pros and cons of appointments based on merit versus appointments based on neutrality. The end result was that coaches and franchises themselves drove the process that resulted in merit-based appointments becoming the norm.

To this end, in May 2009, I became the first official to be appointed to ref a Super Rugby final on merit alone. It was the year the Bulls completely dismantled the Chiefs 61-17 at Loftus in the most lopsided final in the history of the competition.

Finals are often arm-wrestles, because teams prefer low-risk, percentage rugby, and the Bulls and the Chiefs were certainly evenly matched enough for the game to go that way. But after the Chiefs' Lelia Masaga scored a brilliant opening try, the Bulls counter-punched and scored three tries in quick succession, which seemed to just open the floodgates.

By that stage, the stadium was already rocking. And as the Bulls' tally of tries increased – they eventually scored eight – a carnival atmosphere took over. Eventually the public address system was playing "We are marching to Pretoria" and "Liefling" so loudly that I had to ask for the volume to be turned down during play, because the players couldn't hear me say, "touch, pause, engage" at scrum time.

It's hard to say exactly why the Bulls managed to whip the Chiefs so resoundingly, but I was convinced one of the reasons was that the Kiwis were playing the best Bulls side in a decade. Victor Matfield and Fourie du Preez were the brains trust, the pack was very dominant and Habana was freakishly good on the day. It was almost as if the Chiefs were up against a Bok side. Those factors, combined with the fact that everything just clicked for the Bulls on the day, sealed the Chiefs' sorry fate.

One unusual statistic that spoke volumes about the game was that the Chiefs actually made 16 line breaks to the Bulls' five. Whereas everything the Bulls did produced results, for some unknown reason the Chiefs just couldn't convert their line breaks into points.

I felt for the Chiefs – they had been built up steadily by Ian Foster, and the team included such quality leaders as Mils Muliaina and Liam Messam. But it just wasn't their day, although it was one of the important building blocks to the dynasty they created down the track.

I suppose it was almost inevitable in such a helter-skelter match that I would get smashed by a player. It happened when Jaco Pretorius was trying to cover-defend a Chiefs break next to a ruck and tackled me instead. I wasn't hurt, but I had to rise from a crumpled heap and chase after some of the quickest men in the game. I was miles behind play and was bloody grateful afterwards that no infringements took place or that a try was scored.

The incident earned me YouTube notoriety, which was very funny. Although I wasn't hurt at all in the incident, YouTube described the footage as "Ref gets smashed".

A month later I became the only referee to ref the British & Irish Lions on four different tours when they played the Sharks in Durban. The Sharks were by no means a weak side, but on the day they really didn't know how to deal with the presence, power and intensity of the Lions and were blown away 39-3.

Curiously, what still lingers about that match was an incident of foul play towards the end of the game that involved Lions prop Phil Vickery. My view was slightly obscured, but I saw enough to know that he'd stamped on a player's head/neck/shoulder area, and I gave him a yellow card for his troubles.

When I blew the final whistle, Vickery came up alongside, put his arm around me in a friendly manner and congratulated me on a match well reffed. There was no mistaking the knowing look in his eyes; it told me that he knew he had transgressed and was grateful that I had not taken more serious action against him.

But what really astonished me was that the Aussie citing commissioner did absolutely nothing about it. There was no attempt to follow up on the incident, even though I referred it from my change room for further review. By the time I arrived at the cocktail party upstairs, the book had been closed on the incident.

To this day I find it quite perplexing that such an incident is just swept under the carpet. I can only ascribe it to good men working within a flawed system. The judiciary sometimes reach a verdict based purely on whether an incident occurred or not, rather than on an understanding of or insight into the game itself. At times they seem oblivious to the context in which an incident occurred, which can only really be understood when one has been officiating at the coalface for a long time. Perhaps more former referees need to be included on the judiciary panel.

33

Primus inter pares (First among equals)

After my British & Irish Lions match I was back on the road, this time to take part in the IRB Pacific Nations Cup, aimed at strengthening rugby in the Pacific Rim countries. In addition to reffing three Tests in Fiji, I was the tournament's senior referee entrusted with mentoring up-and-coming refs, including Romain Poite, whose company I really enjoyed.

After blowing a pretty one-sided affair between the New Zealand Māoris and Japan, I then took on a Test that I had been looking forward to for a long time. But the pride of Samoa versus Fiji, a team I have always regarded as one of the most potent attacking forces in world rugby, despite limited resources, didn't pan out to be the magical Test I had anticipated.

It started with a bang, with the teams squaring up to deliver their respective war cries (the *cibi* for Fiji and the *siva tau* for Samoa) before the kick-off. It was absolutely hair-raising, and just as the one war cry was ending, the other started up. It was brilliant and sent shivers down my spine. The two teams ended up face to face, so close they could smell their opponents' breath.

Despite the match not living up to expectations, the respect these two teams showed one another after the final whistle blew was nothing short of remarkable. It was a lesson in humility, good sportsmanship and the amateur ethos that rugby has tried so hard to retain.

Rather unexpectedly, it was Japan and Fiji that dished up one of the most memorable Test matches I would ever ref. Thanks to four tries, atypically mauled from line-outs, underdogs Japan had the crowd on the edges of their seats as they hung on to a fairy-tale 36-26 lead with four minutes on the clock. Then Fiji hit back with a typically audacious length-of-the-field try, which they converted to make it 36-33. Two minutes later, Japan's Kiwi import James Arlidge replied with a penalty from far out to stretch his team's lead to 39-33.

By then, with barely enough time for a passage of play, it looked like Japan were about to register a giant-killing performance that would send their fans into orbit. But Fiji attacked with venom, penetrated the Japanese 22, and then launched wave after wave of attack that spanned the breadth of the field. Eventually, well into stoppage time, Fiji's No. 8, Netani Talei, scored the winning try close to the upright.

With a conversion they could not have missed they won a stunning game of rugby that I will never forget. The attitude of the players was fantastic, the spectacle unbelievable and the dramatic ending quite surreal.

The match was a fitting finale to the 2009 Pacific Nations Cup, a tournament that was one of the highlights of my career.

I had quite a time off the field too, island-hopping for miles on a jet ski until my backside ached. And I was also given the opportunity to give something back to the game when I was asked to appear in an IRB-sponsored documentary about Pacific Island rugby. My contribution was to interact with criminals turned referees inside a high-security prison. It was incredibly rewarding to see how rugby had rehabilitated the lives of some pretty violent dudes. Thanks to the sport, they had gone from breaking the law to applying it.

Not a lot of people understand this, but I got as much of a kick out of a rugby moment like my Fiji prison experience as I did reffing a top-flight Test match.

In October I was fortunate enough to be awarded my fifth Currie Cup final, at Loftus, and my third between the Bulls and Free State. The latter had managed to turn their season around after a dismal start that found them stone last on the log without a win after four rounds.

Before the game I could immediately sense that Free State were on a roll and had not come to Loftus just to make up the numbers. They were there to crown a magnificent comeback with the ultimate prize. Their intent was as clear as the embroidered mantra on the inside of the collar of their jerseys: "The Greatest Comeback Ever".

It was not to be. The Bulls went into a big lead and, although Free State made a bit of a comeback, the deficit was too big to overcome and the Bulls bagged yet another Currie Cup with a 36-24 victory.

I've always had a soft spot for the underdog, so I really felt for Naka Drotské, Os du Randt and the rest of the team after the game. I admire and respect Naka for the journey he has made both as a player and as a coach. What he has done at Free State, who have much more limited resources than, say, the Bulls, is remarkable.

Whether it influenced the final result is a moot point, but there was a forward pass from Bryan Habana to Fourie du Preez, who streaked away to score the Bulls' first try. My assistant referees and I were so far behind the play, we couldn't adjudicate accurately. We had the facility of a TV replay, but we were only allowed to go upstairs for in-goal decisions. Once again a classic case of the laws lagging behind the needs of the game.

When I later asked Naka about that decision, he told me that he didn't expect complete accuracy, as he did not expect us to run at the same pace as Habana. As far as he was concerned, it was just one of those unfortunate calls that are part of the game.

It wasn't the only contentious call of the match, though. In the first half, one of my assistant refs judged a pass to Danville Demas as forward, and after charging down the field, Demas was called back. The TV replay showed it had not been forward. On review, I also thought a couple of other calls were contextually inaccurate.

Quite rightly, Naka wasn't too happy about the Demas call. If we had not called the Habana pass forward because we were not in a position to judge it fairly, by the same token we should not have called the Demas pass forward. I agreed. And I have to give credit to Naka, as despite his frustration and disappointment, he wasn't bitter and understood that the system was fallible.

It just goes to show how difficult those 50/50 calls are for any match official, and although TV technology has helped eliminate a lot of human error, I really don't see how we will ever get it 100 per cent right.

I wrapped up my 2009 season with two Tests in November, one in Dublin, where a late converted try by who else but Brian O'Driscoll drew the match 20-20. And this after Australia had dominated much of the game. The other was at Twickenham between England and the All Blacks, which the visitors won comfortably 19-6, Jimmy Cowan scoring the decisive try.

As I didn't ref at Twickenham all that much, I cherished each and every game there. You cannot beat the venue for prestige and the respect it garners from both players and public. For me, it is the Lord's of rugby.

Looking back on my season after that Test, I felt on top of my game. In fact, in retrospect 2009 was probably one of the best years of my career. I'd reffed two Six Nations Tests, one of them for my 50th Test cap, a milestone achieved by no other ref in the history of rugby, a Super Rugby final, a British Lions tour match, the Pacific Nations Cup, which I loved, a Bledisloe Cup Test, a Currie Cup final and two big northern hemisphere Tests. Not bad going for an old bloke.

At the end of the 2007 World Cup, I had felt that I had one more World Cup in me. Two years later, it was still in my sights. Barring a train smash, I was well on track for World Cup 2011.

34

Sidelined

I was on top of my game and raring to go at the start of the 2010 season. So there was no reason to suspect that anything was out of kilter. But when I later looked back at my opening Super Rugby matches of that year, they were almost portents of the season to come.

The first was between the Cheetahs and the Bulls in Bloemfontein, where the game unfolded pretty much as expected. Then, in the second half, with the Bulls attacking in the Free State 22, eighthman Pierre Spies picked up from the base of the scrum and ran into a wall of darkness as the floodlights suddenly went out.

There was a loud groan from the stands. But down on the field some bright spark – to this day I don't know who exactly – showed a great sense of humour in the heat of battle by shouting, "Play on!" Everyone on the pitch packed up laughing.

Fortunately, the delay was brief. The lights came back on and we got the show on the road again for the Bulls to notch up a dominant 51-34 victory. But a few months later, the lights started flickering on my season, and I didn't find anything very funny for quite some time. In fact, for a while I felt as miserable as I did in my second Super Rugby game of that season, when I again reffed the Cheetahs, this time against the Sharks in Durban.

By the time I landed in my old home town, I was feeling as sick as a dog. But André couldn't find a replacement at such short notice and, like the respective coaches, urged me to go ahead with the match and do my best. I took some medication and slept the whole afternoon, but still arrived at Kings Park feeling bloody terrible. Normally, I couldn't wait to get on the pitch, but that Saturday, as the players ran onto the field, I had to summon every ounce of willpower to drag myself out of my change-room chair. My head was pounding and I had no energy whatsoever. And when Free State enforcer Frans Viljoen bumped into me in the early minutes, it was like I'd been hit by a freight train.

One of the most remarkable memories of that match was how surreal it was to be in the midst of a highly competitive Super 14 fixture with professional players fussing over my welfare, looking out for me and encouraging me to hang in there. They could see just how sick I was.

I lasted until half-time, came off and went straight to coaches Naka Drotské and John Plumtree and said, "That's it. I cannot carry on." I was so dizzy, I thought I would black out.

For the second time in my career, the doc in the medical room battled to find my pulse and ordered me to quit the game there and then. Normally I would have protested, but I was too sick to argue. With relief, I lay back on a stretcher with two drips in my arm, grateful for my assistant referee Pro Legoate, who finished the rest of the game with aplomb.

I should have listened to my body; the warning signs were there for all to see, but I didn't like quitting.

Thankfully my season also had its happy moments. In February, I reffed Six Nations favourite France, who beat Wales 26-20 in a thoroughly enjoyable Test in Cardiff. I never went public with it then, but that Test marked a goal I'd set myself in my early years of reffing the Five Nations. To the best of my knowledge, I became the only official to have reffed the complete set of games between all Five Nations teams.

I set myself a similar challenge in domestic rugby, trying to ref every possible South African permutation. In 2010, I added to my already significant list by refereeing Northern Free State against Griquas in Welkom. And by the end of my career, I'd almost pulled it off – I had reffed every single South African rugby team playing against one another with the exception of just two games: Northern Free State versus the Lions and the Falcons versus Free State.

It's not one of rugby's conventional statistics, but I enjoyed coming up with unconventional ways of keeping things fresh and interesting. So decades ago I formulated this eccentric pursuit that picked up momentum and eventually turned into a private challenge. I wanted to pull off something that I thought was remarkable, albeit a little obscure. Who else in their right mind would bother with this? And fortunately my bosses at SARU very kindly tolerated my diversion (which mostly entailed allocating me to lesser fixtures).

It can become very mundane reffing the same high-profile teams in the same stadiums over and over again, and I'd found a way around that. But I also did it for another reason. It was my way of giving back to rugby. The *platteland* unions welcomed me with open arms. They enjoyed having a high-profile ref blowing their games. And I, in turn, loved travelling to the *platteland*, visiting new places and interacting with new faces and different rugby cultures.

As I've said before, travelling solo to Super Rugby fixtures could be massively challenging, and in 2010 that challenge reached ridiculous proportions. It began with a trek halfway around the world to Wellington to ref the Crusaders, who drew 26-all against the Hurricanes. I felt I had reffed the game well in spite of a couple of minor errors, which I ascribed to miscommunication and lapses in concentration rather than lack of reffing expertise.

But my Super Rugby manager Lyndon Bray and selectors Tappe Henning and Andrew Cole had a different take. Not in the best of moods, I headed down to Hamilton to ref the Bulls against the Chiefs. The Bulls won 33-19, and again I felt I had reffed the game well. But this was not reflected in my report. Frustrated, I sought assistance from management, whose diagnosis, however well meaning, did not sit well with me. According to them, I needed to improve my accuracy.

Normally by then I'd be mulling over the problem on a flight back home, but Lyndon had requested that I extend my two-week tour to four. And, against my better judgement, I had agreed. Even though by that stage I was the loneliest and most homesick I had ever been in 15 years of Super Rugby.

If there was a trip that broke the proverbial camel's back, then it was those four weeks in April 2010. I was tired of living out of a suitcase and experiencing the alienation of a hotel room. I was tired of sacrificing my personal life. And somewhere on the long-haul from Hamilton and Auckland to Canberra via Sydney, I began for the first time to really question whether the sacrifices were worth the rewards.

That April, more than ever before in my Super Rugby travels, I wanted to be close to my friends, family and dogs. I wanted to nip out on my scooter to enjoy a mid-week coffee with friends and kick back with a braai on the weekend.

Of course, that kind of stocktaking didn't help me figure out why the hell my game wasn't firing. And it didn't exactly make the criticism from my bosses, who I felt were simply adding to the pressure, more palatable.

I knew they meant well. All former colleagues, Lyndon, Tappe and Andrew were by then also my very close friends. I knew they didn't think I had lost my touch and still considered me one of their elite refs. They were simply trying to help me get back on track so that I could deliver the high-quality games they were accustomed to. But by the time I arrived at Canberra Stadium to ref the Brumbies against the Hurricanes, their call for more accuracy had really brought out my latent obstinacy.

I decided to give my bosses what they wanted, and for the first and only time in my career, I changed my reffing style. I blew the pea out of my whistle. Everything that moved, I blew. And I gave two yellow cards. I made damn sure that after that game, they wouldn't be able to criticise my "accuracy".

The Hurricanes won 23-13, and I was praised for a much better performance. And in that exact moment, I thought, "Fuck that. That is *not* the way I ref."

I vowed never to abandon my reffing philosophy again, no matter what the consequences. My style was unique and had got me to the top of the ladder. To change it at that stage of my career would have been the beginning of the end. It would have been changing the very essence of me. What I should have realised was that I had merely lost a bit of form, something that could have been sorted out easily with a little patience.

So for the last match of that gruelling April tour, I reffed the Force to a well-deserved 24-16 upset victory over the much fancied Crusaders in Perth, using my tried and trusted recipe of flair, judgement and nerve. It was a hard-nosed, gutsy match that had some fine moments. I did my utmost to facilitate the best possible outcome for both teams, creating an environment of trust so that the players were not afraid to execute what they practised so hard week in and week out.

By the time I had reffed my last Super 14 match in mid-May, at Newlands between the Stormers and the Bulls, I had regained enough of my mojo to be ranked one of the top four refs in Super Rugby. I learnt via the grapevine that Craig Joubert was head and shoulders the best and would be rewarded with the final. And the two semis went to two gentlemen of the game, Mark Lawrence and Stuart Dickinson.

I was obviously disappointed that I'd missed out, but at least there was some comfort to be had ahead of the Bulls/Crusaders semi, which had been moved to Orlando Stadium because of FIFA World Cup preparations taking place at Loftus. I was running touch for Stuart Dickinson that day, and when coaches Todd Blackadder and Frans Ludeke heard that Stuey was caught up in traffic and wasn't likely to make it in time for the kick-off, they were emphatic that they wanted me to handle the game – and continue reffing it even if Stuart arrived during the match.

Quite flattering, really ... But I made it clear that I was Stuey's mate. He had flown halfway around the world for this big moment. I agreed to stand in for him until he arrived, but there was no way I was taking his semi away from him. Thankfully, it was all academic. Stuey made it in the nick of time and I ran touch for him as planned.

After the game, I had an interesting discussion with Blackadder and Ludeke about an issue I'd been contemplating for a number of years. And that was, did the current selection policy for refs serve the game? Surely it made more sense to allow the coaches some input and ask both teams which refs they'd prefer for their match? Surely there was nothing to lose if both coaches wanted the same ref? By the end of my career, I had developed a very clear standpoint on this.

But back to the 2010 season, and another milestone, which took place in June in Hamilton, where I broke Welshman Derek Bevan's long-standing record in the Kiwis' 29-10 victory over Wales. Bevan had reffed the All Blacks 16 times, the most that any referee had reffed any international rugby team. Two months later, I had the privilege of extending that record to 18 when I reffed a Bledisloe Cup Test in Christchurch, which the All Blacks won 20-10.

You'd think that my international profile would have counted for something back home, yet come the Currie Cup, I found myself being inexplicably sidelined by a series of low-key appointments that kept me out of the mainstream public eye and the minds of the selectors. So much so that many rugby fans stopped to ask me whether I was injured.

Not only was I appointed to ref far fewer Currie Cup games that season than ever before, but only one of my seven appointments, between the Bulls and the Sharks, which I thought I'd reffed well, was high profile enough to be televised. The rest were out in the sticks – which I always enjoyed. But not when those appointments were at the expense of my career.

I raised my concerns with André and pointed out that it made no sense not to use my reffing experience in some of the Currie Cup's key matches. Moreover, if I was out of sight, out of mind week in and week out, it was almost impossible for the selectors to accurately gauge my form.

But my protest fell on deaf ears, and I tolerated it. Until I heard that I wasn't part of the elite group to ref the play-off games. André and I had a heated argument about this, but in reality all I could do was make my point. He was not known for admitting an error, and he was still the boss.

I didn't mind missing out on selection. I was disappointed, like anyone else would be. I could even gracefully accept that I had been overlooked by the selection panel; after all, there had been times when I had been the beneficiary of their selections.

But what *was* hard to swallow was an appointment process that apparently sidelined me, especially when I was still considered to be one of the best refs in the world. Of course, reffing a semi or a final was not my right. No matter what my international status, I didn't believe I was ever a shoe-in for anything. But I expected the system to be fair, at the very least. And in the 2010 Currie Cup, there was nothing fair about being denied the opportunity to earn selection on merit.

35

Learning from my mistakes

Having been there before, I knew the drill going into my fourth World Cup season. Every Test I reffed in the months leading up to the April selection counted. I had to ref each one well to make sure that I stayed on track for World Cup selection. And I had to build the kind of form that would put me into the space where I could compete hard for the limited number of play-off matches.

The bottom line was that there was a lot at stake, as there always was in the critical months leading up to World Cup selection. It meant months of heightened scrutiny from coaches who were assessing your strengths and weaknesses as they plotted their strategies, and from selectors as they decided who was on song for their World Cup panel of 10.

It might sound like a stressful time, but I enjoy that sort of challenge. So I had no nerves going into my first 2011 Test, between Wales and Ireland at the Millennium Stadium. No other tournament beats the Six Nations for prestige and tradition. I knew both sides well, especially Ireland, who I had reffed a record 16 times. And I had prepared well.

For the first few minutes the Test unfolded pretty much as I had expected. Until Irish flyhalf Jonathan Sexton kicked the ball out on the full. My Scottish assistant referee Peter Allan ran to the mark and raised his flag. I then made my mark and turned my back to the touchline as I walked to take up a good position for the line-out. During those few strides, while watching the players approaching the line-out, I picked up out of the corner of my eye the ball suddenly being thrown in.

The arriving players were less than half a metre from the mark that would have made it a line-out, which meant it didn't matter which ball was used. But in that flash I thought it looked more like a quick throw-in. And that meant that Wales had to use the same ball that was kicked out without it being handled by anyone before the throw-in.

Uncertain about the ball issue as I sprung into action, I glanced over at Peter, who dropped his flag to confirm that it was a play-on situation. Two passes later and Mike Phillips was over in the corner.

The next thing there was a rush of green towards me and I sensed immediately that something was wrong. I had a pretty good idea what it was. But I saw how agitated the players were, so I let them make their point. And then informed Brian O'Driscoll that I wanted to check with my assistant referee that the correct ball was used. If it wasn't the same ball that Sexton had kicked into touch, or if that ball had been handled by someone else before being thrown in by Welsh hooker Matthew Rees, then we would have to go back for the line-out.

By then I had a gut feel that the wrong ball had been used. The Irish would never have rushed me with such conviction if there hadn't been a blunder. The pity was I couldn't go upstairs and settle it there and then, as TV technology had no jurisdiction over this area of the field in 2011. And Craig Joubert, my assistant referee on the other side, also couldn't help me with any additional information. My only recourse then was to ask Peter, who by then had had a chance to clear his head. When he confirmed the correct ball had been used, I had no other alternative but to award the try.

People ask why I didn't act on my gut instinct, but it's simple. I'd rather make a mistake than guess whether or not something had happened. You cannot ref a match on guesswork.

About five minutes later, while watching Ireland kick a penalty, I sensed from the crowd reaction that the incident had been replayed on the big screen. O'Driscoll, who had been watching, came over and asked if I knew that my decision had been incorrect.

I told him I didn't know and suggested that we focus on the game, because even if I had watched the replay, I couldn't reverse my decision. In a bit of gamesmanship, he again emphasised that there had been an error. In a Test match, you cannot afford to be distracted by what appears on the big screen. Replays are constantly being shown, but a ref's mandate is to concentrate on what is happening on the field. Easier said than done, because it takes skill and nerve not to look.

I was embarrassed after the game when the blunder was confirmed, and all the more so because it could be argued that it significantly influenced Wales's 19-13 victory.

Ireland were remarkably dignified and disciplined after the match, and coach Declan Kidney seemed to harbour no grudge when I went to thank him for the game and acknowledge my error.

It may have been a touch-judge call, but there's no question that I had been complicit in the error. Sexton's clearance was into the stands, so the ball could not have arrived in Rees's hands without being handled. I had followed the trajectory of the ball and should have had some sort of awareness of that.

The Irish punters and the press will probably remember that Test match only for the blunder rather than anything else. But not so Welsh coach Warren Gatland, who came to me afterwards to say that I had reffed exceptionally well and that Wales would've won irrespective of the dodgy throw-in.

My assessor and World Cup selector Michael Lamoullie took a similar tack in his match report. My error notwithstanding, he noted, I had delivered a performance that comfortably cemented me as one of the best referees in the world. He acknowledged my skill of not letting an error corrupt my thought processes and allowing the game to unfold.

While I appreciated both Gatland and Lamoullie's endorsements, that didn't stop me from berating myself. My job was to get things right. I was a senior ref representing my country. People in the game looked up to me. And my manager Paddy O'Brien and his panel of selectors had been relying on me to deliver high-quality performances. Likewise Ireland and Wales. And I had gone and let them all down with what I still consider to be my worst Test-match error.

The incident haunted me every day of the following week while I waited to touch-judge for Craig Joubert's France/Wales Test. No matter how hard I tried, I could not put it behind me.

Paddy had decided that the best course of action would be for him to release a media statement acknowledging the error rather than let me talk to journalists directly. But that whole week I felt it was insufficient. Although Paddy had already assured me that I remained one of his elite refs, well on target for the 2011 Rugby World Cup, I felt I needed to take this a step further. I felt I owed Declan and his troops more than a press release.

Eventually, after discussing a number of options, Paddy and I decided together that it would be a good idea for me to call Declan personally and apologise. My voice still crackles with emotion whenever I recount the conversation that followed.

My apology straight after the match had been perfunctory. I didn't hang around after Tests for beers with coaches. My phone call, however, was the real deal. I told Declan that I was calling to apologise unreservedly for my role in the blunder. That it had been a significant error and probably the lowest point in my career.

His response will stay with me forever. "Jonathan, you are one of our referees of choice. Ireland doesn't have a problem with you. I'm sure we will bump into you again at some stage. And we would very much like the opportunity to be reffed by you again. Thirty seconds of madness doesn't change our opinion of you."

That conversation for me was the embodiment of all that is good about rugby. It brimmed with the dignity that graces the game. The fact that it came from a coach under pressure added significance, and for that he will always have my respect and gratitude.

Thankfully my season only got better after that. I reffed a bunch of games around South Africa, including the Sharks/Northern Free State in Empangeni, to add to my quirky list of *platteland* fixtures. And then I went on to ref a really good Super Rugby competition, putting my head down to see if I could earn another final.

Instead, Bryce Lawrence got the nod, which was disappointing for me. But after chatting about it with Craig Joubert, I felt grateful that I had at least been given the semi-final between the Reds and the Blues in Brisbane. Any play-off game was a privilege. And as Paddy pointed out, not being awarded the final hadn't hurt my World Cup chances. He had wanted consistency and I had been delivering.

That reassurance helped me ref a competitive semi that suited my style and turned out to be a fantastic showcase for Super Rugby, brimming with skill, pace, attritional defence and razzmatazz. Scoring four tries to one, the Reds made the finals with a 30-13 victory. And as I left the field ahead of the players, I experienced a very rare standing ovation from the appreciative crowd. I was taken aback because that does not happen often on a rugby field.

Later my manager Lyndon Bray admitted to me that he should not have made his appointment for the final straight after the pool matches. I was the form ref of the tournament, he said, and had reffed my semi well enough to do the final. That little private acknowledgement was unbelievably rewarding and tempered any disappointment I felt. That sort of thing is not reflected in any Super Rugby annals, but it was enormously satisfying, and Lyndon's honesty only increased the respect I had for him.

Confident and buoyant, I returned to South Africa. I had slipped up but had found my groove again and was ready to put my best foot forward at the World Cup. In fact, looking back I reckon I was close to the form I had achieved going into my 2007 campaign.

Physically, I was also in good nick. After being encouraged by sports-injury physiotherapist Benita de Witt, who used her Lyno Method to restore my biomechanical balance, I had hit the road again and competed in a variety of marathons. That feeling when I crossed the finish line reminded me just how much I loved the sport and how much I had missed it.

After reffing my first Currie Cup match, between Western Province and Griquas, I felt I could not put a foot wrong. By then my World Cup selection had been confirmed and all was going according to plan. All that remained was some fine-tuning in my remaining Currie Cup games. Until an idiot behind the wheel of a tractor took me out ...

36

The road to recovery

The biggest challenge after my scooter accident and the emergency surgery to my half-severed patellar tendon was to do absolutely *nothing*. With just six weeks to stage a miracle recovery, time was of the essence. But doctor's orders for the first 10 days were to stay put and do nothing except sleep and watch TV. For me, that was a huge ask. Especially with my calf and quad wasting away before my eyes. But I'd been told that my best chance of making the 2011 RWC was to keep my leg raised as much as possible to reduce the swelling.

The little walking I did do, between bedroom and bathroom and lounge, was a mission. Steps were a huge challenge. I was hesitant on my feet, nervous of blundering head first into something hard.

Most nights I awoke at 3 a.m., drenched in sweat and overwhelmed by unfamiliar panic. My main concern was whether I would have enough time to recover. And the only way I could calm down was to do my exercises.

So there I was, sometimes drilled by my girlfriend Lisa, doing leg raises. Up and down in sets of 20, tensing my quad. Tense. Relax. No stone unturned. Tense, relax. It was exhausting. With my quad wasted to nothing, all of this took a superhuman effort.

After that I would roll onto my right side and do 20 scissor raises with my injured leg straightened as best I could. Up. Down. Up. Down. Then, sweating like a pig from the effort and my anxiety back in its box, I'd lie still and soon drift back to sleep again.

Back in Dr Mark van der Velde's rooms 10 days after my op, he removed some of the stitches, leaving those where the wound had not quite knitted. Then he gave me the lowdown. First increase my walking and then start running as soon as possible.

Still trying to wrap my head around the challenge ahead, I reached for my crutches to leave. But Mark firmly told me to lose them.

"But I can't walk ..." I whinged.

"Do you want to go to the World Cup?" asked the doc.

"Is there any chance I can have them for just a few more days?"

"No. You are walking away without them. I don't care how long it takes you, but you leave the crutches behind."

In that first pathetic hobble from the doctor's rooms to the car, using chairs, doors and the wall for support, I discovered the enormity of the task ahead. I literally didn't know how to walk any more. All the muscles in my foot and leg were useless. My calf was flaccid and my quad non-existent. My ankle was so morbidly obese, it was obscene.

But what was really daunting was that in the short space of 10 days, I had forgotten how to walk. I had forgotten that simple heel-toe movement I had so taken for granted all my life. I was close to 45 and the reality was that I would have to learn how to walk again. And then run again. Well enough to ref a World Cup. And I had 31 days in which to accomplish that.

In the crucial days ahead, the Sea Point promenade became my companion. Six kays. Eight kays. And every step of the way I had to force myself to walk properly. Heel-toe. Heel-toe. No stone unturned ...

I walked hundreds of kilometres. I was never the greatest trainer on the planet, but during that recovery period I was at my most diligent. I put in big distances, watchful all the time that I wasn't moving too quickly, because I'd been warned that it would do more damage.

Speaking to other surgeons, I discovered the consensus around recovery for my type of injury was around 12 weeks. And the question mark was not so much whether I would run again, but whether I'd be able to brake in an instant while running or suddenly switch direction while running, both critical tools of my trade.

The other consensus was unanimously conservative. All the surgeons, with the exception of Mark, said the same thing: "I'm not going to say you can't make it, but your recovery will be touch and go."

For me, that was like a red rag to a bull. No one tells me that something can't be done, because that motivates me even more. There's a reason why I love bulldogs. I was also motivated by the fact that this was not the first time I'd negotiated a serious injury of the same knee. In 1998, after I discovered I had split my articular cartilage while reffing Boland against Griquas in

Wellington, I had carried that crippling injury right through the Currie Cup and Super Rugby season, as well as two World Cup qualifiers, before succumbing to surgery. Nine games in all, and there was no reason why I couldn't rise to the challenge again.

But my 2011 injury was in a different league. I would have to up my game even further.

I also had to keep one eye on the politics of the situation. I couldn't risk divulging the full extent of the injury to anyone. The party line was that I was playing it safe and resting following a minor knee operation.

My official line to Paddy and anyone else who inquired was that I had a flesh wound that needed around 30 stitches. That my ligaments were intact. But I omitted to say that my patellar tendon was cleaved in half. I had to trust that the healing process, an iron resolve and the good grace of a higher power would see me through.

I emailed weekly progress reports to Paddy, telling him that everything was under control. I emphasised the fact that my recovery was exponential week by week and that I'd arrive at the World Cup fully fit.

I will always be grateful to Paddy for the way he handled the situation. For not demanding that I undergo a fitness test. I appreciated that he respected me and my abilities enough to let me be the judge of my own progress. I knew I was taking a calculated risk, but how can you live life without risk? The time to tell the full story about my injury was not then.

In uncertain, seemingly chaotic times, where there are no guarantees, I'd trained myself to embrace whatever unfolded. Because therein lay the opportunity to carve my own destiny. To make the impossible possible. To create the space for miracles. If I didn't think like that, I would have thrown the towel in long ago. Long before I drove into that tractor.

Fear and uncertainty should be celebrated – that's what true courage is all about. And that's what leads to a deeper understanding of ourselves and the world around us.

Three and a half weeks after my op, I called Mark with an update. Immediately, he cut to the chase: "You need to start running now."

I told Lisa and she offered to do my first run with me. We parked at Newport Deli, one of my favourite breakfast spots, and walked towards the Green Point lighthouse. Then I broke into a hobbling run.

A kilometre later my muscles were screaming at me. I stopped and walked until Lisa started screaming at me. And so we went. Walk. Run. Walk. Run. For the last kilometre, it was pure survival. I was in pain. But I dug deep. Eight kilometres later, feeling absolutely blown, I came to a screeching halt. A passing motorist saw me leaning against a wall next to Newport Deli.

"You look like you're in agony. You didn't look comfortable at all. Can we give you a lift to your car?" I can only imagine how bad I must have looked.

After that first run I switched to working the treadmills for a while. It was easier to get going on a treadmill and monitor my progress more accurately. In between I went for intensive physio every second or third day. I was not going to die wondering. And I was certainly not going to give up.

I wasn't daunted by the gut-wrenching news in that emergency room that I only had six weeks to heal a cleaved patellar tendon that normally took around 12 weeks to repair. I'm quite proud that I had the guts to attempt a recovery, the belief it took … And then going at it no matter how many times the voice of doubt dangled the easy way out.

I thought of players in similar situations. Welsh captain Matthew Rees so severely injured his neck the same month I was injured, it cost him the World Cup. And talented Ireland flanker David Wallace got tackled by England centre Manu Tuilagi in a warm-up international four weeks before the World Cup, sustaining a devastating knee ligament injury that not only robbed him of his last World Cup, but put him into early retirement.

As I reflected on the opportunities this challenge presented to me, I used these players to motivate me, as I was aware of the fact that they had not been as fortunate as me. I was lucky that half my tendon remained intact. It could have been totally severed. My entire leg could have been crushed or amputated.

I also became acutely aware of the fact that sometimes all the ability and will in the world are just not enough. Sometimes, despite our best intentions, life has another plan for us, a bigger picture that we cannot grasp at the time.

In the week before I left for New Zealand, I worked out on the Grucox bike at the Sports Science Institute of South Africa in Newlands. Invented by knee guru Dr Willem van der Merwe, the bike reduces stress on your knee joints while it strengthens your muscles with progressive resistance.

I felt I was growing stronger and more confident. From running eight kays, I managed to increase to 10, 11, 12. The week before my departure, I was running four and a half minutes a kay and very soon after that, 4 minutes 15 a kay. I was finding my groove again.

My acid test came three days before my World Cup flight. I could have picked a Currie Cup fixture, but instead I opted for the Bishops/Rondebosch derby on 27 August, as it would not be televised and there would be less scrutiny.

I began as nervous as all hell. It might only have been a school derby, but there were still 10 000 spectators. Trundling through the whole game, I never got out of third gear, but my positional play was good.

My confidence increased as the match progressed. Then, out of the blue, about 11 minutes before the end, the smallest guy on the field, Rondebosch's replacement centre, ran into the back of my left calf with his knee. Bang!

Bishops went on to score a try seconds later and I limped back to the conversion spot thinking, shit, I can hardly walk. I was just getting back into my rhythm and now my calf was in spasm.

For the remaining minutes of play, I was in trouble. Amazingly, though, my knee felt fine. There was no pain there. Mark's handiwork had held. But the *lammie* in my calf hobbled me. And I finished the match worrying about the haematoma that would take several weeks of physio to heal.

But the good news came from my friend Ryan Maron, who reported that he couldn't detect any limp. In my mind, the hard yards were behind me. According to Mark, my recovery rate would be exponential from that point on.

The accident had really tested my resolve, my dogged refusal to accept my fate and my willingness to suffer and grow. The recovery was my greatest physical achievement.

37

Once a chief, always a chief (Native American proverb)

I'm loathe to blow my own trumpet, but I reckon that a lot of other sports-people would have thrown in the towel in the emergency room. They would not have challenged the prognosis. Yet I was fortunate enough to stage a come-back and had the will to see it through. I confronted the challenge and I won.

Two things worked in my favour when I arrived at the World Cup. The one was that Paddy O'Brien did not put me through a fitness test. To his credit, all he wanted was my assessment of my injury. He said to me, "Jonathan, all I want to know is, are you ready? I totally trust you, but are you ready?" I answered "yes". He urged me to keep on training. I will always be very grateful for the way Paddy trusted my judgement.

Something else that was in my favour was that I would have two weeks between arriving and reffing my first match, between Tonga and Canada, on 14 September. Three days before I flew out of South Africa I'd reffed the Bishops/Rondebosch derby and felt okay. Not great, but well enough to know that with two more weeks and the exponential recovery that my surgeon had promised, I'd have enough confidence in my legs to ref a competitive Test match.

My main concern during the initial weeks was that I didn't get bumped or knocked while I was touch-judging Namibia against Fiji on 10 September and then Italy versus Australia a day later. I kept thinking, it's taken so much to get this far, I don't want to get injured before I ref a game. That was my first goal. Ref just one game and take it from there.

I was encouraged that my knee felt good during and after those back-to-back pool matches, even though I did not have any rest days in between. The other plus was that I ran without any of the heavy strapping I had planned on using. Instead, I opted for just a micro-pore dressing to prevent my injury from bursting open if it took a knock. My surgeon had briefed me that although my tendon had knitted and was healing well, my skin was still fragile and might split open on impact. I didn't mind that, just as long as I was fully functional.

Surviving those two touch-judge appointments with such a light dressing built my confidence. But despite everything ticking along nicely, I still felt a lot of trepidation going into my first pool match. Normally Tonga against Canada wouldn't scare an experienced ref like me, but it turned out to be my most emotional start to a World Cup. I was super-proud to run onto the field in Whangarei, New Zealand's northernmost city, after eight weeks of blood, sweat and tears, but I was also a bundle of nerves. Would I get through the match? Would I go on to ref more?

As I ran onto the field to take up my position, no one in the stands could have guessed what a miracle it was for me to be there. No one could share in my triumph over adversity. Not even my touch judges knew about the road I had travelled. Instead, out there in the middle, amid the excitement and expectation that precedes kick-off, in the solitude that's been so integral to my life, I quietly allowed myself a few moments of contemplation about the resolve I had shown to stand on that very spot.

Then, as I blew my first blast of the whistle and took that first step, every ounce of anxiety and anguish I had experienced during the last eight weeks rushed out of my body. It was like someone had opened an emotional valve. That euphoric feeling remained with me for much of the game.

I began tentatively, not wanting to get too close to the action in case I got a knock. But I was soon back in the swing of things, conducting the game as if I had had a seamless season. And it turned out to be a thriller, with Canada coming from behind to beat Tonga, who had all the momentum and a lion's share of the possession up until the last quarter, when they were 20-13 up.

In the dying minutes of the game, with the result still in the balance, the tension was briefly broken by a streaker. Wearing nothing more than a well-endowed thong and a green foam fist, he delighted the crowd as he managed to run the length of the field and "score" before being tackled.

I'd had some weird things happen to me on my rugby journey, but nothing like my encounter with that streaker, whose brief appearance on the field included a swaggering "Mr Universe" pose a few metres in front of me.

Canada managed to snatch the game 25-20 with a last-gasp try.

I had crossed the first hurdle with my knee in one piece and a performance that didn't let anyone down. Normally I would have gone straight back into the tunnel, but I decided to do a cool-down after the game. My body hadn't been active for 90 minutes for quite a while, so I wanted to get rid of some of the stiffness that would inevitably result, as well as the emotions I'd been feeling all the while. As I moved slowly up and down the field with my assistant refs, I said a quiet "thank you" and "well done" to myself. Canada–Tonga wasn't one of the World Cup's headline acts, but it was a big deal for me.

The day after the match I drove back to Auckland, a three-hour trip, and met Lyndon Bray, head of the SANZAR referees, in a bar for a beer. While we were chatting, this bloke walks up to me and asks if I can pose with him for a photo.

"No problem," I told him. He said: "You don't recognise me, do you? I'm the streaker from last night."

What were the chances of that happening? There I was, 24 hours after the match, 180 kilometres from Whangarei, at a random pub in Auckland, and the streaker, who had spent the night in jail and the morning in court, where he had paid a fine, was standing in front of me. This time, thankfully, fully clothed.

What was even stranger was that the bloke, who introduced himself as Connor Irwin, a 24-year-old property analyst from Belfast, was no stranger. He was a mate of a mate of mine. What were the odds of that?

Three days later I reffed England, who managed to smash Georgia 41-10 after a stuttering first half. To my immense relief, my knee was perfect.

Then roll on Japan versus Canada, my third game, which was played in Napier, a small but quite beautiful town on the eastern coast of North Island, known for its numerous art-deco buildings. I had refereed the same fixture four years earlier, and it was another coincidence that the two teams were drawn in the same pool again, with the computer randomly selecting me as the referee!

But this was a much better game than the previous fixture between them. Played in perfect conditions, both teams displayed an ability to use the ball and be creative. Japan deserved their 15-7 half-time lead, as they had put the spirited Canadians under huge pressure with their well-constructed attacking platforms. They also continued to be the better team going into the last quarter, when Canada started to come into the game with increased physicality and self-belief.

Down by eight points with seven minutes to go, they scored a try and then missed an easy conversion. A few minutes before full time, they won and converted a penalty when Japan illegally slowed down the ball. But there was still time for a winner, and Japan attacked relentlessly, wave after wave, until play broke down on the far side of the field. Canada had held on to level the score at 23-all. Another draw, the same two teams, the same referee ...

Bob Francis remarked what a great game of rugby it had been, with Japan perhaps a little unlucky not to have walked away with the spoils (as Canada had been four years previously). As if all of the above was not enough of a coincidence, the match report indicated that two of the try-scorers, Daniel van der Merwe and Kosuke Endo, had both scored tries four years ago too. Crazy. Beautiful.

My last World Cup looked like it was fast becoming one of freakish coincidences. More than two weeks after my accidental pub encounter with my Irish streaker I was relating the story to Lisa, who by then had joined me in New Zealand for the rest of my tournament.

We were in Dunedin, and as I was remarking on the synchronicity, we rounded the corner and bumped into none other than Connor Irwin! What were the chances? Okay, so it stands to reason that my Irish streaker would have been in Dunedin for the final pool match between Ireland and Italy. But so were 30 000 other spectators.

Although the Italians were confident they could beat Ireland if they played their best rugby, the Irish proved too classy, with a deserved 36-6 victory.

Personally, I thought I deserved a medal for finishing that match. And ironically it was not because of my knee. Instead it was my shoulder that went when I got too close to the Irish scrumhalf Conor Murray as he was tackled. The swinging legs of tackler Alessandro Zanni took mine out from underneath me and, as I put my left hand out to break my fall, I dislocated my shoulder.

The searing pain indicated that this was a serious injury, but I jumped up straightaway and carried on running. There was no way I had come that far to lie down and die. If this was going to be my last World Cup game, they would have to carry me off the field on a stretcher. I was determined to finish the match, come hell or high water. So I gritted my teeth and got on with it without anyone being the wiser that I was reffing on *vasbyt*.

After the match, I took time off from training and asked our team physio to strap me up to alleviate the pain and discomfort. But he knew I hadn't just pulled a muscle and sent me for a scan, which revealed that in dislocating my shoulder, I had ripped one third of my cartilage off the bone and ripped off my bicep tendon. It's no wonder that I was in so much pain.

To make matters worse, my name was not among the four referees selected for the quarter-finals. I was massively disappointed. I had sweated bullets to make it to New Zealand and had reffed my pool matches well. And the selectors had always regarded me as their BMT ref, well suited to the tough, attritional wars of the knockout stages.

That said, I had to balance my disappointment with the acknowledgement I had received from Paddy and his selectors while I was top of the tree. They had allowed me to live my dreams. I had no problem with them not picking me. I had been around long enough to know that selection is always a tricky business and that someone will always be disappointed.

So while I thought I had reffed well enough in a tournament where no ref had really stood head and shoulders above the pack, I accepted with all the good grace I could muster that Craig Joubert, Bryce Lawrence, Nigel Owens and Steve Walsh were judged by the selectors to be more deserving of a quarter-final appointment. Nevertheless, I was so disappointed. Had I come this far just to ref four pool matches?

I got a heads-up from Tappe, who looked me in the eye and told me to keep fit, stay focused and remain positive, because my tournament was probably not over. He explained that six refs had been considered for the quarters and intimated that Alain Rolland and I were the two who had just missed out. After the quarters, the best ref of the four was Craig, who had long been groomed for bigger things, so I knew he was also probably in the running for a later appointment. My informed opinion was that I was being pencilled in for the third- and fourth-place play-off match.

One of the other selectors, Michael Lamoullie, sensing my disappointment at not having made the cut, told me in confidence that selection for the quarters had been very, very close. My sense was that I had just missed the cut, which basically corroborated what Tappe had said.

Before Paddy announced his refs for the semis, he requested a meeting that ended up shocking the living daylights out of me. It seemed pretty innocuous at the time. In fact, he had broached the subject of a meeting very casually as we were walking back to our hotel after a relaxed evening out at the pub with the other refs. We were laughing and chatting like two good mates. As far as I was concerned, he wanted the standard talk that we always had towards the end of a World Cup to plot the way ahead.

I did not sense what was coming when he raised the issue of my retirement.

The subject had been on the cards for a while, as I had already started thinking about how I would make my exit. In April, Paddy and I had had a brief discussion about it. "Don't throw me to the wolves," I'd told him. "Let's collaborate and come up with a plan that's reasonable for you and me."

Paddy began our meeting by asking me where my career was headed. I told him frankly that perhaps World Cup 2015 might be a bridge too far for me, but that I could deliver a great product for at least another year or so. Paddy heard me out and then told me that he and his selectors thought that I should end my international career at the end of 2011 with a December Test between Wales and Australia! His reasoning was that he needed to blood his young guard.

I felt as if I'd been punched in the guts. I told Paddy I was not comfortable with such a rushed and unexpected exit. Other refs with less on their CVs and in worse form had hung around for much longer. But Paddy was unmoved. I sensed that his mind was already made up. But he ended the meeting on what seemed like a conciliatory note. "Put your thoughts in writing," he told me, "and I'll consider them."

Sometimes things don't pan out the way you want them to. Moreover, Paddy had a job to do and certainly didn't owe me any favours as a friend. I accepted that and wouldn't have wanted it any other way. So I compromised.

I wrote a humble letter in which I urged Paddy to do the right and reasonable thing, as there was no turning back once the decision was made. There would be only one exit. I requested a six-month exit so that I could retire with dignity. I didn't expect glorious or high-profile appointments during that time – just something reasonable that would befit their most capped international referee. All I wanted was an exit that recognised 14 and half years of unstinting loyalty and professionalism.

When I got no reply, I requested a meeting with Paddy, who, to my surprise, brought Tappe along. Again I was clear about what I wanted. But again Paddy was unmoved. He told me that he had shown my letter to two other selectors and they had both said they would not be dictated to by a ref on when he feels he should retire. I was stunned. As Paddy had requested, I had put my thoughts in writing. And I had compromised. I hadn't dictated or demanded anything. It was a discussion document.

The meeting didn't last much longer. With Tappe looking on, Paddy told me that he and his selectors were not changing their minds. Wales versus Australia was to be my last Test match. Take it or leave it.

"Are you telling me that that is my last international no matter what?" I asked.

"Yes," Paddy said. "That is our decision." And then he added something that was even harder to swallow. "I don't consider you a Six Nations or a Tri-Nations ref any more."

This from a man who was supposed to be my friend. I had been his confidant and most loyal, experienced foot soldier for many years. It was outrageous. I was good enough to be selected for the World Cup, I had been judged by the selection panel to be one of the top six refs at the tournament and had just missed out on a quarter-final. And now, all of a sudden, I wasn't good enough to ref a top-tier Test match?

All this would have made some sense if the selectors were concerned about my shoulder. But they hadn't raised the injury with me at all. What frustrated me the most was that although I was one of the six referees out of 10 to be considered for the quarter-finals, I was the only one to miss out completely. Instead of doing the third/fourth-place match, I was overlooked in favour of someone from outside the top six; Wayne Barnes was chosen to ref that game. I had no idea how they reached that decision, as neither of us had reffed a game since the original decision was made, so there was no new information available to the selectors. Incidentally, all the referees who were rated 7 to 10 at the RWC got appointments in the Six Nations of 2012 – except me.

And the policy of retiring older referees to "make space for youth" did not apply to the two referees, Dave Pearson and Alain Rolland, who were older than me. They could continue with their careers.

Paddy claimed that it had been a committee decision to retire me, but I later discovered that he had submitted a draft of his 2012 Six Nations appointments to the board before we met to discuss my retirement and my name was not on the list.

I played no further part in World Cup 2011 as a referee. And I left feeling so bitter and angry that I could not bring myself to say goodbye to Paddy. I also left with no answer to the recurring question: What would it have cost him to compromise? Allowing me a dignified exit would have offered both him and me a win-win situation, as I certainly was not falling off the edge of the ref panels – as was clearly and repeatedly demonstrated over the next two seasons. I could have done a good job in any Test match.

Seeing my tears and disappointment, which I was battling to hide during our goodbyes, my friends and colleagues commiserated. Romain Poite, in particular, was a true friend. "Jonathan, you are a great referee and I am really sorry for you. I am disappointed for you. But don't let this decision of theirs influence what we all think about you."

Back home in Cape Town, I called my family and told them what had happened and that this was my last dance. They were as shocked and emotional as I was. My dad, who does not normally wear his emotions on his sleeve, was crying. All of them promised that they would be there for my last hurrah in Cardiff. Everywhere I went during the next few weeks, friends and sympathetic colleagues wanted to know what on earth had gone down at the World Cup. To the last man they were dumbstruck that I was being put out to pasture. Many thought it an injustice.

A year later I would meet with Joël Jutge, the newly appointed IRB ref manager, and Mark Egan, the department head, at the Cullinan Hotel in Cape Town and tell them my story. After listening intently, Mark turned to Joël and said that perhaps they needed to pay more attention to referee exit strategy than they had done in the past.

In the absence of answers, all the support I got was hugely uplifting. Like I've said before, the selectors were instrumental in allowing me to achieve many of my dreams. They had a job to do. A very difficult job that could never please everyone all the time. And I had to respect them for that. Like the players, I, too, relied on selectors. They can make and break you. That is the harsh nature of professional sport.

So as hard as it was to get used to the idea that I would not be reffing Test-match rugby again after December, I had to make the best of the occasion I was given. I had to put aside my anger and disappointment and focus on the moment.

Sometimes life is defined not by those times when we are riding the wave, but by the times when we are being dumped and how we deal with it. In this particular case, I had not only been dumped, but was held under the water for a long time. And when I came up, I wasn't in the best of shape. But I was determined to get back on the board and ride one last wave.

My first priority was my shoulder. Paddy had been clear: Wales/Australia was my swansong. My retirement would not be postponed. So, as I had with my knee injuries, I needed to find a way through. Because there was no way in hell I was missing that Test. If necessary, I was prepared to run through a wall to ref it.

Fortunately after I found shoulder guru Dr Steve Roche, who understood my urgency, that was not necessary. "If you were 25, I'd operate," he told me. "But you are 45, so let's leave it, because 90 per cent of the time, with older guys, the injury settles down."

Instead he prescribed a cortisone injection a few days before my departure, administered with an unbelievably big needle. It turned out to be a miracle cure. By the time I landed at Heathrow, my shoulder felt as good as new. Before I departed, Paddy emailed me and asked whether I would announce my retirement before or after the game. "You're the world's most capped Test referee," he added, "and we want to make a big thing about it."

Not in the mood for bullshit, I had a few choice things to say. Basically I was straight. I was not retiring. I was not asked; I was pushed. You're getting rid of me. And you want me to announce my retirement so that your decision looks good. Sorry, no can do.

In the lead-up to the Test, both Australia and Wales presented me with auto-graphed jerseys. The Welsh jersey had special significance, as Shane Williams's autograph at the top stood out from the rest. I completely identified with the Welsh wizard, who had become a legend of the game. We were both on the small side but still packed a punch. Coincidentally, this would also be his last Test appearance, and he went on to top it with a memorable try, after which he did a handstand. His celebration crowned a magnificent career and delighted the crowd.

I was so pleased that my last Test involved Warren Gatland and Robbie Deans, as there was much mutual respect. In our pre-match chat, they both mentioned the contribution I had made to the game over the years, which I appreciated. It was great to get meaningful recognition from the teams I was going to ref.

But the abiding memory of the build-up was the time I spent with my family in Cardiff, reflecting on my wonderful career during our walk from our hotel to the Millennium Stadium on the day of the Test. We joined the crowds and flowed with them to the ground. It was awesome to walk with the people who had walked my journey with me every step of the way.

My 68th Test match went exactly to plan. I delivered what I set out to do, giving the players a platform to deliver an entertaining, world-class perform-ance. The game flowed beautifully and it felt like I had all the time in the world to make decisions. I left the field content that I had proved that I still had plenty of reffing left in me. And I walked away from my last international appointment proud that the match and the players – and not the ref's decisions – were the talking point.

The next day's train journey to Heathrow with my family was a reflective one that eventually became anxious due to numerous delays on the lines. By the time we reached the airport there was little time for goodbyes, especially for Gary, who had to hustle to get his three young sons to check-in on time. David, who was on the same flight back to Canada, hung back long enough to give me a hug. As we hugged, I told him that I had given my everything to reach that point.

He broke down. And when David let go, so did I. With my mom looking on, weeping tears of pride, two brothers wept, knowing that this was the end of a long, proud journey.

This, then, was the last stop after all the triumphs and joys.

38

Winding down

One of the main talking points that emerged during RWC 2011 was the Bryce Lawrence saga. Many South African rugby followers were livid with his performance in South Africa's quarter-final match against Australia, which they felt was the reason the Boks crashed out of the competition.

Bryce had a poor game, there's no getting around that. I doubt whether he was solely responsible for the Boks' loss, but there was certainly a fair body of evidence to suggest that many of the decisions he made, and especially the non-decisions, were not up to standard. In Bryce's own words, he "froze" when he should have been making the big calls.

Many people thought Bryce had been bribed. After all, how could a team so dominant not get the rewards they deserved? While it is true that South Africa played most of the rugby on the day, I am almost certain that the man I know was not remotely susceptible to this sort of influence. Was he the right man for the job? South Africans would have had few complaints about his previous performances in the international arena, where he refereed some big Springbok wins over the Lions and Australia. The selectors thought highly of him, and he was given the appointment on merit.

A more likely scenario is that Bryce himself got carried away with the sideshows and issues peripheral to his main task, which was to concentrate on the micro detail of the game unfolding in front of him. Apparently prior to the quarter-final he was made aware, or became aware, of the protestations of John O'Neill, the CEO of the Australian Rugby Union, about the manner in which he had officiated in Australia's RWC defeat to Ireland a few weeks earlier. The pressure he may have felt as a result could have been the reason why he was not prepared to make the big calls in the Springbok quarter-final. There were certainly instances where transgressions were not penalised, where sanction was not upgraded, and where other incidents were glossed over; in fact, the winning penalty was a touch-judge call. Bryce's profile going into the game was about 20 penalties per match. In that game it was around 10. Fairly indicative of the pressure he was feeling?

The fallout included a Facebook page petitioning that he never be allowed to referee another South African team again, which garnered more than 100 000 signatures. Incidentally, the signatories got their wish, as Bryce never refereed another Test, and he never reffed any of the South African franchises in his final Super Rugby season. So he went from being one of the top six refs in the world, good enough to be chosen to do the plum play-off game, to not being good enough to referee another Test ever again.

People should realise that Bryce didn't choose himself for that game; I am sure that he wanted to do his best on match day. Forget for a minute about being a Saffer, or a Kiwi in the case of Wayne Barnes, or a Welshman if you don't fancy Rolland, or a Frenchman if you don't rate Joubert, or a Samoan if Owens's name comes up, or an Irishman if you get Kaplan ... What has emerged from this episode is the fact that rugby has moved way beyond the point where it can afford to grant one man such huge powers over the outcome of a game.

When I got back home, world-renowned sports scientist Professor Tim Noakes contacted me to discuss what had happened. He was perplexed that rugby in the modern age was still essentially a game of chance.

What started as a brief chat over coffee lasted nearly three hours. Tim wanted to know why so many calls had gone against South Africa. Why the laws had not been applied in a more balanced manner. And how this could have robbed the Boks of the opportunity to defend their title while, at the same time, casting doubt on the legitimacy of the tournament. Noakes could not understand how a professional sport could be so reliant on the performance of one man, with teams having no immediate on-field recourse when things went wrong for them. Could the laws be open to such misinterpretation? And what was being done about it?

By the end of our conversation he had a better grasp of the flawed processes involved, from the referee selection to referee review. I also explained that some of the laws of the game were not being applied at all and others were open to interpretation.

Looking back on my 2011 RWC experience, it certainly helped build character. I had fought so hard to get there, maintaining my standards, delivering a product I felt was right up there with the best on offer, traversing and transcending some unique personal challenges. My accident had complicated my path even further, followed by my shoulder injury, which forced me to grit my teeth yet again, and then there was the massive disappointment of missing out on selection altogether and, with it, the undignified exit from the game I had served for so long and with such passion.

But by the start of the 2012 season my anger began to dissipate and I became quite philosophical about things. After all, I couldn't change the decisions that had been made. And although I felt they were the wrong decisions, I knew that all sportspeople experience tough periods, filled with disappointments and challenges. And that, at the end of the day, they just made you stronger.

That is not to say that it didn't take some time to work through the huge disappointment of no longer being a Test referee. I was intense and passionate about my work, and I still felt that I had so much to offer Test rugby.

And as much as I tried, I could not understand why the investment in the next tier of referees had to work in exact four-year cycles. That was tantamount to saying that older players like Brian O'Driscoll and Andrew Hore should retire directly after RWC 2011, as they probably wouldn't make it to the next World Cup. I considered it to be thoroughly flawed thinking.

But, as always, I picked myself up and focused on the more restricted landscape of provincial rugby. It was challenging at times, especially without the nice juicy carrot of international rugby to motivate me. I had to prove to myself – and others – that despite perceptions in certain quarters that I was no longer the top dog, I still had the skill and confidence of a Test referee. In essence, nothing had changed.

Instead of mourning the loss of the prestige international rugby embodied, I decided to focus on improving those facets of my own game that needed attention. It entailed practising discipline in training and review; moving along with modern trends; paying more attention to detail; and focusing on game-day preparation. These were all areas in which I felt I could improve.

In doing so, I rationalised, I would still be a world-class international referee, albeit operating on a much smaller stage.

While trying to focus on how to deliver my best product, SARU started a restructuring process that dragged on for all but three months of 2012, which placed a huge amount of strain on me and my colleagues and affected our performances.

It got so bad that I was even distracted during kicks at goal in a cracker of a game between the Waratahs and the Crusaders. At times, all I could think about were my contract negotiations and whether I would be around long enough to end my career with dignity.

By the start of negotiations in January, I had made the decision to continue refereeing for another season and, after months of toing and froing, was offered a contract for 2013. It involved a pay cut, which, although difficult to accept, was understandable. No longer an international ref, I was of less value to SARU. They were simply making a logical business decision. Besides, I was caught between a rock and a hard place in respect of my employment opportunities. I had nowhere to turn, nowhere to run to. If I didn't take what was offered, I would not have been able to complete my journey at all.

But I was not happy with the contract term of one year, which would end in September 2013. That was absolutely absurd, given that the Currie Cup season ran until the end of October. André told me that if I was refereeing well, they would extend the contract by a month. I wondered why the extra month was such a burden on the organisation, especially in the twilight of my career. Eventually they succumbed and my contract was extended to October 2013.

As challenging as it was at times to focus on my refereeing while my career hung in the balance, I enjoyed Super Rugby immensely. The result was that by June 2012 I was ranked top of the pile in the competition and ready to kick on. Alas, I didn't referee well enough in the last two rounds, and was given a play-off game in Brisbane, still in contention for the final, but perhaps not the favourite.

Not a month later I got a call from SANZAR ref manager Lyndon Bray saying that he thought I should hang up my whistle. It was a bolt out of the blue. On numerous occasions during the season Lyndon had mentioned that he wanted me on his 2013 team, which was one of the main reasons I had renewed my contract.

I'm not sure whether someone had whispered something in his ear, but Lyndon was now whistling a very different tune. I was really angry with this about-turn, and I told him as much. He said he would get back to me. He did, but only after journeyman Keith Brown retired unexpectedly. Lyndon's offer was another year of Super Rugby, dependent on how I performed.

I took it as a challenge and told Lyndon that I had no reason to believe that 2013 would be any different from my last 15 seasons of Super Rugby, where I had consistently been ranked among the top three or four referees of the tournament.

I also said that if he felt I was underperforming, he could drop me completely, with my blessing, which would end my Super Rugby career in rather poor fashion. He and I also cut a deal that he need not consider me for play-off games no matter how good my performances were. I was quite happy to sit those out so that the so-called up-and-comers could have a chance.

Having sorted out my Super Rugby future, the Currie Cup then turned into a disaster from a personal perspective. Once again I found myself being marginalised when I wasn't given that many big games. André informed me that they were blooding youngsters in line with a committee decision. But when I asked committee members about it, they told me that their intention had not been to implement the policy at the expense of the senior refs.

This made sense to me, and I bet if you asked the other Currie Cup stakeholders – the coaches, the players, the spectators and the media – few would have agreed that it was a good idea to use ref No. 15 on the list when No. 2 was available. The Currie Cup needed all the help it could get, and using inexperienced referees would not only impact negatively on the game from an accuracy perspective, but also in terms of the final product. I disagreed with this policy, and I made my feelings known. The upshot of reffing in the sticks for most of the Currie Cup season was a one-sided promotion/relegation match between the Cheetahs and the Kings in Bloemfontein.

Thankfully my season wasn't devoid of highlights, one of them being my one-thousandth fixture, which I will always treasure. A long time in the making – 29 seasons in all! – it happened in August when I refereed the North West Leopards and the Griffons from Welkom. I posted on Facebook how proud I was of finally achieving this milestone and dedicated the occasion to those rugby people who had supported me throughout my career. The messages of support that flooded in were truly overwhelming.

The Leopards' André Mey and the Griffons' Eugene van Wyk – both great rugby men in their own right and now presidents of their unions – made a special effort for me in Potchefstroom. And as a thank you I donated a signed Test jersey to the host union. But what really gave me goosebumps was the guard of honour the players formed for me when I ran onto the field. It was a unique gesture I had never seen before.

In addition, Western Province Rugby Union also presented me with a plaque to mark the occasion, a gesture only reserved for players who play more than 100 games for their province. It has a very special place among my memorabilia.

Regrettably, I let my conditioning slip towards the end of 2012, and management expressed its concern. Determined to be in the best possible shape for my last season as a professional ref, I went on diet and started running again. By the time the 2013 season started, I had lost 5.5 kilograms and was ready to roll.

Not that that made me any less nervous about the fitness tests we would undergo at our pre-season Super Rugby training camp. But thanks to exceptional referee camaraderie, I made it through with flying colours. Some of my colleagues cheered me on, making sure I didn't quit. Chris Pollock, Glen Jackson, James Leckie, the lot ...

Jaco Peyper was on my right and Craig Joubert on my left, and together they punched me through the finish line. Craig, especially, never allowed my mind to stray from the target (level 18 on the yo-yo), and then even pushed me to do one for joy after I had reached my goal! In a moment of special friendship, Lyndon came over to me afterwards to tell me that I had certainly made a point to my detractors.

It was at that training camp in Sydney that I announced my retirement from Super Rugby. The response from my colleagues was magnificent. To the last man – including those who were still in nappies when I started reffing Super Rugby – they paid special tribute to me. I was very emotional. After all these years, this was it. This was the moment. There was no more injury time. Unbelievably, I was now in the home straight of my long, long career.

Emotionally and physically whacked, I arrived at the South African referees training camp a day later, where André told me that I had to complete the fitness test that I had just passed in Sydney. I was speechless. "Why?" I asked. "I've just passed the test."

"No," he said. "It doesn't count."

I found that very odd, but I decided to show him a carrot. I not only completed the test, but improved on my Sydney performance. Not bad for the oldest ref by five years!

It gave me the kick I needed to carry me through my last Super Rugby season, where I focused on maintaining my high standards and squeezing every last drop of enjoyment out of every fixture. The mid-season, deal-breaking chat with Lyndon never came, as I knew it wouldn't, and by the June window I was still among the elite few at the top of the pile.

During my break I flew to Sri Lanka to assist their rugby union with some domestic issues that they were experiencing. The trip included some fantastic sightseeing with my girlfriend Nicky: the big rock in Sigiriya, the ancient ruins at Polonnaruwa, the Buddhist monasteries in Dambulla, the tea plantations south of Kandy and the rainforest of Singaraja. An amazing experience.

To cap the journey I refereed the annual Bradby Shield Encounter between Trinity College and Royal College in the beautiful mountain city of Kandy. The crowd of 14 000 included none other than Graham Henry, the guest of honour, and former pupils from around the world who converged on Kandy for the match. It created a wonderful atmosphere. It was an experience that, for me, ranks right up there with the best schoolboy fixtures anywhere in the world.

There was another significant schools match that season. Not nearly on the same scale as the one in Kandy, but no less meaningful. I was invited to referee my old school, King David Linksfield, against their sister school, Victory Park, in the annual derby. It was a great feeling to be able to go back to my roots, to the place where it had all begun 30 years previously.

Victory Park defeated King David Linksfield in a well-contested game that Wednesday afternoon, but that didn't diminish the appreciation I was shown by my alma mater, right down to the injured King David player who momentarily forgot his pain when I poked my head into the back of the ambulance to check on his condition. He was so beside himself to see me that he insisted that I pose next to his stretcher for a photograph.

I knew after RWC 2011 that my journey as a professional referee was coming to an end. I had tried my best to continue to do what I loved doing, but the reality was that the challenges just kept increasing. It was never going to last forever, and my exit as a professional referee was more about finding the most opportune moment to go rather than hanging around and milking the last drops from the cow.

39

The end game

The frustration that a ruptured disc caused me on my return from Sri Lanka in June 2013 dealt a heavy blow to my aspirations to finish my career on a high, with a strong legacy intact, refereeing at the highest level and proving not only to myself, but to all and sundry, that not only was I still capable, but also one of the best (despite my advancing years).

Come July, I was not able to complete my Super Rugby commitments in the pool stages of the competition, despite my best efforts and those of my spinal surgeon, Dr Jim Crozier. At one stage I even asked him to administer an injection that would allow me to run out one last time for a match that Lyndon Bray had given me right at the end of the competition, between the Sharks and the Kings. It was in the forlorn hope that I would be ready for a swansong run-out, but Crozier told me in no uncertain terms that my severely weakened leg (as a result of a displaced nerve) would not hold up, but would collapse within the first 20 minutes of the game. I had to rest and trust that the recovery would kick in around 9 to 10 weeks after the diagnosis.

I wasn't that concerned about the fact that there would not be play-off rugby for me (even though Lyndon had told me that I was one of the top four referees by the June break, and in the running for game time in the knock-out stages); what concerned me was that I didn't have the right feeling about my exit and when it should take place. I had made it clear that enjoyment, being a team player and upholding my own high standards for the duration of the competition were my priorities. As the season progressed, it became very clear to me that these three factors were indeed what it was all about and I never deviated from them.

I missed the first few rounds of the Currie Cup in late July while I was recovering, and then made a conscious decision to give it a go after 10 weeks, come what may. I had to fight, and I was ready for a scrap – this time with my own body.

My first game back was pretty nondescript, but I was just happy to be heading to George one last time. South Western Districts versus Northern Free State was never going to make the headlines in the rugby annals, but for me it was a watershed game that would give me enough confidence to take those small steps back to my old self. I took some painkillers and wore a Transact pad on my lower back and a corset around my weakened core to help me get through the game. After a hesitant start, I eventually settled into a decent enough game of B-section Currie Cup rugby, which the hosts won 30-25. I was so grateful to have come through that challenge.

The next day I drove back from George to Cape Town with Nicky, leaving at sparrows as I was going to do the biggest game on the schools calendar in South Africa, Paarl Gym versus Paarl Boys High. Played in Paarl, a country town on the outskirts of Cape Town, the game literally divides families and stops the town dead in its tracks. Old boys from all over the country come down for the game, which has some awesome traditions. The week leading up to it is apparently one big *jôl*, resulting in many needing time out to recover.

This year's derby was one of those magical schoolboy games that come around once every few years. Before the match, both schools got together and gave me a framed memento of my participation in this fixture, with the inscription "Thanks for all the years of service to SA rugby". How special is that!

The game was fast and free-flowing and didn't abate till the end. Paarl Gym ended up winning 37-26. The victors and the vanquished gave their all until the final whistle. It was a naive mixture of bravado, endeavour and abandon. I was exhausted, as it was my second exertion in as many days, and although my left leg suffered from the lack of conditioning, I felt that I had come through with flying colours.

I refereed a few more B-section games and then took a big chance. My first major assignment was WP versus Free State in the pouring winter rain at Newlands. I wasn't quite ready physically, but was helped by the dodgy conditions. Breakaway tries by Rian Smit of Free State, who hightailed it all the way to the try line, resulting in me joining Club 22 (again),* and Michael Rhodes, who snapped up a scrappy ball off the back of a line-out in his own

---

* When the referee doesn't reach the 22-metre line before the try is scored.

half and sprinted through for a fantastic try by a forward (with the same result … alas), made me question whether I wasn't pushing it too soon.

Unfortunately I didn't have the luxury of another year, and while no one else seemed to notice my physical restriction, I wasn't comfortable … But I had come too far to give up now.

I waded through another two games in August, and by the time my two September appointments were due, I was ready to discard the corset. Fortunately I was a lot stronger by then and felt as if I were hitting some form. So much so that come the business end of the Currie Cup, André told me that my form was excellent, and, to his great surprise, I was outperforming even those referees who should have been higher up on the ladder than me.

As he put it, "You are supposed to be put out to pasture." While I was grateful for his acknowledgement, I also knew that you were only as good as your last game. And as I approached my final Currie Cup pool game between the Sharks and WP in Durban, I suddenly realised that this could be it … the last game of my career!

Strangely enough, I felt totally in the zone, at ease and comfortable that I had done everything I could. The game in Durban was a table-topper, but failed to deliver anything special (except a mighty performance by Duane Vermeulen), as WP produced a tremendous defensive performance to top the table and remain unbeaten.

I was told then that I had done enough to continue my career for a couple more weeks, refereeing a warm-up in the promotion/relegation in Kimberley … and then my sixth and final Currie Cup final. What a magnificent end to my career! I cannot describe the deep sense of satisfaction, relief and gratitude I felt as I contemplated the finale, the finish line, that last lunge. My body, nowhere near its peak, had held together.

Tappe called me to say I fully deserved my appointment and that it was a reward for the form I had shown in the competition. I had told him before that I didn't want a hand-out, and that if I wasn't good enough, or at least close to the top, I didn't want the final. He told me that my appointment had hardly merited any discussion and was a unanimous decision. All I could say was, "Thank you!"

I was hugely emotional in the days leading up to the final. Many reporters and news stations had called me to chat about my contribution to the game and to rugby in South Africa, as well as about refereeing in general. The sheer weight of all the messages I received prior to the final started to take its toll.

I was battling to keep it together, and as stoic as I sometimes appear, there is a deep well of emotion that resides within.

There are many examples of the goodwill that was shown at the time, but one event stands out. One evening I attended the WP Referees Black Tie Dinner, where various dignitaries, corporates and sponsors, but mostly referees, were present. Also attending was the referee team for the Springbok–All Black game on the upcoming Saturday, headed by Nigel Owens (who, I might add, refereed so well in that game that I would rate it as one of the top five performances by any referee in any Test in any country – a stunningly accurate performance with just the right mix of management and game understanding, resulting in an epic match).

At the dinner, various items were auctioned off, but one of the more expensive items that attracted a great deal of interest was a signed WP jersey. I was not really concentrating on the bidding, but I know that the item was auctioned off for a decent amount. The successful bidder was Kobus van der Merwe, ex-player and former coach of WP and the Stormers, Griqualand West and Border. After winning the bid, he stood up and told the audience that he would like to donate the framed jersey to me for all I have done for SA rugby. I thought I'd seen it all, but this just blew me away.

Being acknowledged by my own people, by all South Africans, made me feel really special. I had done my best to reach the top, and then to stay there, but there was no mistaking that besides the players and coaches whom I valued most, the public were my next most important stakeholder, and their appreciation meant the world to me.

Nicky was magnificent and supported me throughout. I'm sure I wasn't the best company that week, as for some reason butterflies had got the better of me. Probably because I knew that I would never experience a moment like this ever again. Whatever it was, I was allowed my time and space.

On the day of the final, I drove to the ground on my own, reflecting every second of the way on my life's journey now that the end of my career was in sight. I arrived at Newlands to referee the visiting Sharks against Province. It was a dream match-up: the place where I was born versus the one I now called home – symbolic in every sense of the word. My assistants for the game were Chris du Preez and Stefan Breytenbach, with Deon van Blommenstein supplying crucial inputs from the TV monitor. Jaco Peyper was on standby should my fragile body fail me.

As much as I tried, as the game approached and at various stages of the warm-up, I battled to keep my emotions in check and was often reduced to tears. Then it was time to run onto the hallowed turf one last time. It was one of the only times that I actually looked around the whole stadium before the kick-off. I looked at every corner of the ground, taking it all in.

The anthem was belted out with typical gusto, and I was teetering on the edge of emotion again. Then, just before I was given the go-ahead to start the game from the TV ground staff, Frans Steyn came over and said something really special to me. His words touched me deeply. He said something along the lines that it had been an honour to work with me, and that I could feel rightly proud of my career.

It was ironic that I had started my refereeing career before Frans Steyn was even born; in fact, most of the people on the field that day were not alive then. I had a good blub and was hoping the cameras were not capturing the moment. But I was wrong, because that moment will one day define to others how much that day meant to me: first-class game No. 423, Currie Cup game No. 161, the 65th time I had refereed WP, the 58th time I had refereed the Sharks, and the ninth time WP versus the Sharks. It was my sixth Currie Cup final.

The Sharks, clearly fired up for the occasion – as every team playing for the ultimate prize in SA rugby usually is – took an early lead via an intercept try by Charl McLeod, but WP hit back soon afterwards with a well-worked try of their own through Damien de Allende, a rising star in WP rugby. The rest of the half was hard fought, with Demetri Catrakilis and Pat Lambie respectively converting a few penalties. (Incidentally, I used to play touch rugby with Demetri's dad, George, at the Wanderers when I lived in Johannesburg.)

Province were hanging in despite having to play catch-up rugby for most of the half, while the Sharks were playing a clever brand of tactical rugby, not engaging WP at their strengths, which was their powerful defence. Cleverly worked kicks into space, a good kick chase, pressure at the breakdown with numbers and a rush defence seemed to give them the edge. At half-time there wasn't much in it and the game was there for the taking, but McLeod's second try as the third quarter ended proved to be decisive.

Another try, by Lwazi Mvovo, was disallowed when my excellent TMO, Deon, ruled the Sharks offside, and they went on to stubbornly defend their try line towards the end, neutralising a few strong WP mauls close to their line. They closed out the game with another Lambie penalty to seal the deal and win 33-19. On reflection, I felt the score could have been even bigger, as almost everything seemed to work for the Sharks, and as much as WP wanted this trophy for their brilliant supporters as well as for some of the senior men in the team who had never tasted glory in the Currie Cup, it was the Sharks' day.

I blew an extra-long final whistle, and stood there watching the agony of the WP players and the pure joy of the Sharks team. I had seen what was unfolding before me many times over the years – it was a metaphor for life. There was the victor and the vanquished – the roles would be reversed every weekend thereafter, and for me, how you handled yourself in the good times as well as the bad would often define the quality of the character.

Jannie du Plessis was the first player to come over to shake my hand, saying that it was an absolute privilege to have known me and thanking me for all I had done for SA rugby over the years. He reminded me that I had refereed him in four finals, all of which he had won, and that it was an honour to have shared some time together on the field. My tears started again.

One by one, the players came over. The incredible Schalk Burger (one of the toughest men out there), Keegan Daniel (who has boxed above his weight for years), little Cheslin Kolbe, a rising star with magical feet and a big heart, Charl McLeod (whose name will forever be associated with this final), Deon Fourie (a man of huge courage), Siya Kolisi, who gave me the warmest hug (a player who played a starring role at schoolboy level when Grey PE gave Paul Roos a rugby lesson 41-16 in their own backyard, with me as ref), Jacques Botes (whose dedication and teamwork enabled him to break one of the longest-standing records, for most number of Currie Cup appearances, previously held by Helgard Müller), Duane Vermeulen (a beast of a man, who had to wait so long to get his Bok cap), Bismarck du Plessis (naughty and volatile, yet also engaging and endearing) ... the list goes on.

Matt Proudfoot, Robbie Fleck and Allister Coetzee could not have been more magnanimous in defeat; Brad MacLeod-Henderson, Sean Everitt and Brendan Venter humble in victory. I went up on to the stage to receive my memento from the president of SARU, Oregan Hoskins, and was in tears again ... Years of keeping my emotions in check and I was now having an epic fail. I got to Thelo Wakefield, president of the WP Rugby Union and a man with whom I have much in common, including the same birthday, and just snapped. There was a lot of him to bury my head into, thank God, as I was a gibbering wreck.

Rudolph Straeuli, Hennie le Roux, Breyton Paulse – former players I had reffed for over a decade each, came to offer their warm congratulations while I was on the field. We reminisced about the "old days", and then my greatest confidant and friend in the game, Paul Dobson, trooped all the way down the stairs and onto the field (he is an old fella now) to tell me in his own inimitable way: "That was all right, Jono. That was all right." The moment was captured. I had crossed the finish line with many of my friends around me, though some only in spirit.

We took a couple of snaps, I chatted with some of the crowd who had gathered at the players' entrance, and then I left the field with a big smile, a contented heart and very puffy eyes!

In the change room, Ben Theron, WP referee manager extraordinaire, had organised some champagne for my team. While I was paying tribute to each of my team members, from the water girl to the TMO, in walked Schalk Burger (who, at the time of writing, had never won the Currie Cup and had not always had the best results with me as the ref), who congratulated me on my career, taking off his specially embroidered jersey and handing it to me. A minute or so later Keegan walked in and gave me his. There were also messages from Frans Ludeke, Naka Drotské, Jake White, Alan Solomons, Johan Ackermann, Jimmy Stonehouse and many more. That the people I had chosen to serve had taken the time to show their appreciation for half a lifetime of service meant the world to me.

I also received a text from André, which read: "Hi, *kleinboet*, you have a God-given talent to referee and used it over 20 years and tonight you displayed it magnificently. You are a legend, Kappers!"

Being a part of the Currie Cup for such a long time meant so much to me. I had grown up watching the tournament, and it had become a symbol for me, the very heart of what I was doing. I loved the rivalry and what it meant to the people of the regions I visited, and indeed the people of South Africa.

I refereed a final in each of the five major rugby-playing centres, and each of them added huge value not only to me as a rugby referee, but to me as a person; indeed, to what I had become.

If someone had asked me how I would have liked to end my career, the answer would always have been: "With a Currie Cup final."

I felt truly blessed.

40

Retirement

At the annual SARU awards banquet at the beginning of 2014, I was awarded the Referee of the Year award for 2013. In addition, the organisers had put together a special tribute honouring the role I had played as a referee and an ambassador for the organisation and my country for the better part of two decades. I was humbled to be recognised one last time, but in truth, my work was not done.

As fate would have it, SARU had informed me that there were a couple of Tests in Namibia, which I had been trying to get to for years, and these would be my final dates with international rugby. How fitting then, that I got to referee in the one place I still wanted to visit.

Namibia beat Zim 35-26 in the first game, and then played Kenya, whom they thrashed 55-35 in a 12-try spectacular. I did what I had set out to do: providing the players with a platform to display their skill sets, which allowed the spectators to enjoy some wonderful rugby, and for myself, delivering a performance that included all my trademark ingredients – a hard-nosed contest that included some exhilarating passages of play and wonderful tries.

Something very poignant had happened. I had been superfluous to IRB requirements at the end of 2011, despite still being able to offer an excellent service, and now I was refereeing Test-match rugby two years later, albeit on a much smaller stage (incidentally, on the same weekend that the oldest bloke on the panels, Alain Rolland, announced his retirement from international rugby). The irony was not lost on me. But, more than that, the Namibian people made me feel so welcome, I resolved there and then that I would return one day.

Despite my foray to Namibia, I knew my decision to retire was the right one. While many people in the professional rugby world, as well as some of the public, have urged me to continue fighting for my place, it has become increasingly difficult for me to justify to myself the nomadic lifestyle. Besides running very low on doggie-sitters (thanks in particular to Shirls and Ruth), I have found the travelling really tough over the last few years. I was in my hotel room on my last Super Rugby tour in April 2013 thinking how I had paid my dues, done my time sitting alone in hotel rooms for weeks on end. When you are starting out, it's okay. But 16 years of constant cross-continent travel, putting your life on hold, is enough.

In addition, talented referees like Jason Jaftha, Rasta Rasivhenge, Stu Berry and Marius van der Westhuizen are emerging from South Africa and I feel that, despite wanting to challenge myself one more time, I would just be repeating what I've already done. It was important to me to end my career with the support of my colleagues and the rugby public, and I think I have done that.

There are very few unchartered territories that lie in wait for me in the active refereeing world, but much I would like to do elsewhere. Ultimately, I would like to start a family and have a "normal" life. I am reminded of one of my favourite quotes: "In order to get something you never had, you've got to do something you never did." I am ready for the next challenge that life throws at me. Although this is an uncertain, even anxious, time in my life, it is also one full of hidden opportunities.

It would be remiss of me not to mention how grateful I am for all the support I had along the way from SA Rugby. I served on the South African panels for a record 21 years and would not have been able to live my dreams without the platform of Currie Cup rugby. It is a magnificent competition that has brought me much joy. I am grateful for the opportunities I was given over many, many years. Even the people who did not always fully support me helped to forge the metal required for me to guts it out for as long as I did. I was given nothing on a silver platter, which made all the highlights I enjoyed that much tastier.

The IRB also deserves a mention for the manner in which I was allowed to develop as a referee and proudly represent my country in all the great stadia around the world. I had the time of my life in those 70 Tests, and have such gratitude towards the selectors, on whom I was totally reliant, as well as Paddy O'Brien for the most part, who treated me as one of their own.

So, as I look back on my career of 30 years in rugby, of what am I the proudest? At the time when I announced my retirement, I held the records as the most capped Test, Super Rugby and Currie Cup referee of all time. I am proud of my achievements, but all of those records will go. As I've said, those records don't belong to you, they belong to the game as benchmarks for the next generation to aspire to.

What I am most proud of is the fact that I never deviated from who I am – my character, my background, what I represented, how I felt I could contribute, my fortitude when things were not easy, the way I coped through times of intense loneliness ...

The rugby fans have generously indicated that the matches over which I presided were mostly good spectacles. I had a vision of how the game should be refereed, and for the most part I achieved a great deal of success in executing it. That gives me much satisfaction.

I am also truly grateful for the friendships that I have made all over the world, not just with my fellow referees, but also with players, coaches, administrators and the greater public. These relationships have been very important to me. I have learnt much from travel and the meeting of minds.

My refereeing philosophy was the following: to prove, and keep proving, to myself that I am able, with the correct application, to serve this game with flair, good judgement and nerve; to create and facilitate the best environment for players at all levels to be able to exhibit the widest range of skills and feel at ease doing so; to know that for the most part I have the trust of most of the protagonists in their quest for excellence; to have the courage to make big, bold decisions without fear; to reach the top and always keep improving; to rise again just when others start to doubt; and to inspire the next generation with some sort of benchmark to eclipse in time.

Every man carries a badge. Mine was integrity, serving the game, passion, being true to my core values and being loyal to the people I consider my friends. I can walk into the sunset in the full knowledge that I have given every last drop of energy in this body to the sport that I love.

APPENDIX A

Some thoughts on the game moving forward

Referee assessments

For many years I have wondered about the efficiency of the assessment process. Not whether it's been well thought out, but rather whether it functions at an optimum and in the best interests of the game (rather than just in the best interests of the referee). In my 30 years of doing this work, I don't believe that we have ever quite hit the nail on the head. Call me a perfectionist, but I believe there is much room for improvement in this field, a realm which ultimately not only greatly affects selection, but the confidence of the referees it is supposed to be serving.

After reffing my first ever game of rugby, my assessor (whose job it was to see if I had the right stuff to develop into a good referee) merely discussed a few general points with me in relation to my performance. Most of it centred on positional play, but ultimately it was the hooker of the winning team who made all the difference when he interrupted the reviewer and told us that I was the best referee they had ever had at that level. It was the single defining moment of my day. A stranger had gone out of his way to ensure that I got the message: "Keep at it, we enjoyed the game and your input."

For a long time afterwards I was exposed to subjective whimsical mutterings about my performances, most of which I knew to be inaccurate, but was told to just nod profusely so that I could climb the ladder like everyone else before me had.

When I went on my first exchange match to Newlands in 1992, I was given two reports. One of them rated me 4 out of 5 for everything (clearly a man who put a lot of thought into his work), and the other was an essay written by my long-time friend and confidant Paul Dobson, who tried to give me some food for thought but did not mark my performance.

As the nineties ran their course, the assessment morphed from words into marks, and sometimes quite simple marks. The problem with this system was that it was impossible to distinguish between a good performance and a bad one, as most of the marks we were given fell between 86 and 92 per cent. In addition to the fact that these marks meant very little, it made a lottery of the selection process, because if the selectors were relying on the marks, they could not know who was the best man for the job. It was even worse for the referees, as there was no way of developing your skills and growing in the job.

This does not mean that the men with the pens were not doing their work, merely that the system was faulty. As mentioned earlier, I got higher marks in the 2003 RWC than ever before, but I never achieved my potential in that tournament.

Also, there was far too wide and disparate a group to accurately account for this very important pillar of the game, so it was prudently decided that a smaller group should be used at the elite level – the selectors themselves were tasked with doing the work. This resulted in a lot more efficiency and respect for the system, but it was still insufficient.

Technical proficiency versus an understanding of the game was one aspect that was not being adequately addressed. As far as the technical aspects of the game were concerned, I don't believe we were ever on the same page as the coaches, and we were continually playing catch-up in respect of trends. The implications of making poor decisions were far too vague, and we needed a lot more coaching input. It happened far too often that a referee was given a reasonable mark, but his decisions had resulted in outcomes that had a significant influence on the game.

In addition, some aspects of the game were seldom addressed, sometimes because of vested interests. A classic example of this was the scrum. There was often very little agreement among the foremost scrum doctors of the world on what was and what wasn't allowed, so much so that it once nearly led to blows at a conference in South Africa. The point is, if the experts can't agree, how the hell is the poor referee going to get it right? Added to that is the fact that I have been told that, despite referees getting some decisions technically correct, they were not good in the context of the game.

Some have even suggested that because they are too difficult to judge, scrum infringements should only be awarded free kicks instead of scrums so as not to influence the results of matches. That, my friends, is a sad indictment of the game. How can we penalise post-tackle/ruck infringements with penalties and not scrums? No, the answer lies in agreeing on what is acceptable and then upskilling the referees so that they have a 98 per cent accuracy in this respect.

I refereed a Super 15 match in 2013 in which I penalised Wyatt Crockett for two infringements in a game where the Crusaders clearly had a stronger scrum, but, in my opinion, were attacking the Western Force illegally. When the accuracy of my calls was brought into question, I asked two experts (both international props) in South Africa for their opinions, and both agreed with the calls I had made. Lyndon Bray then consulted another expert in New Zealand, who disagreed and thought the dominant scrum should have been given the rewards.

I then asked Mike Foley, coach of the Western Force, for his opinion. I explained to him that I was trying to grow as a referee and would not mind if he said that I had been in the wrong. However, he not only told me that I was right, but that I should have given *another* penalty against Crockett! So we had the rather ridiculous situation where there was so much disagreement between the major role players that the next time I would referee one of these two teams, I would be none the wiser, and neither would they. Furthermore, if the assessor doesn't know what to make of it, the game, and this facet of the game in particular, suffers. Unacceptable.

But I will give credit where it is due. At SANZAR, the evaluation itself and the process around it have improved immeasurably. They factor in important additional information that helps referees develop.

But there are still question marks hanging over the information the referee receives if the evaluation is not completed fully and accurately. That's where the problem lies. Teams are still not given enough input, and information that could be very helpful is lost. It will be much better for the game if teams were allowed to give their input to the referees, perhaps via a third party, which will force the referees to pay more attention to the needs of the players.

This is the area where I feel there is huge room for improvement. Referee administrators have to acknowledge that the information they are passing on to the referees is not complete and, ultimately, not always in the best interests of the game. Feedback from the players/coaches is critical to bridging the disconnect that has always existed between these role players.

Positives are numerous – I like the role that empathy plays; the role of ref-erees in changing the behaviour of serial offenders (a brewing issue at the top tier of world rugby) and how it is potentially measured; the profiling of referees who stray outside of what is the target range in respect of rewarding the balance between attack and defence; the role that non-decisions play in the outcome of games; how important ball-in-play has become that we even measure it in referee assessments; and plain and simple errors. I enjoy the level of honesty that exists for the most part among the referees in respect of performance, and the role of the manager/coach who is responsible for pulling it all together and getting the best out of the troops at his disposal the following week.

The future of refereeing

Is a referee's job simply too complicated for one man to handle? The game has evolved over many decades and perhaps, instead of tinkering with the laws to produce a better spectacle and create a better product for all role players, the time has come to innovate, so that this previously amateur sport can be run more efficiently. Over the past few decades I have observed a gradual decline in refereeing standards, and this is not my opinion alone. I noticed it in my own performance, too, despite my best efforts to prepare as well as I possibly could. It cannot be that there is such a dearth of quality officials. In my opinion, they are probably as good or bad as at any other stage in rugby history. The answer is simple: we need refined technology and better use of the TMO. We need to improve our communication with the public, as rugby is a very complex game and the public deserves a better deal. They are often left in the dark on how decisions are made, and why. And there is often no accurate follow-up in the public domain. (This is an arena in which I think I could excel. I would very much like to help the public understand what is sometimes called the "grey areas" of the game.)

It needs a facility where on-field challenges become part and parcel of the fabric of the game, either by the coach or the captain. Incidentally, SA Rugby has trialled this with a measure of success. It would, in essence, allow the captain or the coach of a team to have one challenge per half. The result: teams would feel that they are not subjected as much to referee error and rugby would become more professional. The downside is that there would be a few more stoppages, but at least human error – and the resultant frustration felt by the players and the fans – would be largely eliminated.

The idea is that each team has one challenge per half and, as in American football, if it's successful, they get another. That way teams are more in control of their own destiny, and the fact that they have only one chance prevents gamesmanship.

More importantly, though, I believe the time has come for the game to employ a two-referee system, which would facilitate better outcomes for all. To hold on to the notion that this wonderful game can still be controlled by one man is archaic. Far too often, international teams are uncomfortable with referees. Two referees would not allow personality to enter into the fray, i.e. in the case where a referee has built up a rapport with a coach or a team. This will not be a factor if one has a pair of referees.

Furthermore, the level of preparation will greatly improve, as different match officials focus on different aspects of the game (barring the obvious), and they will have the opportunity to discuss their vision of the game. I trialled a two-referee system as far back as 1990 with a bloke called Johan Calitz, whom I had never met before the couple of first-league club matches we reffed together, and the experiment worked exceptionally well.

We found that there was a decrease in the number of penalties we awarded and the teams took fewer chances, as the additional presence on the field discouraged them from transgressing. As with anything new and innovative, the powers that be must be prepared to take the risk. They will have to commit more resources, and there are financial implications involved – for example, two referees would have to be remunerated as opposed to one. The National Rugby League in Australia employs this policy and American gridiron has even more officials who look specifically for infringements in their particular domain. While this system is not without its faults, it does give the public confidence that the authorities are keen to get things right on the pitch.

My mate Craig Joubert was the best referee at the 2011 World Cup and deservedly was given the final as a reward. He did well on the day, but because the score was so close (8-7), the French in particular queried many of his decisions. As in any other close Test match, some of Craig's decisions and non-decisions may have been incorrect and could have had an influence on the final result, but he nevertheless refereed the final as well as any of his predecessors – as various members of the selection committee said at the time – and he can be rightly proud of his achievement. However, the point here is that if the world's best referee, with all his exceptional skills and the support he was given, was not able to get everything right, what does it say about the rest of his colleagues who are not rated as highly as he is? If we are happy to stick to the status quo, then so be it, but I sense that the current situation is not acceptable.

Incidentally, the English were similarly aggrieved at how André Watson handled the scrums in their RWC final against the Wallabies in 2003, but they won the game, so there was limited comeback. Imagine if they'd lost ... One of their reporters, who was livid, told me directly after the game that there would have been an inquiry into Watson's performance had they lost the game. Although André did well on the day, I often wondered what would have happened if things had turned out differently on the scoreboard. Other referees have not been as fortunate as him.

I refereed the 2009 Currie Cup final between the Bulls and Free State. It was a hard-fought final, as was always the case between these two rivals. I made a few calls I regretted, notably missing a forward pass that led to the first try. The fact of the matter was that all three of the officials missed the pass and we didn't have the facility of replay at the time. In addition, I must admit I found it quite difficult to keep up with Bryan Habana!

There were also one or two breakdown decisions that, under closer scrutiny, I thought could have gone either way; and certainly two assistant referee calls, which I felt were very poor in the context of the game. A number of those calls went against the losers, Free State. My case was no different from those above, and merely underlines my theory that the teams deserve better. We now have the television review, which is a help, but I still strongly advocate giving our customers even more.

Assistant referees

The role of assistant referees has always been a talking point. This may stem from match officials needing more help (with a job that is too complex) and from the desire of other stakeholders in rugby for a greater degree of accuracy. This issue will not go away. Many a game has been decided by the input, or lack of it, from sideline officials. The problem stems from the fact that this job, too, is not an exact science. I have had first-hand experience of match officials who were desperate to assist me, but through no lack of preparation or desire have missed some important calls or made mistakes.

The reality is that there needs to be a devolution of power and a delineation of responsibilities so that all match officials, including the TMO, act as a unit in order for the correct outcomes to be achieved. The error I made in the 2011 Six Nations match, which led to a try, is evidence of this. I would love to have had the opportunity to check a replay of the incident, but at the time it wasn't protocol and I could not correct what I suspected was an on-field error.

Some referees do not want to utilise the assistant referees, as they feel that some of them are not adequately equipped to contribute effectively. My point then, as it always has been, is that there needs to be a constant level of trust and it matters not the level of achievement of the assistant referees. At times this has negatively impacted on games I have reffed, but that has not changed my mind. The solution is to improve the officials' skills and give them the confidence to contribute effectively.

I once ran touch for a friend of mine in a Six Nations Test where I contributed in excess of 20 times, in a variety of areas, but all my suggestions were ignored. Eventually I asked him if he could hear me, and he said yes. "Do you want me to carry on giving you information?" I asked him. Again, he said yes. So I carried on, but there was little point. That happens.

Make no mistake, it is not good for the game. There has been an abject failure to be accountable in this respect. There are also assistant referees who hardly contribute at all – either because they are intimidated, or because they lack confidence. There is much room for improvement in this area. The officials need to work as a team and get more of it right, no matter the great strides that have already been made in this regard.

Preparation

How great a role does preparation play? I cannot emphasise enough how critical this is. It is not so much going into a game with preconceived ideas, but rather arming yourself with information that will allow you to get the right outcomes for the game. Sometimes seeing things beforehand definitely helps to get it right in the heat of battle. Obviously this only applies to major matches, where referees are able to study behavioural trends and the various skill sets of the players and the teams before the game.

The pre-match talks I had with the coaches of the various teams were especially useful as a means of gathering information and developing an understanding of the upcoming game. No matter how much preparation I did beforehand, there were always new points that were raised in these talks, which I appreciated.

So I didn't just use the pre-match chat as an ice-breaker, as has been suggested by some, but rather as a way of gathering information. Some experts believe that the pre-match meeting is harmful, as it might influence a referee's decision-making on the pitch, for example to favour one team over the other. I don't subscribe to that rubbish. If referees don't have the nous to deliver a fair product on the day, then they shouldn't be there in the first place. We are, after all, talking about the top tier of referees in world rugby here.

Art versus science

It is vitally important that a referee maintain the right balance between technical competence and artistic input, as it is an area with hidden pitfalls. With so many grey areas at the different facets of play, it is important that the referee understands what the game needs from both perspectives and then tries to achieve the balance as a lawman, facilitator and perhaps even as an entertainer. To simply blow the pea out of the whistle is not going to satisfy anyone.

In addition, I have found that both verbal and non-verbal cues often help players to understand what is expected when they are attempting a contentious play. I always considered myself to be more of an artist, as that came more naturally to me, but the reality is that it is vitally important for the referee to maintain the right balance.

One thing I have found in the last few years is that the ability to deliver punitive sanction to ensure a fairer contest cannot be valued too highly. Teams at the top flight will always try to push the referee and see how far they can go. If the referee is not well prepared, both physically and mentally, he stands no chance of getting it right on match day. After all, it only takes one or two decisions to affect the outcome of a major Test match. But more than that, handing out timely and appropriate cards can have dramatic results.

The exacting and demanding public does not want to see match officials overreacting to a situation. On the other side of the coin are the players and coaches, who want officials to have a deeper understanding of what is happening on the field in order to ensure that the best team wins fair and square. I don't feel referees are doing well in this regard at the moment. The issuing of cards is haphazard at times and has had huge implications in major Test matches of late.

Fitness

The role that fitness plays in the life and career of a professional referee cannot be underestimated. As South African refs, we have prided ourselves on ensuring that we deliver in this regard. We have undergone rigorous testing since I got onto the panels in 1993. On some occasions I felt the tests were even tougher than those the players undergo. At the time when we were just learning about this field, we would do phosphate decrement testing, speed testing, speed endurance testing, agility testing, the Cooper test (a 12-minute run test used for measuring aerobic fitness) and a 6 x max meterage all in one session.

It has been proven time and again that, in general, the fittest referees are the ones who are able to think clearly when fatigue sets in. Without trying to stir up controversy, I don't believe that similar testing was always done in other parts of the world, or that it was done to the same extent, and perhaps standards were compromised on occasion. However, under the guidance of Matt Blair, the IRB started measuring the fitness levels of match officials more stringently before the 2011 RWC in New Zealand. It is, however, a constantly evolving area of the game.

Coaching the ref

One bizarre tidbit of information is that in my 30 years as a referee, I have never had a coach. Ever. More often than not, I was left to my own devices, unless I had concerns about an element of my game or some trend was brought to my attention. There were times where I didn't hit the right buttons in games, but I did feel that, by and large, most of my managers trusted my ability to get to grips with whatever was presented on match day.

I was arrogant enough to think that I was the best, but humble enough to keep working at my game. As a result of this, I really feel that there is a big opportunity to explore the use of a specialist referee coach, with credibility, to ensure that standards of excellence are defined and maintained.

People often talk to me about the differences between northern hemisphere and southern hemisphere referees. These differences are not reflected in the statistics; rather what may differ is how referees like to manage games and what aspects of the game are emphasised by their bosses and employers. I have spoken to managers at the elite level and the problem lies in not having all the senior referees under one umbrella.

At the time of writing, we have a situation where the international referees are all being paid by their unions, even though the IRB can use them for all the major Test matches. Surely this must change. The IRB should employ the top eight referees, as in cricket, where the top umpires adjudicate most of the high-level games. This would allow the managers to have far more control over their resource pool. This smaller pool of officials would allow a greater degree of consistency and standards would be much easier to maintain. Furthermore, and critically important, is that any trend that crops up from time to time with players and in teams would be able to be discussed more regularly and fixed quicker and with greater efficiency. This has to happen – it's a no-brainer.

Training camps

For one of our early-season camps in South Africa, we went to the bush, which, I must say, I always found to be a ball-breaker of note. I am not one for wasting time with getaways, and prefer to cut to the chase and get to grips with business. The general object of these camps was to refresh our knowledge and understanding, and set standards so that we would all be on the same page as the season approached. Some of these camps were used as team-building opportunities. At one of them, we were told to carry heavy logs around for the duration of the day, which I found demeaning and of absolutely no value. Grown men carrying logs was tantamount to "*sien jy daardie boom?*" in the army. What a joke.

On occasion I found some of the activities to be quite stimulating, especially if they were cerebral, but some of the other referees remarked to me that we were not troops in the army. I challenged this nonsense on more than one occasion, which predictably went down like a lead balloon, but that didn't dissuade me from keeping at it.

Match-day habits

I generally kept things very simple on match day. I never got a special haircut or wore flashy boots or clothing that hugged my shapely body, as my thinking was that we were there to do a job, not draw attention to ourselves.

I have been known to get my timing wrong on more than one occasion, but I never missed a flight in all my years of reffing, nor did I ever miss a game. Due to misjudging traffic bottlenecks I nearly missed my first Currie Cup final in 2002 (see Chapter 19) and also pushed it close for a Super Rugby semi in Canberra, when a liaison officer misjudged our departure time. I had my driver, Brett Bowden, driving on the wrong side of the road to ensure that we arrived in time. No sweat – the adrenaline actually helped to punch me into game mode.

I used the same black plastic Acme Thunderer for 17 years and can't really remember having a reserve whistle in my kitbag. It was a hand-me-down from my colleague Richard Every when he retired.

I never had a change-room routine and my warm-up was pretty non-existent, consisting of the odd stretch here and there, but only really because I saw some other guys doing it and I wanted to be part of the team.

I always had very basic instructions for my team: mostly, it was "give me relevant information that will help the final product". I trusted them the whole way through, sometimes to my own detriment. But as brief as my instructions sometimes were, I was known for giving the players quite a long window to express last-minute concerns and to remind them of my standards. So I pretty much had zero change-room protocol, and while I am sure I looked like lastminute.com getting ready, it was for a good reason. Keeping it simple with no frills was my motto. I often came across as much more carefree than some of the others.

Referee selection

The IRB gave me many, many opportunities over a long period of time. I was rewarded by the selectors and lived my dreams all over the world at all the great stadiums with all the great players and coaches. However, during that time, even while riding the wave, it struck me how important it was that the selections for each game were credible. It would be so beneficial to the sport if the teams involved could agree on match officials for each game they play. I am suggesting a process whereby a list comprising, let's say, the names of four or five referees, is suggested to teams for each Test match in the Six Nations, for example. If their choices, made anonymously, reveal a strong preference for one or two referees, then the appointment is simple. Give the customers what they want!

By allowing the coaches and/or teams to have an increased say in the selection of the referee, it would ensure that the best referees get more games and the best interests of the game are served. There have been too many instances where teams were not comfortable with a referee; he knew it, they knew it, but everyone pretended how happy they were to see one another again, and it did not always result in a good game. Although the selectors may become less important if the coaches and teams choose the referee, they would still initiate and facilitate the process.

Retirement age

When I announced my retirement, I was 46 years old, five years older than the next oldest referee at Super Rugby level. I was never much of a speed merchant, but I had always prided myself on looking after myself physically. It was during my last year that many a player and coach remarked that I was retiring too early, and that they couldn't give a rat's arse about my age.

This was at odds with some managers, who seemed intent on delivering the next tier of younger referees at the expense of the older set. The fact of the matter is that experience and the ability to hold one's nerve in the heat of battle is the domain of a select few and we don't grow on trees.

In France, they retire their referees at the age of 45. Needless to say, in the rugby world, this is a hotly debated topic: do you choose experience over the potential that youth offers (but doesn't necessarily deliver on)? Yes, the ball may be in play for longer these days, but sometimes the pace of the game is overrated. Once again, a two-referee system would allow on-field personnel to get into better positions to accurately adjudicate play and largely eliminate age as a factor.

Crowd control

The most hostile crowds I have encountered over the past 30 years? Personally, I have been very lucky. I have never really felt that intimidated by big crowds, vitriol or booing. I found the Canberra crowd quite feral at times, whereas Suncorp in Brisbane is very loud and the crowd get right into the game. They gave me a standing ovation when the Reds won the semi against the Blues in 2012 and booed me when they got hammered by the Sharks in 2013. I got "frone wif a borrel" at the Cake Tin in Welly in 2000 by a select few. The spectators at Stade Vélodrome in Marseille were vociferous when France played New Zealand, but were positively outstanding when they realised they were going to win, and I got to hear quite a few amazing renditions of "La Marseillaise".

At the River Plate in Buenos Aires, running touch for Scotty Young in the early 2000s, I was genuinely concerned that the stadium might have been built on shaky foundations, as it appeared to be bouncing!

I never really had many dramas back home except those I have alluded to, for example some club rugby in Joburg, as well as some really dodgy club venues in the Western Cape, where players' and match officials' safety did not appear to be of paramount importance.

No-score draws and low-scoring thrillers

Throughout my career I prided myself on getting the players to deliver games that were easy on the eye. Sometimes, though, there were anomalies, for which

I initially felt responsible. I've mentioned one already, a no-score draw first-team schoolboy fixture between Swartland and Hugenote played in a swamp in Wellington in 2004. Another that comes to mind is the 12-6 Bledisloe arm-wrestle played in the frozen tundra of Christchurch in 2002, where neither team really wanted possession for the full 80 minutes.

Other notable Test-match non-thrillers include Scotland versus England in 2008 (15-9), where I felt hardly a blow was landed in real anger; and two Tests involving France and Argentina in 2008 and 2011, where I had real difficulty encouraging anything expansive at all. France won 12-6 and 15-9, but in reality I didn't really feel that the crowd got their money's worth. I understood that the win was all important and that the players were very familiar with one another, most playing their rugby in France, but was less than enthused doing the review and battled to find anything for the highlights reel.

In Super Rugby I had the unusual score of 9-8 when the Highlanders smashed the Brumbies in 1999 on a cold day in Carisbrook when points were hard to come by, and 14 years later another, 12-6, when the Sharks battled past the Stormers in a bruising slugfest in very poor conditions in Durban.

In my last Currie Cup season I had the pleasure of refereeing the Eastern Cape derby between Border and Eastern Province, which finished 9-6 thanks to a late flurry of points, and in 2008 a thrilling 9-all draw between Boland and Griquas played in hurricane-like conditions.

Really only a handful, but interesting nevertheless.

Scoring

Innovations in respect of scoring are not new, but what they do achieve is to change the face of the game. There is no question that increasing the value of the try was the right move and, in time, it will be increased again. Quite whether the timing is right at present I am not sure, but it is tries that put bums on seats, which is all important for the future of the game.

Previous RWCs have often failed to produce spectacular play-off matches, with games featuring a predominance of kicking and percentage rugby. Perhaps there are opportunities here, too, for innovation, so that these games can provide the public with more entertainment.

The clock

If scrums and line-outs are eating the clock so dramatically, then why don't we start the clock only once the ball has been fed into these two facets of the game? It makes sense, and the public won't have to suffer the enormous amount of dead time that is dished up on occasion (incidentally, the scrum innovations over the past few years have helped to reduce the amount of dead time in matches by just under 20 per cent, allowing the public to enjoy the ball in play for longer). I think that the game will become more dynamic, athletic and spectacular if we do this, resulting in more enjoyment for all concerned.

Rugby memorabilia

Over the years I have kept a lot of memorabilia from my 30 seasons in the game. From programmes of every game I officiated and around 600 ties given to me by a variety of players' clubs and rugby unions to cups and medals, cultural pieces of interest, plates, tossing coins, pennants, photos, rugby balls, blazers, prizes and various other collectables of games I was involved in. It has been a wonderful pursuit, and most of the memories are displayed in a room in my house. Sure, they provide a snapshot of achievements from days gone by, but, more than that, they are wonderful memories of my involvement in this sport.

Undoubtedly my single biggest joy was accumulating jerseys; not my own, but those of the teams and players I was involved with. In the beginning, I was given the odd jersey by a player or a team, but as I started to think about retirement, I wondered if I could complete the sets. I am hugely grateful to all the legendary players who parted with their own. By the time I announced my retirement I had accumulated signed jerseys from most of the top international teams I had refereed, the Super Rugby teams, as well as the 14 South African unions. Their worth cannot be measured in monetary terms.

APPENDIX B

The people who most influenced my rugby career

Who has had the most significant influence on my rugby career?

1. To start with, **my mother**, for discouraging me as a player and then encouraging me to start refereeing. She was the one who made the call to the Transvaal Referees Society, and she was the one who drove me to my first meeting in the south of Johannesburg. For 30 years and with a great deal of interest she watched how my career was progressing, through all the highs and lows. She was continually supportive of my involvement in the game, and held a belief only slightly less strong than mine that I would succeed at the top end. She loved to attend the games I reffed, sometimes even coming on her own to watch schools games.

    At various points I had to ban her from coming to watch what I considered to be lesser games in the smaller towns of the country, but she did accompany me on some of my trips abroad for major Test matches, which was the very least I could do for her. Her driving energy was so much a part of my overall ambition to walk in the footsteps of giants. She was always there for me. I cannot begin to repay her for all the love and support she has given me.

2. **My father**, who used to take me to watch club rugby on weekends at Kings Park. This was undoubtedly where the seeds were sown and my dreams had their origin. In the end it was more like *me* dragging *him* to the rugby, and once I realised that my playing skills were limited, I was keen to find another niche in the sport.

My dad took a backseat for many years, but I always knew he supported me in my chosen career. He enjoyed my rise to fame as a Test referee and would often beam with pride when his friends or the media commented on my competence. I invited him and his wife Terry to watch the England versus New Zealand game at Twickenham in 2002. It turned out to be one of my best supported matches of all time, with most of my family and numerous friends making the big trek across the world to share the special day with me.

3. **My brothers Gary and David** were also there for me from the very beginning. Both of them followed in my footsteps and started their rugby careers as hookers, Gary going on to represent Rhodes, even though rugby was not his game, and David going on to play that one mighty game for the Sharks. What a privilege for me to be able to share my life with such special people. The fact that they are my brothers has enriched me.

    Gary took up refereeing like his big brother until I told him that his 100-kilogram frame and flat feet were not conducive to this profession, and David supported me on and off the field, allowing us to share many special memories. Their living in Canada proved no obstacle and we still managed to find the time to get together at all my major overseas Test matches.

    I will never forget black-belt Gary keeping a watchful eye on me after the 2000 Test in Wellington, where he made sure that I did not get into trouble with the masses, as well as the way he brought his boys at different times to watch me and ensure that our family would forever remember those very special times; and David for staying connected to me throughout my journey, loyal to the bone and willing me to go where no other had gone before.

    I cannot describe in words that hug we shared in the tunnel at Heathrow as we realised that it was the end of my journey as a Test referee, and the sheer outpouring of emotion from all those pent-up years of being in control. It was a a moment that absolutely broke me – my little brother brought to tears as we realised we would never be back. I can only say how grateful I am that my mother was there to witness the special love we have for each other. Better wingmen I could not have wished for.

4. **Ian Anderson** lived a short life, but in that time he achieved a great deal. Not many will remember his special talent as a referee or his kind and gentle

nature. He was a man of honour, and one whose style inspired me. His death was a jolt to me in my formative years, as I lost a formidable ally and close refereeing friend. He had such an uncomplicated style of officiating and made everything look so easy. And he had no ego on the field, always seeming to get games going for the benefit of those watching. I have no doubt he would have gone on to become one of the greatest referees of all time.

5. **Paul Dobson** has been a giant of a friend to me. From our first interaction in 1992, when he assessed me in my first exchange game between Western Province B and Northern Transvaal B at Newlands, I got the feeling that he was a true rugby man who was genuinely interested in furthering the careers of those youngsters whom he came across. Besides writing about 20-odd books and being one of the greatest rugby historians the country has ever produced, and being the deserving recipient of the IRB Lifetime Achievement Award for service to the game, he was my confidant, a true friend at all times and a great guide who helped me through some tough times.

   He never asked for a thing in all the time I have known him besides the odd programme to help with some match reports. He is my favourite older bloke of all time. I hope I am able to inspire and assist youngsters in the same humble and selfless manner as he has me, and I hope that I will be privileged enough to stay involved in the game for as long as he has.

6. **Paddy O'Brien** was my colleague in the late-90s. We were both intensely passionate about the game and loved being involved in it. A half-decent referee himself, he refereed many important Test matches and finals. Even though he was half a generation ahead of me, I was still able to appreciate him as a referee and a friend. I was very angry with him about the rubbish surrounding my exit from the international arena, but I cannot describe how important he was as a friend and a manager during the decade or so that I was at the top of the tree. As I have often stated, we are just little cogs in a machine, and though I may have performed well over a long period of time, I was as fortunate as anyone to be the beneficiary of many, many world-class Test matches during his tenure as manager of referees. My gratitude for his and his selectors' faith in me is limitless.

7. **Phil Botha** – what a breath of fresh air! A big man with a granite jaw but a gentle heart. Feeling stifled in the *verkrampte* environment in Joburg until

CALL IT LIKE IT IS

1993, I was fortunate to end up with a manager who encouraged me to be myself. I blossomed under Phil, and he was almost certainly the catalyst who was able to bring out the best in me, both in my innate skills set and my leadership potential. He did this with most of the other up-and-comers too, and to this day he has the respect of most of the people whose lives he touched during his time as manager of referees in Natal.

The likes of Joubert, Jonker, Berry and I all owe much of our success to the friendship, leadership and unselfish attitude of Phil Botha. Indeed, his sidekicks, Roger Hay and Mark Howard-Browne, good rogues in their own right, ensured that the Sharks region produced a fair amount of quality referees during their tenure. I was proud to have Phil by my side in my first Six Nations match, and I know Stu Berry invited Phil and Roger over for his first Test, at the end of 2013 in Japan.

8. **Nick Mallett** – the story has been well documented, but his respect for me as a referee and his willingness to go out on a limb when things were not moving quickly enough really helped to kick-start my Test career. What turned out to be a casual conversation with no vested interest and certainly no gain for him resulted in me being given my first big break as a referee, in the first Six Nations match, between Italy and Scotland in Rome, after which there was no looking back. I have maintained a friendship with him ever since our first interaction, in 1995 when he was coaching Boland, and I refereed many of the provincial teams he coached, as well as Italy.

APPENDIX C

My top 10 referees

Ian Anderson (South Africa) – I met Ian when I went to my first referees' meeting in 1984. He was friendly, kind and wise. He made his mark in an era when youth was not valued. He stood out like a beacon among the mediocrity of his generation and was deservingly awarded first provincial and then Test colours in the early nineties. I liked him because he was a kind and thoughtful man, but that's not why he stood out as a referee. Often with rolled-up sleeves, he was an empathetic referee who had a great feel for the game, and in his short career was well respected by players and the public. He refereed three Test matches and would have done many more – probably even become iconic in the South African refereeing world. I was overseas when he was appointed to his dream game at Murrayfield between Scotland and the All Blacks in 1992 (Ian being of Scottish descent). However, someone decided that he was too green for that arena at that point and awarded the game to Freek Burger instead. Ian was driving back from a wedding in Natal when he was involved in a fatal car accident on 9 January 1993. He was in his early thirties. My mom called me in Israel to give me the news and I was too shocked to talk. It wasn't until 2005 that I refereed my first Test match at Murrayfield (between Scotland and Wales). In my kitbag was an Anderson-clan scarf that I had bought for Ian 12 years earlier. It felt like he was with me the whole day.

Kerry Fitzgerald (Australia) – legendary referee who did the first RWC final between New Zealand and France in 1987. I never got to meet him (he, too, died young) and so can't comment on him as a person. But what impressed me most about his refereeing was his style. Unobtrusive, he floated around the field with what appeared to be a magic wand. Players were rarely seen questioning his calls, and consequently there were very few incidents of note in his career; he always seemed to referee fixtures which had good flow to them. He was the forerunner of a whole slew of world-class international referees that Australia produced in the 1990s (their golden era), namely Scott Young, Andrew Cole, Stuart Dickinson, Gus Erikson and Peter Marshall.

Derek Bevan (Wales) – an absolutely world-class referee with a character to boot. Slightly different in style to my preference, he was a strong communicator and very demonstrative. Always in control of his matches, he often produced memorable fixtures (too many to mention here). He refereed the 1991 RWC final between England and Australia, and the semi-finals of the following two RWCs (between South Africa and France in 1995 and South Africa and Australia in 1999). He seemed to have heaps of nerve and was able to bring his character onto the field with humour and assuredness. In 1999, when he was clearly reaching the end of the road in his career, I remember being at a dinner given in his honour, which I thought was a lovely touch by the Welsh. I also recall the younger referees pushing him through the fitness test prior to the 1999 RWC, literally carrying him to the finish line. And, most importantly, I remember a chance meeting I had with him at a bar during the tournament (when I was having a tough time with some South African colleagues of mine) when he looked me in the eye and said, "I know exactly what's going on here." And he did! At one stage, he held the record for most number of Test matches refereed (44). He was one of the most charismatic referees of his era.

Colin Hawke (New Zealand) – one of the standout referees to ever come out of New Zealand, he was generally seen as a no-nonsense referee. He had great voice projection and clarity in decision-making and was immaculate in his hand signals and mannerisms (the best, in my opinion). He was also a straight-down-the-line bloke who was simple and honest in his everyday life, which translated to similar efficiency on the field. No frills. Colin had a long and successful international career. He was always very supportive of me when I was coming through the ranks and equally so after I had "arrived". Colin reminded me a lot of Dave Bishop, who I feel should be categorised in the same league. Very strong-willed and definite in his communication, Bishop was a very direct ref who took no prisoners, players and teams were left in no doubt as to what he was thinking. He was at the top of the New Zealand refereeing tree for quite some time and represented his country for the better part of a decade in the international arena (RWCs included). Like Colin, he was always in good nick and portrayed an air of confidence.

Craig Joubert (South Africa) – of all of them, probably the bloke of whom I am the most proud and to whom I am the closest. I met him when I moved down to Durban in the late-90s and found him to be bright, willing, competitive, respectful and, ultimately, an outstanding friend. After working with him a few times in the early 2000s, I quickly realised that he could, and probably would, be my natural successor (although he wasn't the greatest touch judge around). He impressed me no end when he walked into the referees' room after the Currie Cup final of 2000 and told André Watson that he hadn't learnt much from his (Watson's) performance. It was said tongue-in-cheek, but I found it quite refreshing amid all the ego-stroking that goes on in that type of environment. Craig paid his dues, narrowly missing out on the RWC of 2007 in France, but then made rapid progress through the international ranks. By the time the next RWC arrived he was at the top of his game, and was duly rewarded with the final. I feel extra proud, as I mentored him and gave him all the knowledge I had accumulated (while I was active) so that the next legitimate South African flag-bearer would be in a better position than I was when I started out. He still has some way to go in his career and, if correctly managed, will almost certainly become another iconic South African referee in the international arena.

Ed Morrison (England) – The first RWC I attended was in 1995 at Ellis Park in Johannesburg. It was a typical final with not much give, and was decided (once again) by kicks. But it was also an iconic final, as Nelson Mandela was present and there was the awesome and very low flyover by a Boeing 747. I was slightly inebriated and was wearing a cap that said: "Who the f*ck is Jonah?" The referee on that pressure-filled day was Ed. He did a great job on what must have been the most demanding of occasions. I didn't know him personally, but I knew enough of his accomplished manner on the field, which suggested that he was indeed one of the premier referees of his generation. He seemed to be an affable man with time for everybody. He refereed many of the important fixtures during the 1990s and was without a doubt one of the finest referees England ever produced. He was exceptionally helpful to me when I reffed my first BIG Test, between New Zealand and Australia, settling me before the game and making a couple of crucial calls during it too.

Nigel Owens (Wales) – another world-class referee produced by Wales. He paid his dues over a number of years, scraping into the 2007 RWC in France. By the time the 2011 RWC came, he was ready to step up to the plate. He refereed the quarter-final clash between New Zealand and Argentina, after overcoming a horror show in the South Africa versus Samoa match. His progression since has been nothing short of phenomenal. His manner of communication is very clear, he has great on-field presence and, more importantly, he has grown with the game as it has evolved. He has refereed many finals in his time and generally does them with aplomb. He refereed two of the best-refereed matches I have seen for some time, namely South Africa versus New Zealand at Ellis Park, one of the best Test matches I've ever watched as a neutral spectator, and then Ireland versus New Zealand a few months later, where New Zealand came back from the dead to keep their impressive, unbeaten record intact. Owens recently passed 50 Tests and will go on to do many more. I really enjoy how he tries to keep the game flowing; no doubt the experience he has gained over time has played a huge role in this. He should have a big 2015 RWC!

André Watson (South Africa) – no doubting his ability on the field, he was entrusted to referee many a final in his time at the top, including the 1999 and 2003 RWC finals. He generally maintained a good balance between punitive sanction and the rhythm of the game. He could often get a game moving along at pace, and the powers-that-be clearly had faith in him to handle the pressures of big occasions. Despite occasional run-ins with players like George Gregan, Andrew Mehrtens, Justin Marshall and Balie Swart, he achieved much success for South Africa.

Chris White (England) – another fine English referee who was almost certainly top of the tree around the time of the 2003 RWC in Australia. I met Chris when I was doing my first major Test series, between England and Argentina in 1997. He was travelling with the English tour party as an advisor of sorts and we quickly became good friends. Chris was a very considered referee who embraced the sport as a student of the game; he also had a good feel for what was happening in front of him, and I know that he was the Boks' favourite ref during his time at the top.

Paddy O'Brien (New Zealand) – one of the best refs to come out of the land of the long white cloud. From the same era as Hawke, his greatest asset was the rapport he built with the players, his athletic ability and his good understanding of the game. This encouraged the players to play ball, and his games were often good to watch. Paddy refereed quite a few finals of the National Provincial Championship in New Zealand, and also three Super Rugby finals. He was very unlucky not to be awarded the 2003 RWC final. He refereed the crucial third Test of the British & Irish Lions series when they toured Australia in 2001, holding his nerve right till the end of an absorbing, winner-takes-all fixture.

APPENDIX D

My World XV

My World XV is comprised only of players whom I reffed at some time or another.

World XV

15 – Christian Cullen
14 – Rupeni Caucaunibuca
13 – Tim Horan
12 – Brian O'Driscoll
11 – Jonah Lomu
10 – Dan Carter
9 – George Gregan
8 – Kieran Read
7 – Richie McCaw
6 – George Smith
5 – Martin Johnson
4 – Victor Matfield
3 – Carl Hayman
2 – Keith Wood
1 – Os du Randt

Bench

Olo Brown
John Smit
Paul O'Connell
Juan Smith
Joost van der Westhuizen
Jonny Wilkinson
Joe Roff

Fullback – when I was growing up, I was a massive fan of Gysie Pienaar. He wasn't scared to take risks, and he often pulled it off. I will never forget his contribution during the British & Irish Lions tour of 1980. That iconic photo after he beat Bruce Hay to score the defining try of the match will forever remain one of my favourite childhood rugby memories.

Serge Blanco was probably the best of his generation, but I never had the pleasure of refereeing him. There were many other good fullbacks – Percy Montgomery of South Africa, whose kicking skills improved immeasurably as his career progressed, was a vital component of the successful 2007 Springbok RWC squad; and Jason Robinson of England was lethal on the counter-attack and often breached the kick-chase line with his elusive running skills. But unquestionably the greatest attacking force for me was Christian Cullen. When he was at his peak, he was devastating and could quite easily flummox opponents. A good defender, he was much stronger and tougher than he looked.

Wings – growing up, I loved watching Carel du Plessis, who was one of the most fluid runners with the ball in hand. Ray Mordt, too, was a beast of a man for a wing. Internationally, I think Bryan Williams was combative and a great finisher, and David Campese had a huge X-factor. There are many good candidates here. Little Shane Williams of Wales, a man of astonishing skill and courage, with a good step that could beat most; Joe Roff, who was as skilful a component of the back three as you could ask for and adept at playing pretty much anywhere among the backs; Bryan Habana, a superb finisher and a great opportunist, but more than that, a great team man; and Joeli Vidiri, a huge chunk of a man who was a nice weapon to wield from broken play.

But I will settle for the incomparable Jonah Lomu who, at his best, was pretty much unstoppable; and a player of whom I think the world never really got to see the best – Rupeni Caucaunibuca. What an attacking force! He had power, speed and confidence, and could side-step a bus. While he almost certainly did not fulfil his potential, I saw enough of him in just a short time to rank him up there with the best.

Centres – Danie Gerber was one of the standouts for me. A brilliant stepper and a top finisher, he always seemed to be jogging his way past opponents. Frank Bunce – all power and a difficult man to get past, he seemed to enjoy putting others into space. Philippe Sella was the cornerstone of the French team for over a decade and was a great all-rounder. Tana Umaga had huge *mana* (presence) on the pitch, was a good captain and a very good playmaker. In South Africa, Jaque Fourie is one of the best finishers we have produced. He can cover a variety of positions, having started out as a fullback, and he scored the series clincher in the second Test against the Lions in 2009 from a seemingly improbable position. He is very confident and a strong presence on the field. The Horan/Little era was special too, with Horan just edging his counterpart for his superb effort at the 1999 RWC and for coming back from a complete knee reconstruction.

But the standout centre has to be Brian O'Driscoll. A fantastic leader with a great sense of humour (sometimes he lost his with me), he was quite simply the best centre of his time. He inspired Irish rugby to reach greater heights for a decade and a half, and was the fulcrum not only of the Irish team, but of several Lions tours. And he had an uncanny ability to score tries.

Flyhalf – I refereed a few really good ones. Pity I didn't get to ref Naas Botha, as he was the best general of his time. Joel Stransky was excellent and an accomplished footballer; I enjoyed Henry Honiball, as he brought something different to the party with his devastating tackling exploits; Andrew Mehrtens, a flawed genius, was similarly excellent at controlling a game and was one of my favourites for his chirpy nature and incisive mind; Carlos Spencer was a supremely talented footballer; Stephen Larkham was very understated but a good reader of the game and a very tough competitor; and Ronan O'Gara was very successful with all the teams he played for, but I probably rate him just below some of the above-mentioned.

In the end, it is a two-horse race between Jonny Wilkinson and Dan Carter. Wilkinson may have ended his Test career more prematurely than Carter, but his metronomic boot, iconic kicking style and fabulous defence were right up there with the best. My vote goes to Carter, however, for his ability to attack and breach the defensive line. He has set numerous benchmarks along the way but remains one of the most humble human beings playing rugby today.

Scrumhalf – once again, it is difficult to decide who is the best No. 9. I was a big fan of Agustín Pichot, appreciating how he contributed to the success of Argentina in the 2007 RWC. But in the end it was between Justin Marshall, Joost van der Westhuizen and George Gregan. Marshall was a supremely combative halfback who did the basics well but was always in the thick of things. Very knowledgeable, he complemented his partner, Andrew Mehrtens, exceptionally well. Joost was a great athlete, and was the best try-scoring scrumhalf in the history of the game, excluding Gareth Edwards (perhaps). He was always prepared to have a go, and was very successful too. He was also instrumental in stopping Lomu a few times in the 1995 RWC final. Gregan was the brains behind most of the teams he played for. He wasn't the quickest, the biggest, or the strongest, and didn't have the best pass, but he was super-smart and had an uncanny way of irritating the opposition, which often threw them off their game. He could put others into space around the fringes, which worked well for the Brumbies and Australia. His ability to get the best for his teams (though not always) resulted in many successes. Not shy to have a little sledge every now and again, he was heard shouting "Four more years, mate, four more years" to Byron Kelleher as the clock was winding down and New Zealand was again exiting the RWC prematurely. So a close call, but I choose who, for me, was the most influential figure of them all: George Gregan.

Looseheads – Jason Leonard was the ultimate team man who played over 100 Tests for England on both sides of the scrum. Rodrigo Roncero of Argentina was an enthusiastic and passionate loosie with an all-round game to match. He had a really big engine and a very high work rate. But at the end of the day (as Naas would say), Os du Randt was the standout. He was a good scrummager and carrier of the ball, but, most importantly, he could be an incredibly destructive tackler. He also came back from a knee injury to lift and inspire South Africa to RWC success in 2007.

Hookers – Keven Mealamu for his incredible endurance; Andrew Hore for his Farmer Brown attitude and always having a crack at the ball, even when he wasn't supposed to; Jeremy Paul, who was probably one of the most gifted; and John Smit for his incredible exploits as a captain. However, I decided on Keith Wood, a dynamic, inspiring player who always put his body on the line. He had a tremendous work rate and scored many tries during his rugby career. I think Bismarck du Plessis may well go on to eclipse all of these gents – he is a super talent in broken play, has powerful defence, can pilfer the ball and carry it. And he is a more than adequate scrummager.

Tightheads – Olo Brown was an excellent tighthead prop, as was All Black Greg Somerville, Martin Castrogiovanni of Italy and Phil Vickery, the bedrock of England's efforts in their RWC success of 2003. But I rate Carl Hayman as the most destructive tighthead I ever refereed. Quite reliant on a big hit (in those days it was still allowed), he used that impetus to crush opponents. As a tall man, he was very useful in the line-outs. He eventually went on to play in Europe and thus didn't win as many Test caps as he could have.

Locks – really tough to pick the best here, as there are so many good ones. Paul O'Connell struck me as a colossus in the Irish set-up. He is a man of substance and a tough nut on the field, too. John Eales could do just about everything (I will never forget him keeping his nerve to slot over the winning kick in what was without doubt one of *the* Bledisloe Cup series of modern times) – what an ambassador for his country! His fantastic attitude and leadership ability belied his fighting spirit. Fabien Pelous played some great rugby for his country over a very long period of time. Mark Andrews was the mongrel in the Bok team for a decade, and Bakkies Botha provided the brute force required to subdue one's opponents (I often used to think it quite odd that Bakkies used to say a prayer on the field, and then less than a minute later was capable of borderline brutality).

Martin Johnson was the backbone of the successful RWC-winning England team. He was a fantastic captain, but also a tough man who understood what it took to win the big games. Victor Matfield redefined the role of the line-out forward, and in his era, only Nathan Sharpe appeared to be able to compete with him. Victor was exceptional in nearly every match I refereed him. His all-round skills were not too bad for such a big man and he was surprisingly quick when he needed to be. The slight edge, therefore, to Victor Matfield and Martin Johnson.

Flanker (openside) – Richie McCaw is a standout selection and, for me, has no peer. He is very astute, a tremendous leader and an avid student of the game. His breakdown skills are testament to his understanding of the laws, but it is his all-round game that sets him apart from the others. He does get away with some marginal tactics every now and again, but he also has the courage and understanding to push the envelope.

The blindside was more vexing, with many candidates. André Venter was a workhorse of note; Thierry Dusautoir is a man with a quiet manner but a will of steel; and Juan Smith had the respect of all around him and did a lot of the cleaning up in and around the tackle area. But eventually I decided on George Smith, who I feel had many of the attributes I mentioned above. His technique in and around the tackle in stealing possession or winning his side a penalty is self-evident. He was not the biggest man, but he had a huge heart and his contribution to the team won him many Player of the Year awards in Australia (and he likes the ponies too).

Eighthman – only two candidates: the emerging Kieran Read, who is hard-nosed, tough and rangy and seems to be getting better with time, his competitive nature and leadership ability making him a really tough adversary; and Lawrence Dallaglio, who was also central to England winning the RWC in Australia in 2003, was very strong, with a big engine, and always seeming to be central to the good organisation of the England pack. My tentative vote goes to Read, as I think he will kick on and have many more good years at the top.

The "Nice Guys" XV

15 Mils Muliaina/Chris Latham
14 Christophe Dominici
13 Wynand Olivier/Jaque Fourie
12 Aaron Mauger
11 Cabous van der Westhuizen
10 Dan Carter
9 Andy Ellis
8 Gary Teichmann
7 Dave Pocock
6 George Smith/Todd Blackadder
5 Nathan Sharpe/Donncha O'Callaghan
4 John Eales
3 Adrian Garvey
2 Keven Mealamu/Jeremy Paul
1 Jason Leonard

APPENDIX E

My most memorable games

	MATCH	SCORE	YEAR	REASONS WHY	CITY/VENUE
1	New Zealand v Australia	23-24	2000	Eales's last-minute penalty to win game; high quality of fixture; big Test for me in terms of experience; first Bledisloe Cup	Wellington
2	Bulls v Free State	25-29	2005	The most dramatic of Currie Cup finals. Memorable!	Pretoria
3	England v Samoa	35-22	2003	One of *the* games of the 2003 RWC where Samoa held England for 60 minutes; great pace to the game; awesome support both ways	Melbourne
4	Australia v British & Irish Lions	35-14	2001	Australia under the pump the whole of the first half; one error and the complexion of the game changes. And the series!	Melbourne
5	Western Province v Sharks	19-33	2013	My sixth and last Currie Cup final, this game meant the world to me and it showed; I was a gibbering wreck prior to kick-off but managed to get back in the zone when play distracted me	Cape Town
6	France v England	9-14	2007	Semi-final of the 2007 RWC; didn't referee at my best in the tournament; redemption; dramatic game	Paris
7	France v New Zealand	42-33	2000	France repeat heroics of RWC the previous year; Lamaison's three drops the difference; France 17-0 after 10 minutes; atmosphere in Marseille unreal	Marseille
8	Italy v Scotland	34-20	2000	Newcomers to Six Nations beat the 1999 champions; Domínguez drop goals; my first ever Six Nations match	Flaminio

	MATCH	SCORE	YEAR	REASONS WHY	CITY/VENUE
9	England v New Zealand	31-28	2002	One of the rare games where England matched New Zealand in almost every department; ripper of a game that was not decided until the final whistle	Twickenham
10	Scotland v Ireland	15-22	2009	Very tense Test match with Ireland aiming for much-sought-after Grand Slam; my 50th Test; Peter Stringer makes the play of the game to set up the only try and keep Ireland's hopes alive	Murrayfield
11	Ireland v England	6-42	2003	Winner-takes-all Six Nations decider; both teams very strong; England romp home in dominant form setting the tone for 2003 RWC and achieve Grand Slam	Lansdowne Road
12	Canada v Japan	12-12	2007	Canada always won at least one game in the RWC, while Japan had never won one; Canada hold the whip in hand going into final minutes but Japan score try and convert to draw; grown men crying; standing ovation	Bordeaux
13	Australia v New Zealand	24-28	2008	High-paced match; Australia forge a big lead but cannot hold on in the face of New Zealand counterpunch in the second half; exhausting for all participants	Brisbane
14	New Zealand v British & Irish Lions	38-19	2005	New Zealand score five tries to one, even though Lions have plenty of ball; always an honour to get the third Test in a Lions series	Eden Park
15	France v Argentina	12-6	2008	World-record game but no pomp and ceremony; have just gone where no one else had been before	Marseille
16	Western Province v Bulls	52-34	1997	Best Currie Cup match refereed	Cape town
17	Fiji v Japan	40-39	2009	Fiji the favourite but Japan unstoppable on the drive; score four almost identical tries to lead 36-26 with four minutes to play; awarded penalty close to full time, which they convert to lead 39-33; Fiji score to win!	Fiji
18	Boland v Western Province	25-39	1998	The country bumpkins are in town; five tries to them in 27 minutes in the first half!	Cape Town

	MATCH	SCORE	YEAR	REASONS WHY	CITY/VENUE
19	Bulls v Free State	26-26	2006	My third Currie Cup final, this one in Bloem again; great atmosphere; last drawn match in a final; the end of an epic battle over three years between the Bulls and Free State	Bloemfon-tein
20	New Zealand v Australia	12-6	2002	Bitterly cold; 180+ kicks out of hand; Andy Turner frostbite; Paddy O'Brien saying this will look good on my CV	Christchurch
21	Sharks v Bulls	14-9	2008	My fourth Currie Cup final; hugely emotional occasion and a return to the place it had all started; a tough, bruising game that could have gone either way right up until the end	Durban
22	Lions v Bulls	7-31	2002	My first Currie Cup final, so long in the making! Got caught in a huge traffic jam prior to kick-off; amazing feeling running out for that first final, big heart pump	Ellis Park
23	Russia v Spain	22-38	2002	Russia expelled; Krasnodar experience	Krasnodar
24	Tonga v Fiji	19-24	2005	First Island experience; after-match singing; Bill Cavubati – the biggest man ever made; Island rivalry	Tonga
25	Crusaders v Waratahs	96-19	2002	Best half of rugby by anyone anywhere	Christchurch
26	France v Ireland	43-21	2003	RWC quarter-final; France dominant 37-0 after 43 minutes – game over; Galthié v Woods; Maggs by 2	Melbourne
27	Zimbabwe v Namibia	18-19	1996	First ever Test match	Harare
28	Bulls v Chiefs	61-17	2008	First referee to ever ref a final in Super Rugby on merit alone; annihilation of a very good team by one who played their best rugby in a final	Pretoria
29	Springboks v Namibia	105-13	2007	Rare to ref your own national team in this era; score 15-13 after 20 minutes; Percy breaks SA record	Cape Town
30	Crusaders v Hurricanes	19-12	2006	The final in the fog, no one saw what was coming and no one saw it when it came; only memorable for the actual participants; a throwback to the time when there were no cameras	Christchurch
31	Scotland v France	20-16	2006	Classic Six Nations Test match; Sean Lamont the hero as huge underdogs Scotland manage to hold off the French	Murrayfield

	MATCH	SCORE	YEAR	REASONS WHY	CITY/VENUE
32	Wales v New Zealand	9-29	2008	Wales attempt to outstare New Zealand after the haka, which adds huge drama to the occasion; play a snorter of a first half, making New Zealand look only average	Millennium Stadium
33	Scotland v Wales	22-46	2005	Unbelievable ball-in-play stat; one of the great tries in Welsh rugby history; best half of rugby by a team in a Test match I refereed; Wales take the Grand Slam	Murrayfield
34	Ireland v Scotland	20-23	2009	John Beattie scores breakaway try emulating his father and setting the tone for defeat of Ireland; Scotland first away-win in Six Nations for 10 years (outside of Italy)	Croke Park

APPENDIX F

My match statistics

	SUPER RUGBY			
	MATCH AND FINAL SCORE			**YEAR**
1	Cheetahs	20-24	Lions	1997
2	Lions	35-37	Hurricanes	1997
3	Bulls	23-22	Crusaders	1997
4	Highlanders	26-19	Reds	1998
5	Blues	47-25	Waratahs	1998
6	Waratahs	36-32	Hurricanes	1998
7	Bulls	19-42	Stormers	1999
8	Crusaders	23-36	Reds	1999
9	Waratahs	20-21	Blues	1999
10	Highlanders	9-8	Brumbies	1999
11	Blues	16-22	Brumbies	1999
12	Cats	22-18	Stormers	2000
13	Blues	31-17	Waratahs	2000
14	Chiefs	17-45	Brumbies	2000
15	Reds	33-26	Blues	2000
16	Stormers	24-29	Cats	2001
17	Highlanders	39-20	Waratahs	2001
18	Reds	33-22	Highlanders	2001
19	Waratahs	20-25	Reds	2001
20	Brumbies	30-6	Reds	2001
21	Reds	27-13	Chiefs	2002
22	Crusaders	33-32	Brumbies	2002
23	Chiefs	15-42	Brumbies	2002
24	Crusaders	96-19	Waratahs	2002
25	Waratahs	18-31	Blues	2003
26	Chiefs	43-27	Reds	2003
27	Hurricanes	42-26	Waratahs	2003

	MATCH AND FINAL SCORE			**YEAR**
28	Hurricanes	27-35	Brumbies	2003
29	Brumbies	21-28	Crusaders	2003
30	Blues	42-21	Brumbies	2003
31	Bulls	18-23	Sharks	2004
32	Reds	20-3	Blues	2004
33	Blues	22-17	Waratahs	2004
34	Bulls	62-52	Cats	2004
35	Brumbies	32-17	Chiefs	2004
36	Blues	17-0	Brumbies	2005
37	Hurricanes	26-24	Waratahs	2005
38	Hurricanes	49-37	Brumbies	2005
39	Crusaders	35-25	Waratahs	2005
40	Sharks	26-27	Cheetahs	2006
41	Blues	26-15	Brumbies	2006
42	Crusaders	17-11	Waratahs	2006
43	Chiefs	37-33	Waratahs	2006
44	Crusaders	33-3	Brumbies	2006
45	Hurricanes	16-14	Waratahs	2006
46	Crusaders	19-12	Hurricanes	2006
47	Reds	25-16	Hurricanes	2007
48	Brumbies	15-17	Blues	2007
49	Hurricanes	23-22	Blues	2007
50	Highlanders	3-38	Crusaders	2007
51	Sharks	33-3	Lions	2007
52	Force	6-33	Blues	2007
53	Cheetahs	22-23	Lions	2008
54	Brumbies	28-42	Chiefs	2008
55	Blues	11-16	Brumbies	2008

	MATCH AND FINAL SCORE			YEAR
56	Reds	22-35	Blues	2008
57	Hurricanes	21-10	Force	2008
58	Sharks	25-10	Lions	2009
59	Stormers	8-14	Blues	2009
60	Lions	25-17	Brumbies	2009
61	Lions	32-38	Hurricanes	2009
62	Waratahs	6-20	Bulls	2009
63	Hurricanes	34-11	Stormers	2009
64	Lions	20-32	Crusaders	2009
65	Reds	28-37	Hurricanes	2009
66	Bulls	61-17	Chiefs	2009
67	Cheetahs	34-51	Bulls	2010
68	Sharks	20-25	Cheetahs	2010
69	Bulls	50-35	Highlanders	2010
70	Hurricanes	26-26	Crusaders	2010
71	Chiefs	19-33	Bulls	2010
72	Brumbies	13-23	Hurricanes	2010
73	Force	24-16	Crusaders	2010
74	Bulls	27-19	Sharks	2010
75	Stormers	38-10	Bulls	2010
76	Brumbies	28-20	Chiefs	2011
77	Rebels	25-24	Brumbies	2011
78	Lions	32-41	Blues	2011
79	Sharks	6-16	Stormers	2011
80	Sharks	27-3	Lions	2011
81	Waratahs	28-9	Rebels	2011

	MATCH AND FINAL SCORE			YEAR
82	Hurricanes	11-17	Blues	2011
83	Reds	37-31	Blues	2011
84	Sharks	26-21	Waratahs	2011
85	Stormers	16-19	Bulls	2011
86	Bulls	23-26	Sharks	2011
87	Reds	30-13	Blues	2011
88	Bulls	18-13	Sharks	2012
89	Sharks	27-22	Reds	2012
90	Bulls	61-8	Reds	2012
91	Lions	13-23	Crusaders	2012
92	Cheetahs	33-39	Chiefs	2012
93	Waratahs	30-21	Rebels	2012
94	Waratahs	33-37	Crusaders	2012
95	Cheetahs	20-34	Sharks	2012
96	Bulls	14-19	Stormers	2012
97	Reds	19-13	Highlanders	2012
98	Hurricanes	28-25	Chiefs	2012
99	Reds	17-30	Sharks	2012
100	Cheetahs	22-29	Sharks	2013
101	Sharks	12-6	Stormers	2013
102	Sharks	10-29	Brumbies	2013
103	Chiefs	23-16	Blues	2013
104	Hurricanes	41-29	Waratahs	2013
105	Force	16-14	Crusaders	2013
106	Kings	10-72	Waratahs	2013
107	Sharks	16-18	Bulls	2013

CURRIE CUP				
	MATCH AND FINAL SCORE		VENUE	YEAR
1	NW Cape	15-65 Lowveld	Upington	1994
2	Stellaland	29-26 Vaal Triangle	Lichtenburg	1994
3	NE Cape	44-5 N Natal	Cradock	1994
4	SWD	19-8 Far North	Oudtshoorn	1994
5	Stellaland	17-28 Vaal Triangle	Lichtenburg	1995
6	W Transvaal	25-50 Western Province	Potchefstroom	1995
7	Vaal Triangle	35-13 Zimbabwe	Sasolburg	1995
8	W Transvaal	47-10 E Transvaal	Potchefstroom	1995
9	N Free State	20-20 Namibia	Welkom	1995
10	Border	52-10 W Transvaal	East London	1995
11	Vaal Triangle	22-21 SE Transvaal	Sasolburg	1995
12	Western Province	73-12 N Free State	Cape Town	1996
13	W Transvaal	22-32 Boland	Potchefstroom	1996
14	Free State	27-25 N Transvaal	Bloemfontein	1996
15	Transvaal	32-12 Border	Johannesburg	1996
16	Transvaal	29-26 SE Transvaal	Johannesburg	1996
17	N Transvaal	147-8 SWD	Pietersburg	1996
18	N Transvaal	55-23 Boland	Pretoria	1996
19	Western Province	75-32 Falcons	Cape Town	1997
20	Border	20-39 N Transvaal	East London	1997
21	Western Province	52-34 N Transvaal	Cape Town	1997
22	Griquas	87-14 Border	Kimberley	1998
23	Eastern Province	26-35 Blue Bulls	Port Elizabeth	1998
24	N Free State	34-33 Free State	Welkom	1998
25	Falcons	39-17 Boland	Brakpan	1998
26	Boland	17-13 Griquas	Wellington	1998
27	Western Province	25-39 Boland	Cape Town	1998
28	Lions	12-20 Blue Bulls	Johannesburg	1998
29	SWD	14-33 Griquas	George	1998
30	Free State	34-18 Lions	Bloemfontein	1998
31	Blue Bulls	33-19 Free State	Pretoria	1998
32	Griquas	11-27 Western Province	Kimberley	1998
33	Eastern Province	16-22 Lions	Port Elizabeth	1999
34	Western Province	24-33 Blue Bulls	Cape Town	1999
35	Blue Bulls	19-28 Lions	Pretoria	1999
36	Falcons	19-41 SWD	Brakpan	1999
37	Griquas	13-15 Eastern Province	Kimberley	1999
38	SWD	102-0 N Free State	George	1999

	CURRIE CUP				
	MATCH AND FINAL SCORE			**VENUE**	**YEAR**
39	Border	21-5	Griquas	East London	1999
40	N Free State	23-49	Western Province	Welkom	1999
41	Boland	33-42	Border	Wellington	1999
42	Blue Bulls	56-49	Pumas	Pretoria	2000
43	Eastern Province	48-37	N Free State	Port Elizabeth	2000
44	Blue Bulls	38-33	North West	Pretoria	2000
45	Pumas	32-51	Western Province	Witbank	2000
46	Free State	50-32	Griquas	Bloemfontein	2000
47	Boland	22-52	SWD	Wellington	2000
48	SWD	18-30	Free State	George	2000
49	Western Province	43-22	Lions	Cape Town	2000
50	Lions	51-46	Boland	Johannesburg	2001
51	Free State	75-21	Eastern Province	Bloemfontein	2001
52	Border	22-32	Western Province	East London	2001
53	Blue Bulls	19-22	Western Province	Pretoria	2001
54	Boland	47-36	SWD	Wellington	2001
55	Lions	49-29	Pumas	Johannesburg	2001
56	Blue Bulls	23-15	Falcons	Pretoria	2001
57	Western Province	40-18	Free State	Cape Town	2001
58	SWD	44-39	Lions	George	2002
59	Free State	31-33	Border	Bloemfontein	2002
60	Lions	20-33	Blue Bulls	Johannesburg	2002
61	Griquas	24-68	Western Province	Kimberley	2002
62	Lions	46-37	Sharks	Johannesburg	2002
63	Free State	35-29	Blue Bulls	Bloemfontein	2002
64	SWD	83-16	N Free State	George	2002
65	Griquas	28-29	Blue Bulls	Kimberley	2002
66	Lions	50-13	Western Province	Johannesburg	2002
67	Lions	7-31	Blue Bulls	Johannesburg	2002
68	Eastern Province	21-24	Falcons	Port Elizabeth	2003
69	North West	28-27	Falcons	Potchefstroom	2003
70	Eastern Province	40-64	North West	Port Elizabeth	2003
71	Blue Bulls	64-29	Western Province	Pretoria	2003
72	Pumas	55-46	Free State	Witbank	2003
73	Griquas	24-47	SWD	Kimberley	2003
74	Free State	22-40	Lions	Bloemfontein	2003
75	Blue Bulls	15-19	Griquas	Pretoria	2003
76	SWD	41-59	Western Province	George	2003

	CURRIE CUP				
	MATCH AND FINAL SCORE			**VENUE**	**YEAR**
77	Griquas	19-75	Free State	Kimberley	2003
78	Sharks	48-15	Griquas	Durban	2003
79	Sharks	33-30	Griquas	Durban	2004
80	Lions	32-28	Western Province	Johannesburg	2004
81	Sharks	16-17	Free State	Durban	2004
82	Pumas	37-25	SWD	Witbank	2004
83	Sharks	23-27	Blue Bulls	Durban	2004
84	SWD	5-47	Blue Bulls	George	2004
85	Lions	49-35	Sharks	Johannesburg	2004
86	Free State	27-27	Blue Bulls	Bloemfontein	2004
87	Pumas	27-44	Lions	Witbank	2004
88	Sharks	37-23	Boland	Durban	2005
89	Boland	56-20	SWD	Wellington	2005
90	Lions	46-17	Blue Bulls	Johannesburg	2005
91	Boland	29-22	Western Province	Wellington	2005
92	Blue Bulls	69-24	North West	Pretoria	2005
93	Blue Bulls	39-3	Western Province	Pretoria	2005
94	Lions	37-36	Free State	Johannesburg	2005
95	Blue Bulls	25-29	Free State	Pretoria	2005
96	Sharks	33-22	Lions	Durban	2006
97	Western Province	25-28	Sharks	Cape Town	2006
98	Pumas	17-48	Blue Bulls	Witbank	2006
99	Sharks	19-31	Free State	Durban	2006
100	Boland	59-0	N Free State	Wellington	2006
101	Sharks	16-6	Western Province	Durban	2006
102	Lions	39-28	Free State	Johannesburg	2006
103	Falcons	17-32	Lions	Brakpan	2006
104	Border	36-57	Eastern Province	East London	2006
105	Western Province	55-17	Griquas	Cape Town	2006
106	Free State	28-28	Blue Bulls	Bloemfontein	2006
107	Western Province	18-13	Lions	Cape Town	2007
108	Sharks	32-16	Western Province	Durban	2007
109	Boland	12-26	Sharks	Wellington	2007
110	Free State	45-13	Western Province	Bloemfontein	2007
111	Boland	10-15	Lions	Wellington	2007
112	Boland	9-9	Griquas	Wellington	2008
113	Sharks	28-10	Falcons	Durban	2008
114	Sharks	16-11	Lions	Durban	2008

	CURRIE CUP				
	MATCH AND FINAL SCORE			VENUE	YEAR
115	Western Province	10-32	Sharks	Cape Town	2008
116	Griquas	59-19	Falcons	Kimberley	2008
117	Boland	7-41	Sharks	Wellington	2008
118	Border	45-40	Pumas	East London	2008
119	Western Province	30-18	Griquas	Cape Town	2008
120	Griquas	22-58	Blue Bulls	Kimberley	2008
121	Sharks	66-12	Griquas	Durban	2008
122	Boland	54-15	N Free State	Wellington	2008
123	Sharks	14-9	Blue Bulls	Durban	2008
124	Falcons	27-39	N Free State	Kempton Park	2009
125	Eastern Province	25-27	Pumas	Uitenhage	2009
126	Lions	19-23	Griquas	Johannesburg	2009
127	N Free State	63-45	Border	Welkom	2009
128	Lions	19-30	Sharks	Johannesburg	2009
129	Sharks	9-21	Western Province	Durban	2009
130	North West	33-34	Griquas	Potchefstroom	2009
131	Blue Bulls	23-29	Sharks	Pretoria	2009
132	Sharks	34-20	North West	Durban	2009
133	Sharks	19-17	Lions	Durban	2009
134	Boland	36-35	Pumas	Wellington	2009
135	Blue Bulls	36-24	Free State	Pretoria	2009
136	N Free State	43-8	Falcons	Welkom	2010
137	Sharks	27-17	Pumas	Durban	2010
138	Border	37-38	Falcons	East London	2010
139	Sharks	48-30	Griquas	Durban	2010
140	Blue Bulls	40-34	Sharks	Pretoria	2010
141	Pumas	31-61	Griquas	Witbank	2010
142	Griquas	36-48	Blue Bulls	Kimberley	2010
143	Eastern Province	28-46	Pumas	Port Elizabeth	2010
144	Western Province	26-26	Griquas	Cape Town	2011
145	N Free State	34-67	Pumas	Welkom	2012
146	North West	32-38	N Free State	Potchefstroom	2012
147	Free State	22-29	Western Province	Bloemfontein	2012
148	Blue Bulls	26-13	Western Province	Pretoria	2012
149	Western Province	36-15	Free State	Cape Town	2012
150	Free State	53-14	Eastern Province	Bloemfontein	2012
151	SWD	30-25	N Free State	George	2013
152	Eastern Province	9-6	Border	Port Elizabeth	2013

CURRIE CUP				
	MATCH AND FINAL SCORE		VENUE	YEAR
153	Western Province	15-14	Free State	Cape Town	2013
154	Blue Bulls	23-62	Lions	Pretoria	2013
155	Sharks	34-18	Blue Bulls	Durban	2013
156	N Free State	24-19	Border	Welkom	2013
157	Boland	19-40	Eastern Province	Wellington	2013
158	Griquas	21-52	Free State	Kimberley	2013
159	Sharks	13-17	Western Province	Durban	2013
160	Griquas	21-19	Pumas	Kimberley	2013
161	Western Province	19-33	Sharks	Cape Town	2013

TESTS			
	MATCH AND FINAL SCORE		**YEAR**
1	Zimbabwe	18-19	Namibia	1996
2	Gulf States	53-13	Botswana	1997
3	Argentina	33-13	England	1997
4	Fiji	32-15	Tonga	1998
5	Romania	27-23	Georgia	1998
6	Italy	34-20	Scotland	2000
7	New Zealand	23-24	Australia	2000
8	France	42-33	New Zealand	2000
9	Italy	22-41	Ireland	2001
10	Australia	35-14	British Lions	2001
11	Wales	6-36	Ireland	2001
12	New Zealand	12-6	Australia	2002
13	England	31-28	New Zealand	2002
14	Russia	22-38	Spain	2002
15	Ireland	6-42	England	2003
16	New Zealand	21-17	Australia	2003
17	Ireland	45-17	Romania	2003
18	Scotland	39-15	USA	2003
19	England	35-22	Samoa	2003
20	France	43-21	Ireland	2003
21	New Zealand	36-3	England	2004
22	Australia	23-18	New Zealand	2004
23	France	14-24	Argentina	2004
24	Ireland	19-13	England	2005
25	Scotland	22-46	Wales	2005
26	New Zealand	38-19	British Lions	2005
27	Tonga	19-24	Fiji	2005
28	Ireland	7-45	New Zealand	2005
29	Scotland	20-16	France	2006
30	Ireland	31-5	Wales	2006
31	New Zealand	27-17	Ireland	2006
32	New Zealand	32-12	Australia	2006
33	England	26-18	France	2007
34	Italy	24-51	Ireland	2007
35	Australia	29-23	Wales	2007

	MATCH AND FINAL SCORE		**YEAR**
36	Springboks	105-13	Namibia	2007
37	England	28-10	USA	2007
38	Samoa	15-19	Tonga	2007
39	Canada	12-12	Japan	2007
40	Scotland	18-16	Italy	2007
41	France	9-14	England	2007
42	Ireland	16-11	Italy	2008
43	Scotland	15-9	England	2008
44	New Zealand	44-12	England	2008
45	Kenya	39-20	Uganda	2008
46	Australia	24-28	New Zealand	2008
47	France	12-6	Argentina	2008
48	Wales	9-29	New Zealand	2008
49	Wales	23-15	England	2009
50	Scotland	15-22	Ireland	2009
51	Fiji	19-14	Samoa	2009
52	Fiji	40-39	Japan	2009
53	Australia	18-19	New Zealand	2009
54	Ireland	20-20	Australia	2009
55	England	6-19	New Zealand	2009
56	Wales	20-26	France	2010
57	Ireland	20-23	Scotland	2010
58	New Zealand	29-10	Wales	2010
59	Zimbabwe	84-10	Botswana	2010
60	Zimbabwe	28-22	Madagascar	2010
61	New Zealand	20-10	Australia	2010
62	France	15-9	Argentina	2011
63	Wales	19-13	Ireland	2011
64	Tonga	20-25	Canada	2011
65	England	41-10	Georgia	2011
66	Canada	23-23	Japan	2011
67	Ireland	36-6	Italy	2011
68	Wales	18-24	Australia	2011
69	Namibia	35-26	Zimbabwe	2013
70	Namibia	55-35	Kenya	2013

Index

The abbreviation "J.K." is used for Jonathan Kaplan

Do you have any comments, suggestions or
feedback about this book or any other Zebra Press titles?
Contact us at **talkback@zebrapress.co.za**

*

Visit **www.randomstruik.co.za** and subscribe
to our newsletter for monthly updates and news